ONE OF THE MOST REMARKABLE BOOKS
EVER WRITTEN ON ACHIEVEMENT . . .

"Illuminating . . . Inspiration for non-geniuses everywhere." —*PEOPLE*

"Persuasive and fascinating . . . Reminds us that it is character and perseverance that set the successful apart." —MALCOLM GLADWELL, author of *The Tipping Point* and *Outliers*

"What sticks with you are the testimonials, collected from sources as disparate as Will Smith, William James, and Jeff Bezos's mom, that relentlessly deflate the myth of the natural." —*THE ATLANTIC*

"A contemporary classic . . . For anyone hoping to work smarter or live better, *Grit* is an essential—and perhaps life-changing—read." —DANIEL H. PINK, author of *Drive* and *When*

"A fascinating tour of the psychological research on success." —*THE WALL STREET JOURNAL*

"I kept wanting to read this book aloud—to my child, my husband, to everyone I care about. There are no shortcuts to greatness, it's true. But there is a road map, and you are holding it." —AMANDA RIPLEY, author of *The Smartest Kids in the World*

"A pop-psych smash." —*THE NEW YORKER*

"Utterly captivating, inspiring, and original . . . Once you pick up *Grit*, you won't be able to tear yourself away." —AMY CUDDY, Harvard Business School professor and author of *Presence*

"A useful guide for parents or teachers looking for confirmation that passion and persistence matter, and for inspiring models of how to cultivate these important qualities." —*THE WASHINGTON POST*

GRIT

THE POWER *of* PASSION
and PERSEVERANCE

ANGELA
DUCKWORTH

SCRIBNER
New York London Toronto Sydney New Delhi

Scribner
An Imprint of Simon & Schuster, Inc.
1230 Avenue of the Americas
New York, NY 10020

First Scribner trade paperback edition August 2018

SCRIBNER and design are registered trademarks of The Gale Group, Inc.,
used under license by Simon & Schuster, Inc., the publisher of this work.

For information about special discounts for bulk purchases,
please contact Simon & Schuster Special Sales at 1-866-506-1949
or business@simonandschuster.com.

The Simon & Schuster Speakers Bureau can bring authors to your
live event. For more information or to book an event, contact the
Simon & Schuster Speakers Bureau at 1-866-248-3049 or visit
our website at www.simonspeakers.com.

Interior design by Jill Putorti

Manufactured in the United States of America

10   9

Library of Congress Cataloging-in-Publication Data

Names: Duckworth, Angela.
Title: Grit : the power of passion and perseverance / Angela Duckworth.
Description: New York : Scribner, 2016. | Includes bibliographical references and index.
Identifiers: LCCN 2015042880 (print) | LCCN 2015044753 (ebook)
Subjects: LCSH: Success | Perseverance (Ethics) | Expectation (Psychology) |
Diligence. | BISAC: PSYCHOLOGY / Personality. | EDUCATION / Professional
Development.
Classification: LCC BF637.S8 D693 2016 (print) | LCC BF637.S8 (ebook) | DDC
158.1—dc23

ISBN 978-1-5011-1110-5
ISBN 978-1-5011-1111-2 (pbk)
ISBN 978-1-5011-1112-9 (ebook)

For Jason

CONTENTS

PREFACE

Growing up, I heard the word *genius* a lot.

It was always my dad who brought it up. He liked to say, apropos of nothing at all, "You know, you're no genius!" This pronouncement might come in the middle of dinner, during a commercial break for *The Love Boat*, or after he flopped down on the couch with the *Wall Street Journal*.

I don't remember how I responded. Maybe I pretended not to hear.

My dad's thoughts turned frequently to genius, talent, and who had more than whom. He was deeply concerned with how smart he was. He was deeply concerned with how smart his family was.

I wasn't the only problem. My dad didn't think my brother and sister were geniuses, either. By his yardstick, none of us measured up to Einstein. Apparently, this was a great disappointment. Dad worried that this intellectual handicap would limit what we'd eventually achieve in life.

Two years ago, I was fortunate enough to be awarded a MacArthur Fellowship, sometimes called the "genius grant." You don't apply for the MacArthur. You don't ask your friends or colleagues to nominate you. Instead, a secret committee that includes the top people in your field decides you're doing important and creative work.

When I received the unexpected call telling me the news, my first reaction was one of gratitude and amazement. Then my thoughts turned to my dad and his offhand diagnoses of my intellectual potential. He wasn't wrong; I didn't win the MacArthur because I'm leagues smarter than my fellow psychologists. Instead, he had the right answer ("No, she's not") to the wrong question ("Is she a genius?").

There was about a month between the MacArthur call and its official announcement. Apart from my husband, I wasn't permitted to tell anyone. That gave me time to ponder the irony of the situation. A girl who is told repeatedly that she's no genius ends up winning an award for being one. The award goes to her because she has discovered that what we eventually accomplish may depend more on our passion and perseverance than on our innate talent. She has by then amassed degrees from some pretty tough schools, but in the third grade, she didn't test high enough for the gifted and talented program. Her parents are Chinese immigrants, but she didn't get lectured on the salvation of hard work. Against stereotype, she can't play a note of piano or violin.

The morning the MacArthur was announced, I walked over to my parents' apartment. My mom and dad had already heard the news, and so had several "aunties," who were calling in rapid succession to offer congratulations. Finally, when the phone stopped ringing, my dad turned to me and said, "I'm proud of you."

I had so much to say in response, but instead I just said, "Thanks, Dad."

There was no sense rehashing the past. I knew that, in fact, he *was* proud of me.

Still, part of me wanted to travel back in time to when I was a young girl. I'd tell him what I know now.

I would say, "Dad, you say I'm no genius. I won't argue with that. You know plenty of people who are smarter than I am." I can imagine his head nodding in sober agreement.

"But let me tell you something. I'm going to grow up to love my work as much as you love yours. I won't just have a job; I'll have a calling. I'll challenge myself every day. When I get knocked down, I'll get back up. I may not be the smartest person in the room, but I'll strive to be the grittiest."

And if he was still listening: "In the long run, Dad, grit may matter more than talent."

All these years later, I have the scientific evidence to prove my point. What's more, I know that grit is mutable, not fixed, and I have insights from research about how to grow it.

This book summarizes everything I've learned about grit.

When I finished writing it, I went to visit my dad. Chapter by chapter, over the course of days, I read him every line. He's been battling Parkinson's disease for the last decade or so, and I'm not entirely sure how much he understood. Still, he seemed to be listening intently, and when I was done, he looked at me. After what felt like an eternity, he nodded once. And then he smiled.

Part I

WHAT GRIT IS AND WHY IT MATTERS

Chapter 1

SHOWING UP

By the time you set foot on the campus of the United States Military Academy at West Point, you've earned it.

The admissions process for West Point is at least as rigorous as for the most selective universities. Top scores on the SAT or ACT and outstanding high school grades are a must. But when you apply to Harvard, you don't need to start your application in the eleventh grade, and you don't need to secure a nomination from a member of Congress, a senator, or the vice president of the United States. You don't, for that matter, have to get superlative marks in a fitness assessment that includes running, push-ups, sit-ups, and pull-ups.

Each year, in their junior year of high school, more than 14,000 applicants begin the admissions process. This pool is winnowed to just 4,000 who succeed in getting the required nomination. Slightly more than half of those applicants—about 2,500—meet West Point's rigorous academic and physical standards, and from that select group just 1,200 are admitted and enrolled. Nearly all the men and women who come to West Point were varsity athletes; most were team captains.

And yet, one in five cadets will drop out before graduation. What's more remarkable is that, historically, a substantial fraction of dropouts leave in their very first summer, during an intensive seven-week train-ing program named, even in official literature, Beast Barracks. Or, for short, just Beast.

Who spends two years trying to get into a place and then drops out in the first two months?

Then again, these are no ordinary months. Beast is described in the West Point handbook for new cadets as "the most physically and emo-tionally demanding part of your four years at West Point . . . designed to help you make the transition from new cadet to Soldier."

A Typical Day at Beast Barracks

5:00 a.m.	Wake-up
5:30 a.m.	Reveille Formation
5:30 to 6:55 a.m.	Physical Training
6:55 to 7:25 a.m.	Personal Maintenance
7:30 to 8:15 a.m.	Breakfast
8:30 to 12:45 p.m.	Training/Classes
1:00 to 1:45 p.m.	Lunch
2:00 to 3:45 p.m.	Training/Classes
4:00 to 5:30 p.m.	Organized Athletics
5:30 to 5:55 p.m.	Personal Maintenance
6:00 to 6:45 p.m.	Dinner
7:00 to 9:00 p.m.	Training/Classes
9:00 to 10:00 p.m.	Commander's Time
10:00 p.m.	Taps

The day begins at 5:00 a.m. By 5:30, cadets are in formation, stand-ing at attention, honoring the raising of the United States flag. Then follows a hard workout—running or calisthenics—followed by a non-stop rotation of marching in formation, classroom instruction, weapons training, and athletics. Lights out, to a melancholy bugle song called "Taps," occurs at 10:00 p.m. And on the next day the routine starts over again. Oh, and there are no weekends, no breaks other than meals, and virtually no contact with family and friends outside of West Point.

One cadet's description of Beast: "You are challenged in a variety of ways in every developmental area—mentally, physically, militarily, and socially. The system will find your weaknesses, but that's the point—West Point toughens you."

———

So, who makes it through Beast?

It was 2004 and my second year of graduate school in psychology when I set about answering that question, but for decades, the U.S. Army has been asking the same thing. In fact, it was in 1955—almost fifty years before I began working on this puzzle—that a young psychologist named Jerry Kagan was drafted into the army, ordered to report to West Point, and assigned to test new cadets for the purpose of identifying who would stay and who would leave. As fate would have it, Jerry was not only the first psychologist to study dropping out at West Point, he was also the first psychologist I met in college. I ended up working part-time in his lab for two years.

Jerry described early efforts to separate the wheat from the chaff at West Point as dramatically unsuccessful. He recalled in particular spending hundreds of hours showing cadets cards printed with pictures and asking the young men to make up stories to fit them. This test was meant to unearth deep-seated, unconscious motives, and the general idea was that cadets who visualized noble deeds and courageous accomplishments should be the ones who would graduate instead of dropping out. Like a lot of ideas that sound good in principle, this one didn't work so well in practice. The stories the cadets told were colorful and fun to listen to, but they had absolutely nothing to do with decisions the cadets made in their actual lives.

Since then, several more generations of psychologists devoted themselves to the attrition issue, but not one researcher could say with much certainty why some of the most promising cadets routinely quit when their training had just begun.

Soon after learning about Beast, I found my way to the office of Mike Matthews, a military psychologist who's been a West Point faculty member for years. Mike explained that the West Point admissions process successfully identified men and women who had the potential to thrive there. In particular, admissions staff calculate for each applicant something called the Whole Candidate Score, a weighted average of SAT or ACT exam scores, high school rank adjusted for the number of students in the applicant's graduating class, expert appraisals of leadership potential, and performance on objective measures of physical fitness.

You can think of the Whole Candidate Score as West Point's best guess at how much talent applicants have for the diverse rigors of its four-year program. In other words, it's an estimate of how easily cadets will master the many skills required of a military leader.

The Whole Candidate Score is the single most important factor in West Point admissions, and yet it *didn't* reliably predict who would make it through Beast. In fact, cadets with the highest Whole Candidate Scores were just as likely to drop out as those with the lowest. And this was why Mike's door was open to me.

From his own experience joining the air force as a young man, Mike had a clue to the riddle. While the rigors of his induction weren't quite as harrowing as those of West Point, there were notable similarities. The most important were challenges that exceeded current skills. For the first time in their lives, Mike and the other recruits were being asked, on an hourly basis, to do things they couldn't yet do. "Within two weeks," Mike recalls, "I was tired, lonely, frustrated, and ready to quit—as were all of my classmates."

Some did quit, but Mike did not.

What struck Mike was that rising to the occasion had almost nothing to do with talent. Those who dropped out of training rarely did so from lack of ability. Rather, what mattered, Mike said, was a "never give up" attitude.

Around that time, it wasn't just Mike Matthews who was talking to me about this kind of hang-in-there posture toward challenge. As a graduate student just beginning to probe the psychology of success, I was interviewing leaders in business, art, athletics, journalism, academia, medicine, and law: *Who are the people at the very top of your field? What are they like? What do you think makes them special?*

Some of the characteristics that emerged in these interviews were very field-specific. For instance, more than one businessperson mentioned an appetite for taking financial risks: "You've got to be able to make calculated decisions about millions of dollars and still go to sleep at night." But this seemed entirely beside the point for artists, who instead mentioned a drive to create: "I like making stuff. I don't know why, but I do." In contrast, athletes mentioned a different kind of motivation, one driven by the thrill of victory: "Winners love to go head-to-head with other people. Winners hate losing."

In addition to these particulars, there emerged certain commonalities, and they were what interested me most. No matter the field, the most successful people were lucky and talented. I'd heard that before, and I didn't doubt it.

But the story of success didn't end there. Many of the people I talked to could also recount tales of rising stars who, to everyone's surprise, dropped out or lost interest before they could realize their potential.

Apparently, it was critically important—and not at all easy—to keep going after failure: "Some people are great when things are going well, but they fall apart when things aren't." High achievers described in these interviews really stuck it out: "This one guy, he wasn't actually the best writer at the beginning. I mean, we used to read his stories and have a laugh because the writing was so, you know, clumsy and melodramatic. But he got better and better, and last year he won a Guggenheim." And they were constantly driven to improve: "She's never satisfied. You'd think she would be, by now, but she's her own harshest critic." The highly accomplished were paragons of perseverance.

Why were the highly accomplished so dogged in their pursuits? For most, there was no realistic expectation of ever catching up to their ambitions. In their own eyes, they were never good enough. They were the opposite of complacent. And yet, in a very real sense, they were satisfied being unsatisfied. Each was chasing something of unparalleled interest and importance, and it was the chase—as much as the capture—that was gratifying. Even if some of the things they had to do were boring, or frustrating, or even painful, they wouldn't dream of giving up. Their passion was enduring.

In sum, no matter the domain, the highly successful had a kind of ferocious determination that played out in two ways. First, these exemplars were unusually resilient and hardworking. Second, they knew in a very, very deep way what it was they wanted. They not only had determination, they had *direction*.

It was this combination of passion and perseverance that made high achievers special. In a word, they had grit.

———

For me, the question became: How do you measure something so intangible? Something that decades of military psychologists hadn't been able to quantify? Something those very successful people I'd interviewed said they could recognize on sight, but couldn't think of how to directly test for?

I sat down and looked over my interview notes. And I started writing questions that captured, sometimes verbatim, descriptions of what it means to have grit.

Half of the questions were about perseverance. They asked how much you agree with statements like "I have overcome setbacks to conquer an important challenge" and "I finish whatever I begin."

The other half of the questions were about passion. They asked whether your "interests change from year to year" and the extent to which you "have been obsessed with a certain idea or project for a short time but later lost interest."

What emerged was the Grit Scale—a test that, when taken honestly, measures the extent to which you approach life with grit.

———

In July 2004, on the second day of Beast, 1,218 West Point cadets sat down to take the Grit Scale.

The day before, cadets had said good-bye to their moms and dads (a farewell for which West Point allocates exactly ninety seconds), gotten their heads shaved (just the men), changed out of civilian clothing and into the famous gray and white West Point uniform, and received their footlockers, helmets, and other gear. Though they may have mistakenly thought they already knew how, they were instructed by a fourth-year cadet in the proper way to stand in line ("Step up to my line! Not on my line, not over my line, not behind my line. Step up *to* my line!").

Initially, I looked to see how grit scores lined up with aptitude. Guess what? Grit scores bore absolutely no relationship to the Whole Candidate Scores that had been so painstakingly calculated during the admissions process. In other words, how talented a cadet was said nothing about their grit, and vice versa.

The separation of grit from talent was consistent with Mike's observations of air force training, but when I first stumbled onto this finding it came as a real surprise. After all, why *shouldn't* the talented endure? Logically, the talented should stick around and try hard, because when they do, they do phenomenally well. At West Point, for example, among cadets who ultimately make it through Beast, the Whole Candidate Score is a marvelous predictor of every metric West Point tracks. It not only predicts academic grades, but military and physical fitness marks as well.

So it's surprising, really, that talent is no guarantee of grit. In this book, we'll explore the reasons why.

———

By the last day of Beast, seventy-one cadets had dropped out.

Grit turned out to be an astoundingly reliable predictor of who made it through and who did not.

The next year, I returned to West Point to run the same study. This time, sixty-two cadets dropped out of Beast, and again grit predicted who would stay.

In contrast, stayers and leavers had indistinguishable Whole Candidate Scores. I looked a little closer at the individual components that make up the score. Again, no differences.

So, what matters for making it through Beast?

Not your SAT scores, not your high school rank, not your leadership experience, not your athletic ability.

Not your Whole Candidate Score.

What matters is grit.

———

Does grit matter beyond West Point? To find out, I looked for other situations so challenging that a lot of people drop out. I wanted to know whether it was just the rigors of Beast that demanded grit, or whether, in general, grit helped people stick to their commitments.

The next arena where I tested grit's power was sales, a profession in which daily, if not hourly, rejection is par for the course. I asked hundreds of men and women employed at the same vacation time-share company to answer a battery of personality questionnaires, including the Grit Scale. Six months later, I revisited the company, by which time 55 percent of the salespeople were gone. Grit predicted who stayed and who left. Moreover, no other commonly measured personality trait— including extroversion, emotional stability, and conscientiousness— was as effective as grit in predicting job retention.

Around the same time, I received a call from the Chicago Public Schools. Like the psychologists at West Point, researchers there were eager to learn more about the students who would successfully earn their high school diplomas. That spring, thousands of high school juniors completed an abbreviated Grit Scale, along with a battery of other questionnaires. More than a year later, 12 percent of those students failed to graduate. Students who graduated on schedule were grittier, and grit was a more powerful predictor of graduation than how much students cared about school, how conscientious they were about their studies, and even how safe they felt at school.

Likewise, in two large American samples, I found that grittier adults were more likely to get further in their formal schooling. Adults who'd earned an MBA, PhD, MD, JD, or another graduate degree were grittier than those who'd only graduated from four-year colleges, who were in turn grittier than those who'd accumulated some college credits but no degree. Interestingly, adults who'd successfully earned degrees from two-year colleges scored slightly higher than graduates of four-year colleges. This puzzled me at first, but I soon learned that the dropout rates at community colleges can be as high as 80 percent. Those who defy the odds are especially gritty.

In parallel, I started a partnership with the Army Special Operations Forces, better known as the Green Berets. These are among the army's best-trained soldiers, assigned some of the toughest and most dangerous missions. Training for the Green Berets is a grueling, multistage affair. The stage I studied comes *after* nine weeks of boot camp, four weeks of infantry training, three weeks of airborne school, and four weeks of a preparation course focused on land navigation. All these preliminary training experiences are very, very hard, and at every stage there are men who don't make it through. But the Special Forces Selection Course is even harder. In the words of its commanding general, James Parker, this is "where we decide who will and who will not" enter the final stages of Green Beret training.

The Selection Course makes Beast Barracks look like summer vacation. Starting before dawn, trainees go full-throttle until nine in the evening. In addition to daytime and nighttime navigation exercises, there are four- and six-mile runs and marches, sometimes under a sixty-five-pound load, and attempts at an obstacle course informally known as "Nasty Nick," which includes crawling through water under barbed wire, walking on elevated logs, negotiating cargo nets, and swinging from horizontal ladders.

Just getting to the Selection Course is an accomplishment, but even so, 42 percent of the candidates I studied voluntarily withdrew before it was over. So what distinguished the men who made it through? Grit.

What else, other than grit, predicts success in the military, education, and business? In sales, I found that prior experience helps—novices are less likely to keep their jobs than those with experience. In the Chicago public school system, a supportive teacher made it more likely that students would graduate. And for aspiring Green Berets, baseline physical fitness at the start of training is essential.

But in each of these domains, when you compare people matched on these characteristics, grit still predicts success. Regardless of specific attributes and advantages that help someone succeed in each of these diverse domains of challenge, grit matters in all of them.

———

The year I started graduate school, the documentary *Spellbound* was released. The film follows three boys and five girls as they prepare for and compete in the finals of the Scripps National Spelling Bee.

To get to the finals—an adrenaline-filled three-day affair staged annually in Washington, DC, and broadcast live on ESPN, which normally focuses its programming on high-stakes sports matchups—these kids must first "outspell" thousands of other students from hundreds of schools across the country. This means spelling increasingly obscure words without a single error, in round after round, first besting all the other students in the contestant's classroom, then in their grade, school, district, and region.

Spellbound got me wondering: To what extent is flawlessly spelling words like *schottische* and *cymotrichous* a matter of precocious verbal talent, and to what extent is grit at play?

I called the Bee's executive director, a dynamic woman (and former champion speller herself) named Paige Kimble. Kimble was as curious as I was to learn more about the psychological makeup of winners. She agreed to send out questionnaires to all 273 spellers just as soon as they qualified for the finals, which would take place several months later. In return for the princely reward of a $25 gift card, about two-thirds of the spellers returned the questionnaires to my lab. The oldest respondent was fifteen years old, the absolute age limit according to competition rules, and the youngest was just seven.

In addition to completing the Grit Scale, spellers reported how much time they devoted to spelling practice. On average, they practiced more than an hour a day on weekdays and more than two hours a day on weekends. But there was a lot of variation around these averages: some spellers were hardly studying at all, and some were studying as much as nine hours on a given Saturday!

Separately, I contacted a subsample of spellers and administered a verbal intelligence test. As a group, the spellers demonstrated unusual verbal ability. But there was a fairly wide range of scores, with some kids scoring at the verbal prodigy level and others "average" for their age.

When ESPN aired the final rounds of the competition, I watched all the way through to the concluding suspenseful moments when, at last, thirteen-year-old Anurag Kashyap correctly spelled A-P-P-O-G-G-I-A-T-U-R-A (a musical term for a kind of grace note) to win the championship.

Then, with the final rankings in hand, I analyzed my data.

Here's what I found: measurements of grit taken months before the final competition predicted how well spellers would eventually perform. Put simply, grittier kids went further in competition. How did they do it? By studying many more hours and, also, by competing in more spelling bees.

What about talent? Verbal intelligence also predicted getting further in competition. But there was no relationship at all between verbal IQ and grit. What's more, verbally talented spellers did not study any more than less able spellers, nor did they have a longer track record of competition.

The separation of grit and talent emerged again in a separate study I ran on Ivy League undergraduates. There, SAT scores and grit were, in fact, inversely correlated. Students in that select sample who had higher SAT scores were, on average, just slightly less gritty than their peers. Putting together this finding with the other data I'd collected, I came to a fundamental insight that would guide my future work: *Our potential is one thing. What we do with it is quite another.*

Chapter 2

DISTRACTED BY TALENT

Before I was a psychologist, I was a teacher. It was in the classroom— years before I'd even heard of Beast—that I began to see that talent is not all there is to achievement.

I was twenty-seven when I started teaching full-time. The month before, I'd quit my job at McKinsey, a global management consulting firm whose New York City office occupied several floors of a blue-glass skyscraper in midtown. My colleagues were a bit bewildered by my decision. Why leave a company that most of my peers were dying to join—one regularly singled out as one of the world's smartest and most influential?

Acquaintances assumed I was trading eighty-hour workweeks for a more relaxed lifestyle, but of course, anyone who's been a teacher knows that there's no harder job in the world. So why leave? In some ways, it was consulting, not teaching, that was the detour. Throughout college, I'd tutored and mentored kids from the local public schools. After graduation, I started a tuition-free academic enrichment program and ran it for two years. Then I went to Oxford and completed a degree in neuroscience, studying the neural mechanisms of dyslexia. So when I started teaching, I felt like I was back on track.

Even so, the transition was abrupt. In a single week, my salary went from *Seriously? I actually get paid this much?* to *Wow! How the heck do teachers in this city make ends meet?* Dinner was now a sandwich eaten hurriedly while grading papers, not sushi ordered in at the client's expense. I commuted to work on the same subway line but stayed on the train past midtown, getting off six stops farther south: the Lower East Side. Instead of pumps, pearls, and a tailored suit, I wore sensible shoes I could stand in all day and dresses I wouldn't mind getting covered in chalk.

My students were twelve and thirteen years old. Most lived in the housing projects clustered between Avenues A and D. This was before the neighborhood sprouted hip cafés on every corner. The fall I started teaching there, our school was picked for the set of a movie about a rough-and-tumble school in a distressed urban neighborhood. My job was to help my students learn seventh-grade math: fractions and decimals and the rudimentary building blocks of algebra and geometry.

Even that first week, it was obvious that some of my students picked up mathematical concepts more easily than their classmates. Teaching the most talented students in the class was a joy. They were, quite literally, "quick studies." Without much prompting, they saw the underlying pattern in a series of math problems that less able students struggled to grasp. They'd watch me do a problem once on the board and say, "I get it!" and then work out the next one correctly on their own.

And yet, at the end of the first marking period, I was surprised to find that some of these very able students weren't doing as well as I'd expected. Some did very well, of course. But more than a few of my most talented students were earning lackluster grades or worse.

In contrast, several of the students who initially struggled were faring better than I'd expected. These "overachievers" would reliably come to class every day with everything they needed. Instead of playing around and looking out the window, they took notes and asked questions. When they didn't get something the first time around, they tried again and again, sometimes coming for extra help during their lunch period or during afternoon electives. Their hard work showed in their grades.

Apparently, aptitude did *not* guarantee achievement. Talent for math was different from excelling in math class.

This came as a surprise. After all, conventional wisdom says that math is a subject in which the more talented students are expected to excel, leaving classmates who are simply "not math people" behind. To be honest, I began the school year with that very assumption. It seemed a sure bet that those for whom things came easily would continue to outpace their classmates. In fact, I expected that the achievement gap separating the naturals from the rest of the class would only widen over time.

I'd been distracted by talent.

Gradually, I began to ask myself hard questions. When I taught a lesson and the concept failed to gel, could it be that the struggling student needed to struggle just a bit longer? Could it be that I needed to find a different way to explain what I was trying to get across? Before jumping to the conclusion that talent was destiny, should I be considering the importance of effort? And, as a teacher, wasn't it my responsibility to figure out how to sustain effort—both the students' and my own—just a bit longer?

At the same time, I began to reflect on how smart even my weakest students sounded when they talked about things that genuinely interested them. These were conversations I found almost impossible to follow: discourses on basketball statistics, the lyrics to songs they really liked, and complicated plotlines about who was no longer speaking to whom and why. When I got to know my students better, I discovered that all of them had mastered any number of complicated ideas in their very complicated daily lives. Honestly, was getting x all by itself in an algebraic equation all that much harder?

My students weren't equally talented. Still, when it came to learning seventh-grade math, could it be that if they and I mustered sufficient effort over time, they'd get to where they needed? Surely, I thought, they were all talented *enough*.

―――

Toward the end of the school year, my fiancé became my husband. For the sake of his own post-McKinsey career, we packed up and moved from New York to San Francisco. I found a new job teaching math at Lowell High School.

Compared to my Lower East Side classroom, Lowell was an alternate universe.

Tucked away in a perpetually foggy basin near the Pacific Ocean, Lowell is the only public high school in San Francisco that admits students on the basis of academic merit. The largest feeder to the University of California system, Lowell sends many of its graduates to the country's most selective universities.

If, like me, you were raised on the East Coast, you can think of Lowell as the Stuyvesant of San Francisco. Such imagery might bring to mind whiz kids who are leaps and bounds smarter than those who lack the top-notch test scores and grades to get in.

What I discovered was that Lowell students were distinguished more by their work ethic than by their intelligence. I once asked students in my homeroom how much they studied. The typical answer? Hours and hours. Not in a week, but in a single day.

Still, like at any other school, there was tremendous variation in how hard students worked and how well they performed.

Just as I'd found in New York, some of the students I expected to excel, because math came so easy to them, did worse than their classmates. On the other hand, some of my hardest workers were consistently my highest performers on tests and quizzes.

One of these very hard workers was David Luong.

David was in my freshman algebra class. There were two kinds of algebra classes at Lowell: the accelerated track led to Advanced Placement Calculus by senior year, and the regular track, which I was teaching, didn't. The students in my class hadn't scored high enough on Lowell's math placement exam to get into the accelerated track.

David didn't stand out at first. He was quiet and sat toward the back of the room. He didn't raise his hand a lot; he rarely volunteered to come to the board to solve problems.

But I soon noticed that every time I graded an assignment, David had turned in perfect work. He aced my quizzes and tests. When I marked one of his answers as incorrect, it was more often my error than his. And, wow, he was just so hungry to learn. In class, his attention was rapt. After class, he'd stay and ask, politely, for harder assignments.

I began to wonder what the heck this kid was doing in *my* class.

Once I understood how ridiculous the situation was, I marched David into the office of my department chair. It didn't take long to explain what was going on. Fortunately, the chair was a wise and wonderful teacher who placed a higher value on kids than on bureaucratic rules. She immediately started the paperwork to switch David out of my class and into the accelerated track.

My loss was the next teacher's gain. Of course, there were ups and downs, and not all of David's math grades were A's. "After I left your class, and switched into the more advanced one, I was a little behind," David later told me. "And the next year, math—it was geometry—continued to be hard. I didn't get an A. I got a B." In the next class, his first math test came back with a D.

"How did you deal with that?" I asked.

"I did feel bad—I did—but I didn't dwell on it. I knew it was done. I knew I had to focus on what to do next. So I went to my teacher and asked for help. I basically tried to figure out, you know, what I did wrong. What I needed to do differently."

By senior year, David was taking the harder of Lowell's two honors calculus courses. That spring, he earned a perfect 5 out of 5 on the Advanced Placement exam.

After Lowell, David attended Swarthmore College, graduating with dual degrees in engineering and economics. I sat with his parents at his graduation, remembering the quiet student in the back of my classroom who ended up proving that aptitude tests can get a lot of things wrong.

Two years ago, David earned a PhD in mechanical engineering from UCLA. His dissertation was on optimal performance algorithms for the thermodynamic processes in truck engines. In English: David used math to help make engines more efficient. Today, he is an engineer at the Aerospace Corporation. Quite literally, the boy who was deemed "not ready" for harder, faster math classes is now a "rocket scientist."

During the next several years of teaching, I grew less and less convinced that talent was destiny and more and more intrigued by the returns generated by effort. Intent on plumbing the depths of that mystery, I eventually left teaching to become a psychologist.

———

When I got to graduate school, I learned that psychologists have long wondered why some people succeed and others fail. Among the earliest was Francis Galton, who debated the topic with his half cousin, Charles Darwin.

By all accounts, Galton was a child prodigy. By four, he could read and write. By six, he knew Latin and long division and could recite passages from Shakespeare by heart. Learning came easy.

In 1869, Galton published his first scientific study on the origins of high achievement. After assembling lists of well-known figures in science, athletics, music, poetry, and law—among other domains—he gathered whatever biographical information he could. Outliers, Galton concluded, are remarkable in three ways: they demonstrate unusual "ability" in combination with exceptional "zeal" and "the capacity for hard labor."

After reading the first fifty pages of Galton's book, Darwin wrote a letter to his cousin, expressing surprise that talent made the short list of essential qualities. "You have made a convert of an opponent in one sense," wrote Darwin. "For I have always maintained that, excepting fools, men did not differ much in intellect, only in zeal and hard work; and I still think this is an *eminently* important difference."

Of course, Darwin himself was the sort of high achiever Galton was trying to understand. Widely acknowledged as one of the most influential scientists in history, Darwin was the first to explain diversity in plant and animal species as a consequence of natural selection. Relatedly, Darwin was an astute observer, not only of flora and fauna, but also of people. In a sense, his vocation was to observe slight differences that lead, ultimately, to survival.

So it's worth pausing to consider Darwin's opinion on the determinants of achievement—that is, his belief that zeal and hard work are ultimately more important than intellectual ability.

On the whole, Darwin's biographers don't claim he possessed supernatural intelligence. He was certainly intelligent, but insights didn't come to him in lightning flashes. He was, in a sense, a plodder. Darwin's own autobiography corroborates this view: "I have no great quickness of apprehension [that] is so remarkable in some clever men," he admits. "My power to follow a long and purely abstract train of thought is very limited." He would not have made a very good mathematician, he thinks, nor a philosopher, and his memory was subpar, too: "So poor in one sense is my memory that I have never been able to remember for more than a few days a single date or a line of poetry."

Perhaps Darwin was too humble. But he had no problem praising his power of observation and the assiduousness with which he applied it to understanding the laws of nature: "I think I am superior to the common run of men in noticing things which easily escape attention, and in observing them carefully. My industry has been nearly as great as it could have been in the observation and collection of facts. What is far more important, my love of natural science has been steady and ardent."

One biographer describes Darwin as someone who kept thinking about the same questions long after others would move on to different—and no doubt easier—problems:

> The normal response to being puzzled about something is to say,"I'll think about this later," and then, in effect, forget about it. With Darwin, one feels that he deliberately did not engage in this kind of semi-willful forgetting. He kept all the questions alive at the back of his mind, ready to be retrieved when a relevant bit of data presented itself.

———

Forty years later, on the other side of the Atlantic, a Harvard psychologist named William James took up the question of how people differ in their pursuit of goals. Toward the end of his long and distinguished career, James wrote an essay on the topic for *Science* (then and now the premier academic journal, not just for psychology but for all of the natural and social sciences). It was titled "The Energies of Men."

Reflecting on the achievements and failures of close friends and colleagues, and how the quality of his own efforts varied on his good and bad days, James observed:

> Compared with what we ought to be, we are only half awake. Our fires are damped, our drafts are checked. We are making use of only a small part of our possible mental and physical resources.

There is a gap, James declared, between potential and its actualization. Without denying that our talents vary—one might be more musical than athletic or more entrepreneurial than artistic—James asserted that "the human individual lives usually far within his limits; he possesses powers of various sorts which he habitually fails to use. He energizes below his maximum, and he behaves below his optimum."

"Of course there *are* limits," James acknowledged. "The trees don't grow into the sky." But these outer boundaries of where we will, eventually, stop improving are simply irrelevant for the vast majority of us: "The plain fact remains that men the world over possess amounts of resource, which only very exceptional individuals push to their extremes of use."

These words, written in 1907, are as true today as ever. So, why do we place such emphasis on talent? And why fixate on the extreme limits of what we might do when, in fact, most of us are at the very beginning of our journey, so far, far away from those outer bounds? And why do we assume that it is our talent, rather than our effort, that will decide where we end up in the very long run?

———

For years, several national surveys have asked: Which is more important to success—talent or effort? Americans are about twice as likely to single out effort. The same is true when you ask Americans about athletic ability. And when asked, "If you were hiring a new employee, which of the following qualities would you think is most important?" Americans endorse "being hardworking" nearly five times as often as they endorse "intelligence."

The results of these surveys are consistent with questionnaires that psychologist Chia-Jung Tsay has given to musical experts, who, when asked, reliably endorse effortful training as more important than natural talent. But when Chia probes attitudes more indirectly, she exposes a bias that tips in exactly the opposite direction: we love naturals.

In Chia's experiments, professional musicians learn about two pianists whose biographies are identical in terms of prior achievements. The subjects listen to a short clip of these individuals playing piano; unbeknownst to the listeners, a single pianist is, in fact, playing different parts of the same piece. What varies is that one pianist is described as a "natural" with early evidence of innate talent. The other is described as a "striver" with early evidence of high motivation and perseverance. In direct contradiction to their stated beliefs about the importance of effort versus talent, musicians judge the natural to be more likely to succeed and more hirable.

As a follow-up study, Chia tested whether this same inconsistency would be evident in a very different domain where hard work and striving are celebrated: entrepreneurship. She recruited hundreds of adults with varying levels of experience in business and randomly divided them into two groups. Half of her research subjects read the profile of a "striver" entrepreneur, described as having achieved success through hard work, effort, and experience. The other half read the profile of a "natural" entrepreneur, described as having achieved success through innate ability. All participants listened to the same audio recording of a business proposal and were told the recording was made by the specific entrepreneur they'd read about.

As in her study of musicians, Chia found that naturals were rated higher for likelihood of success and being hirable, and that their business proposals were judged superior in quality. In a related study, Chia found that when people were forced to choose between backing one of two entrepreneurs—one identified as a striver, the other a natural—they tended to favor the natural. In fact, the point of indifference between a striver and a natural was only reached when the striver had four more years of leadership experience and $40,000 more in start-up capital.

Chia's research pulls back the curtain on our ambivalence toward talent and effort. What we *say* we care about may not correspond with what—deep down—we actually *believe* to be more valuable. It's a little like saying we don't care at all about physical attractiveness in a romantic partner and then, when it comes to actually choosing whom to date, picking the cute guy over the nice one.

The "naturalness bias" is a hidden prejudice against those who've achieved what they have because they worked for it, and a hidden preference for those whom we think arrived at their place in life because they're naturally talented. We may not admit to others this bias for naturals; we may not even admit it to ourselves. But the bias is evident in the choices we make.

———

Chia's own life is an interesting example of the natural versus striver phenomenon. Now a professor at University College London, she publishes her scholarly work in the most prestigious of academic journals. As a child, she attended classes at Juilliard, whose pre-college program invites students "who exhibit the talent, potential, and accomplishment to pursue a career in music" to experience "an atmosphere where artistic gifts and technical skills can flourish."

Chia holds several degrees from Harvard. Her first was a bachelor's degree in psychology; she graduated magna cum laude with highest honors. She also has two master's degrees: one in the history of science and the other in social psychology. And, finally, while completing her PhD in organizational behavior and psychology at Harvard, she also picked up a secondary PhD in music.

Impressed? If not, let me add that Chia also has degrees from the Peabody Conservatory in piano performance and pedagogy—and yes, she's performed at Carnegie Hall, not to mention Lincoln Center, the Kennedy Center, and at the palace recital commemorating the presidency of the European Union.

If you only saw her credentials, you might leap to the conclusion that Chia was born more gifted than anyone you know: "My god! What an extraordinarily talented young woman!" And, if Chia's research is right, that explanation would embellish her accomplishments with more luster, more mystery, and more awe than the alternative: "My god! What an extraordinarily dedicated, hardworking young woman!"

And then what would happen? There's a vast amount of research on what happens when we believe a student is especially talented. We begin to lavish extra attention on them and hold them to higher expectations. We expect them to excel, and that expectation becomes a self-fulfilling prophecy.

I've asked Chia what she makes of her own musical accomplishments. "Well, I guess I may have some talent," Chia said. "But I think, more than that, I loved music so much I practiced four to six hours a day all throughout childhood." And in college, despite a punishing schedule of classes and activities, she made time to practice almost as much. So, yes, she has some talent—but she's a striver, too.

Why did Chia practice so much? I wondered. Was it forced on her? Did she have any choice in the matter?

"Oh, it was *me*. It was what I wanted. I wanted to get better and better and better. When I practiced piano, I pictured myself onstage in front of a crowded audience. I imagined them clapping."

———

The year I left McKinsey for teaching, three of the firm's partners published a report called "The War for Talent." The report was widely read and eventually became a best-selling book. The basic argument was that companies in the modern economy rise and fall depending on their ability to attract and retain "A players."

"What do we mean by *talent*?" the McKinsey authors ask in the book's opening pages. Answering their own question: "In the most general sense, talent is the sum of a person's abilities—his or her intrinsic gifts, skills, knowledge, experience, intelligence, judgment, attitude, character, and drive. It also includes his or her ability to learn and grow." That's a long list, and it reveals the struggle most of us have when we try to define talent with any precision. But it doesn't surprise me that "intrinsic gifts" are mentioned first.

When *Fortune* magazine put McKinsey on its cover, the lead article began: "When in the presence of a young McKinsey partner, one gets the distinct impression that if plied with a cocktail or two, he might well lean across the table and suggest something awkward, like comparing SAT scores." It's almost impossible, the journalist observed, to overestimate "the premium placed within the McKinsey culture on analytic ability, or as its denizens say, on being 'bright.'"

McKinsey is famous for recruiting and rewarding smart men and women—some with MBAs from places like Harvard and Stanford, and the rest, like me, who possess some other credential that suggests we must have very big brains.

My interviews with McKinsey unfolded as most do, with a series of brainteasers designed to test my analytic mettle. One interviewer sat me down and introduced himself, then asked: "How many tennis balls are manufactured in the United States per year?"

"I guess there are two ways to approach that question," I responded. "The first way is to find the right person, or maybe trade organization, to tell you." My interviewer nodded, but gave me a look that said he wanted the other kind of answer.

"Or you could take some basic assumptions and do some multiplying to figure it out."

My interviewer smiled broadly. So I gave him what he wanted.

"Okay, assume there are about two hundred fifty million people in the United States. Let's say the most active tennis players are between the age of ten and thirty. That's got to be, roughly speaking, one-fourth of the population. I guess that gives you a little over sixty million potential tennis players."

Now my interviewer was really excited. I continued the logic game, multiplying and dividing by numbers according to my completely uninformed estimates of how many people actually play tennis, and how often they play on average, and how many balls they would use in a game, and then how often they would need to replace dead or lost ones.

I got to some number, which was probably wildly off, because at every step I was making another uninformed assumption that was, to some degree or another, incorrect. Finally, I said: "The math here isn't that hard for me. I'm tutoring a little girl who is practicing her fractions right now, and we do a lot of mental math together. But if you want to know what I'd *really* do if I needed to know the answer to that question, I'll tell you: I'd just call someone who actually knows."

More smiling, and then an assurance that he'd learned all he needed to from our interaction. And also from my application—including my SAT scores, which McKinsey heavily relies on to do their early sorting of candidates. In other words, if the advice to corporate America is to create a culture that values talent above all else, McKinsey practices what it preaches.

———

Once I accepted the offer to join the New York City office, I was told that my first month would be spent in a fancy hotel in Clearwater, Florida. There I joined about three dozen other new hires who, like me, lacked any training in business. Instead, each of us had earned some other academic badge of honor. I sat next to a guy with a PhD in physics, for example. On my other side was a surgeon, and behind me were two lawyers.

None of us knew much about management in general, or about any industry in particular. But that was about to change: in a single month, we would complete a crash course called the "mini-MBA." Since we were all vetted to be superfast learners, there was no question that we would successfully master a massive amount of information in a very short amount of time.

Newly equipped with a casual acquaintance with cash flow, the difference between revenue and profit, and some other rudimentary facts about what I now knew to call "the private sector," we were shipped off to our designated offices around the world, where we would join teams of other consultants and be matched up with corporate clients to solve whatever problems they threw our way.

I soon learned that McKinsey's basic business proposition is straightforward. For a very large sum of money per month, companies can hire a McKinsey team to solve problems too thorny to be solved by the folks who are already working on them. At the end of this "engagement," as it was called in the firm, we were supposed to produce a report that was dramatically more insightful than anything they could have generated in-house.

It occurred to me, as I was putting together slides summarizing bold, sweeping recommendations for a multibillion-dollar medical products conglomerate, that, really, I had no idea what I was talking about. There were senior consultants on the team who may have known more, but there were also more junior consultants who, having just graduated from college, surely knew even less.

Why hire us, then, at such an exorbitant cost? Well, for one thing, we had the advantage of an outsider's perspective untainted by insider politics. We also had a method for solving business problems that was hypothesis and data driven. There were probably lots of good reasons CEOs brought in McKinsey. But among them, I think, was that we were supposed to be sharper than the people who were already on-site. Hiring McKinsey meant hiring the very "best and brightest"—as if being the brightest also made us the best.

———

According to *The War for Talent*, the companies that excel are those that aggressively promote the most talented employees while just as aggressively culling the least talented. In such companies, huge disparities in salary are not only justified but desirable. Why? Because a competitive, winner-take-all environment encourages the *most* talented to stick around and the *least* talented to find alternative employment.

Duff McDonald, the journalist who's done the most in-depth research on McKinsey to date, has suggested that this particular business philosophy would be more aptly titled *The War on Common Sense*. McDonald points out that the companies highlighted in the original McKinsey report as exemplars of their endorsed strategy didn't do so well in the years after that report was published.

Journalist Malcolm Gladwell has also critiqued the *The War for Talent*. Enron, he points out, epitomized the "talent mindset" approach to management advocated by McKinsey. As we all know, the Enron story doesn't have a happy ending. Once one of the largest energy trading companies in the world, Enron was named America's Most Innovative Company by *Fortune* magazine six years in a row. Yet, by the end of 2001, when the business filed for bankruptcy, it had become clear that the company's extraordinary profits were attributable to massive and systematic accounting fraud. When Enron collapsed, thousands of its employees, who had no hand at all in the wrongdoing, lost their jobs, health insurance, and retirement savings. At the time, it was the largest corporate bankruptcy in U.S. history.

You can't blame the Enron debacle on a surfeit of IQ points. You can't blame it on a lack of grit, either. But Gladwell argues convincingly that demanding Enron employees prove that they were smarter than everyone else inadvertently contributed to a narcissistic culture, with an overrepresentation of employees who were both incredibly smug and driven by deep insecurity to keep showing off. It was a culture that encouraged short-term performance but discouraged long-term learning and growth.

The same point comes through in the postmortem documentary on Enron called, appropriately enough, *The Smartest Guys in the Room*. During the company's ascendency, it was a brash and brilliant former McKinsey consultant named Jeff Skilling who was Enron's CEO. Skilling developed a performance review system for Enron that consisted of grading employees annually and summarily firing the bottom 15 percent. In other words, no matter what your absolute level of performance, if you were weak, relative to others, you got fired. Inside Enron, this practice was known as "rank-and-yank." Skilling considered it one of the most important strategies his company had. But ultimately, it may have contributed to a work environment that rewarded deception and discouraged integrity.

———

Is talent a bad thing? Are we all equally talented? No and no. The ability to quickly climb the learning curve of any skill is obviously a very good thing, and, like it or not, some of us are better at it than others.

So why, then, is it such a bad thing to favor "naturals" over "strivers"? What's the downside of television shows like *America's Got Talent*, *The X Factor*, and *Child Genius*? Why shouldn't we separate children as young as seven or eight into two groups: those few children who are "gifted and talented" and the many, many more who aren't? What harm is there, really, in a talent show being named a "talent show"?

In my view, the biggest reason a preoccupation with talent can be harmful is simple: By shining our spotlight on talent, we risk leaving everything else in the shadows. We inadvertently send the message that these other factors—including grit—don't matter as much as they really do.

Consider, for example, the story of Scott Barry Kaufman. Scott's office is just two doors down from mine, and he's a lot like the other academic psychologists I know: He spends most of his waking hours reading, thinking, collecting data, doing statistics, and writing. He publishes his research in scientific journals. He knows a lot of polysyllabic words. He has degrees from Carnegie Mellon, Cambridge University, and Yale. He plays the cello *for fun*.

But as a child, Scott was considered a slow learner—which was true. "Basically, I got a lot of ear infections as a kid," Scott explains. "And that led to this problem with processing information from sound in real time. I was always a step or two behind the other kids in my class." So halting was his academic progress, in fact, that he was placed in special education classes. He repeated third grade. Around the same time, he met with a school psychologist to take an IQ test. In an anxiety-ridden test session he describes as "harrowing," Scott performed so poorly that he was sent to a special school for children with learning disabilities.

It was not until age fourteen that an observant special education teacher took Scott aside and asked why he wasn't in more challenging classes. Until then, Scott had never questioned his intellectual status. Instead, he'd assumed that his lack of talent would put a very low ceiling on what he might do with his life.

Meeting a teacher who believed in his potential was a critical turning point: a pivot from *This is all you can do* to *Who knows what you can do?* At that moment, Scott started wondering, for the very first time: *Who am I? Am I a learning disabled kid with no real future? Or maybe something else?*

And then, to find out, Scott signed up for just about every challenge his school had to offer. Latin class. The school musical. Choir. He didn't necessarily excel in everything, but he *learned* in all. What Scott learned is that he wasn't hopeless.

Something that Scott found he *did* learn fairly easily was the cello. His grandfather had been a cellist in the Philadelphia Orchestra for nearly fifty years, and Scott had the idea that his grandfather could give him lessons. He did, and the summer that Scott first picked up the cello, he began practicing eight or nine hours a day. He was fiercely determined to improve, and not only because he enjoyed the cello: "I was so driven to just show someone, anyone, that I was intellectually capable of anything. At this point I didn't even care what it was."

Improve he did, and by the fall, he earned a seat in his high school orchestra. If the story ended there and then, it might not be about grit. But here's what happened next. Scott kept up—and even increased—his practicing. He skipped lunch to practice. Sometimes he skipped classes to practice. By senior year, he was second chair—he was the second-best cellist in the orchestra—and he was in the choir, too, and winning all kinds of awards from the music department.

He also started doing well in his classes, many of which were now honors classes. Almost all of his friends were in the gifted and talented program, and Scott wanted to join them. He wanted to talk about Plato and do mental puzzles and learn more than he was already learning. Of course, with his IQ scores from childhood, there was no such possibility. He remembers the school psychologist drawing a bell-shaped curve on the back of a napkin and pointing to its peak—"This is average"—then moving to the right—"This is where you'd have to be for gifted and talented classes"—and then moving to the left—"And this is where you are."

"At what point," Scott asked, "does achievement trump potential?"

The school psychologist shook his head and showed Scott the door.

That fall, Scott decided he wanted to study this thing called "intelligence" and come to his own conclusions. He applied to the cognitive science program at Carnegie Mellon University. And he was rejected. The rejection letter did not specify why, of course, but given his stellar grades and extracurricular accomplishments, Scott could only conclude that the impediment was his low SAT scores.

"I had this grit," Scott recalls. "I said, 'I'm going to do it. I don't care. I'm going to find a way to study what I want to study.' " And then Scott auditioned for Carnegie Mellon's opera program. Why? Because the opera program didn't look very hard at SAT scores, focusing instead on musical aptitude and expression. In his first year, Scott took a psychology course as an elective. Soon after, he added psychology as a minor.

Next, he transferred his major from opera to psychology. And then he graduated Phi Beta Kappa.

———

Like Scott, I took an IQ test early in my schooling and was deemed insufficiently bright to benefit from gifted and talented classes. For whatever reason—maybe a teacher asked that I be retested—I was evaluated again the following year, and I made the cut. I guess you could say I was borderline gifted.

One way to interpret these stories is that talent is great, but *tests* of talent stink. There's certainly an argument to be made that tests of talent—and tests of anything else psychologists study, including grit— are highly imperfect.

But another conclusion is that the focus on talent distracts us from something that is at least as important, and that is effort. In the next chapter, I'll argue that, as much as talent counts, effort counts twice.

Chapter 3

EFFORT COUNTS TWICE

Not a day goes by that I don't read or hear the word *talent*. In every section of the newspaper—from the sports page to the business section, from profiles of actors and musicians in the weekend supplement, to front-page stories of rising stars in politics—allusions to talent abound. It seems that when anyone accomplishes a feat worth writing about, we rush to anoint that individual as extraordinarily "talented."

If we overemphasize talent, we underemphasize everything else. In the extreme, it's as if, deep down, we hold the following to be true:

For instance, I recently listened to a radio commentator draw a comparison between Hillary and Bill Clinton. He observed that both are unusually good communicators. But while her husband, Bill, is a gifted politician, Hillary has to contort herself into the role. Bill is a natural; Hillary merely a striver. The unsaid but obvious implication is that she'll never quite be his equal.

I've caught myself doing it, too. When someone really, really impresses me, I might reflexively say to myself: *What a genius!* I should know better. I do. So what's going on? Why does an unconscious bias toward talent persist?

———

A few years ago, I read a study of competitive swimmers titled "The Mundanity of Excellence." The title of the article encapsulates its major conclusion: the most dazzling human achievements are, in fact, the aggregate of countless individual elements, each of which is, in a sense, ordinary.

Dan Chambliss, the sociologist who completed the study, observed: "Superlative performance is really a confluence of dozens of small skills or activities, each one learned or stumbled upon, which have been carefully drilled into habit and then are fitted together in a synthesized whole. There is nothing extraordinary or superhuman in any one of those actions; only the fact that they are done consistently and correctly, and all together, produce excellence."

But mundanity is a hard sell. When finishing up his analyses, Dan shared a few chapters with a colleague. "You need to jazz it up," his friend said. "You need to make these people more interesting. . . ."

When I called Dan to probe a few of his observations, I learned that he'd become fascinated with the idea of talent—and what we really mean by it—as a swimmer himself and, for several years afterward, as a part-time coach. As a young assistant professor, Dan decided to do an in-depth, qualitative study of swimmers. In total, Dan devoted six years to interviewing, watching, and sometimes living and traveling with swimmers and coaches at all levels—from the local swim club to an elite team made up of future Olympians.

"Talent," he observed, "is perhaps the most pervasive lay explanation we have for athletic success." It is as if talent were some invisible "substance behind the surface reality of performance, which finally distinguishes the best among our athletes." And these great athletes seem blessed "with a special gift, almost a 'thing' inside of them, denied to the rest of us—perhaps physical, genetic, psychological, or physiological. Some have 'it,' and some don't. Some are 'natural athletes,' and some aren't."

I think Dan is exactly right. If we can't explain how an athlete, musician, or anyone else has done something jaw-droppingly amazing, we're inclined to throw up our hands and say, "It's a gift! Nobody can teach you that." In other words, when we can't easily see how experience and training got someone to a level of excellence that is so clearly beyond the norm, we default to labeling that person a "natural."

Dan points out that the biographies of great swimmers reveal many, many factors that contribute to their ultimate success. For instance, the most accomplished swimmers almost invariably had parents who were interested in the sport and earned enough money to pay for coaching, travel to swim meets, and not the least important: access to a pool. And, crucially, there were the thousands of hours of practice in the pool over years and years—all spent refining the many individual elements whose sum create a single flawless performance.

Though it seems wrong to assume that talent is a complete explanation for dazzling performance, it's also understandable. "It's easy to do," Dan explained, "especially if one's only exposure to top athletes comes once every four years while watching the Olympics on television, or if one only sees them in performances rather than in day-to-day training."

Another point he makes is that the minimal talent needed to succeed in swimming is lower than most of us think.

"I don't think you mean to say that any of us could be Michael Phelps," I said. "*Do* you?"

"No, of course not," Dan replied. "To begin with, there are certain anatomical advantages that you really can't train for."

"And," I continued, "wouldn't you say that some swimmers improve more than others, even if they're trying equally hard and getting the same coaching?"

"Yes, but the main thing is that greatness is doable. Greatness is many, many individual feats, and each of them is doable."

Dan's point is that if you had a time-lapse film of the hours and days and weeks and years that produced excellence, you could see what he saw: that a high level of performance is, in fact, an accretion of mundane acts. But does the incremental mastery of mundane individual components explain everything? I wondered. Is that all there is?

"Well, we all love mystery and magic," he said. "I do, too."

Then Dan told me about the day he got to watch Rowdy Gaines and Mark Spitz swim laps. "Spitz won seven gold medals in the '72 Olympics and was the big thing before Michael Phelps," he explained. "In '84, twelve years after retirement, Spitz showed up. He's in his mid-thirties. And he gets into the water with Rowdy Gaines, who at that time held the world record in the one hundred free. They did some fifties—in other words, two lengths of the pool, just sprints, like little races. Gaines won most of them, but by the time they were halfway through, the entire team was standing around the edge of the pool just to watch Spitz swim."

Everyone on the team had been training with Gaines, and they knew how good he was. They knew he was favored to win Olympic gold. But because of the age gap, nobody had swum with Spitz.

One swimmer turned to Dan and said, pointing to Spitz, "My god. He's a fish."

I could hear the wonder in Dan's voice. Even a student of mundanity, it seems, is easily lulled into talent explanations. I pressed him a bit. Was that sort of majestic performance something divine?

Dan told me to go read Nietzsche.

Nietzsche? The *philosopher*? What would a nineteenth-century

German philosopher have to say that might explain Mark Spitz? As it turns out, Nietzsche, too, had thought long and hard about the same questions.

———

"With everything perfect," Nietzsche wrote, "we do not ask how it came to be." Instead, "we rejoice in the present fact as though it came out of the ground by magic."

When I read that passage, I thought of the young swimmers watching their icon Spitz exhibit form that almost didn't seem human.

"No one can see in the work of the artist how it has *become*," Nietzsche said. "That is its advantage, for wherever one can see the act of becoming one grows somewhat cool." In other words, we *want* to believe that Mark Spitz was born to swim in a way that none of us were and that none of us could. We don't want to sit on the pool deck and watch him progress from amateur to expert. We prefer our excellence fully formed. We prefer mystery to mundanity.

But why? What's the reason for fooling ourselves into thinking Mark Spitz didn't *earn* his mastery?

"Our vanity, our self-love, promotes the cult of the genius," Nietzsche said. "For if we think of genius as something magical, we are not obliged to compare ourselves and find ourselves lacking. . . . To call someone 'divine' means: 'here there is no need to compete.'"

In other words, mythologizing natural talent lets us all off the hook. It lets us relax into the status quo. That's what undoubtedly occurred in my early days of teaching when I mistakenly equated talent and achievement, and by doing so, removed effort—both my students' and my own—from further consideration.

So what is the reality of greatness? Nietzsche came to the same conclusion Dan Chambliss did. Great things are accomplished by those "people whose thinking is active in *one* direction, who employ everything as material, who always zealously observe their own inner life and that of others, who perceive everywhere models and incentives, who never tire of combining together the means available to them."

And what about talent? Nietzsche implored us to consider exemplars to be, above all else, craftsmen: "Do not talk about giftedness, inborn talents! One can name great men of all kinds who were very little gifted. They *acquired* greatness, became 'geniuses' (as we put it). . . . They all possessed that seriousness of the efficient workman which first learns to construct the parts properly before it ventures to fashion a great whole; they allowed themselves time for it, because they took more pleasure in making the little, secondary things well than in the effect of a dazzling whole."

———

In my second year of graduate school, I sat down to a weekly meeting with my advisor, Marty Seligman. I was more than a little nervous. Marty has that effect on people, especially his students.

Then in his sixties, Marty had won just about every accolade psychology has to offer. His early research led to an unprecedented understanding of clinical depression. More recently, as president of the American Psychological Association, he christened the field of Positive Psychology, a discipline that applies the scientific method to questions of human flourishing.

Marty is barrel-chested and baritone-voiced. He may study happiness and well-being, but *cheerful* is not a word I'd use to describe him.

In the middle of whatever it was I was saying—a report on what I'd done in the past week, I suppose, or the next steps in one of our research studies—Marty interrupted. "You haven't had a good idea in two years."

I stared at him, openmouthed, trying to process what he'd just said. Then I blinked. Two years? I hadn't even been in graduate school for two years!

Silence.

Then he crossed his arms, frowned, and said: "You can do all kinds of fancy statistics. You somehow get every parent in a school to return their consent form. You've made a few insightful observations. But you don't have a theory. You don't have a theory for the psychology of achievement."

Silence.

"What's a theory?" I finally asked, having absolutely no clue as to what he was talking about.

Silence.

"Stop reading so much and go think."

I left his office, went into mine, and cried. At home with my husband, I cried more. I cursed Marty under my breath—and aloud as well—for being such a jerk. Why was he telling me what I was doing wrong? Why wasn't he praising me for what I was doing right?

You don't have a theory. . . .

Those words rattled around in my mind for days. Finally, I dried my tears, stopped my cursing, and sat down at my computer. I opened the word processor and stared at the blinking cursor, realizing I hadn't gotten far beyond the basic observation that talent was not enough to succeed in life. I hadn't worked out how, exactly, talent and effort and skill and achievement all fit together.

———

A theory is an explanation. A theory takes a blizzard of facts and observations and explains, in the most basic terms, what the heck is going on. By necessity, a theory is incomplete. It oversimplifies. But in doing so, it helps us understand.

If talent falls short of explaining achievement, what's missing?

I have been working on a theory of the psychology of achievement since Marty scolded me for not having one. I have pages and pages of diagrams, filling more than a dozen lab notebooks. After more than a decade of thinking about it, sometimes alone, and sometimes in part-nership with close colleagues, I finally published an article in which I lay down two simple equations that explain how you get from talent to achievement.

Here they are:

talent x *effort* = skill

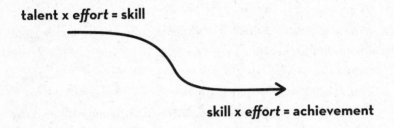

skill x *effort* = achievement

Talent is how quickly your skills improve when you invest effort. Achievement is what happens when you take your acquired skills and use them. Of course, your opportunities—for example, having a great coach or teacher—matter tremendously, too, and maybe more than anything about the individual. My theory doesn't address these outside forces, nor does it include luck. It's about the psychology of achieve-ment, but because psychology isn't all that matters, it's incomplete.

Still, I think it's useful. What this theory says is that when you consider individuals in identical circumstances, what each achieves depends on just two things, talent and effort. Talent—how fast we improve in skill—absolutely matters. But effort factors into the calcu-lations *twice*, not once. Effort builds skill. At the very same time, effort makes skill *productive*. Let me give you a few examples.

———

There's a celebrated potter named Warren MacKenzie who lives in Minnesota. Now ninety-two years old, he has been at his craft, with-out interruption, for nearly his entire adult life. Early on, he and his late wife, also an artist, tried a lot of different things: "You know, when you're young, you think you can do anything, and we thought, oh, we'll be potters, we'll be painters, we'll be textile designers, we'll be jewelers, we'll be a little of this, a little of that. We were going to be the renaissance people."

It soon became clear that doing one thing better and better might be more satisfying than staying an amateur at many different things: "Eventually both of us gave up the drawing and painting, gave up the silk-screening, gave up the textile design, and concentrated on ceramic work, because that was where we felt our true interest lay."

MacKenzie told me "a good potter can make forty or fifty pots in a day." Out of these, "some of them are good and some of them are mediocre and some of them are bad." Only a few will be worth selling, and of those, even fewer "will continue to engage the senses after daily use."

Of course, it's not just the number of good pots MacKenzie makes that has brought the art world to his door. It's the beauty and form of the pots: "I'm striving to make things which are the most exciting things I can make that will fit in people's homes." Still, as a simplification, you might say that the number of enduringly beautiful, exquisitely useful pots MacKenzie is able to produce, in total, will be what he accomplishes as an artist. It would not satisfy him to be among the most masterful potters but only produce, say, one or two pieces in his lifetime.

MacKenzie still throws clay on the wheel every day, and with effort his skill has improved: "I think back to some of the pots we made when we first started our pottery, and they were pretty awful pots. We thought at the time they were good; they were the best we could make, but our thinking was so elemental that the pots had that quality also, and so they don't have a richness about them which I look for in my work today."

"The first 10,000 pots are difficult," he has said, "and then it gets a little bit easier."

As things got easier, and as MacKenzie improved, he produced more good pots a day:

talent x *effort* = skill

At the same time, the number of good pots he's brought into the world increased:

skill x *effort* = achievement

With effort, MacKenzie has gotten better and better at making "the most exciting things I can make that will fit in people's homes." At the same time, with the same invested effort, he has become more accomplished.

————

"Garp was a natural storyteller."

This is a line from John Irving's fourth novel, *The World According to Garp*. Like that novel's fictional protagonist, Irving tells a great story. He has been lauded as "the great storyteller of American literature today." To date, he's written more than a dozen novels, most of which have been best sellers and half of which have been made into movies. *The World According to Garp* won the National Book Award, and Irving's screenplay for *The Cider House Rules* won an Academy Award.

But unlike Garp, Irving was not a natural. While Garp "could make things up, one right after the other, and they seemed to fit," Irving rewrites draft after draft of his novels. Of his early attempts at writing, Irving has said, "Most of all, I rewrote everything . . . I began to take my lack of talent seriously."

Irving recalls earning a C− in high school English. His SAT verbal score was 475 out of 800, which means almost two-thirds of the students who took the SAT did better than him. He needed to stay in high school an extra year to have enough credits to graduate. Irving recalls that his teachers thought he was both "lazy" and "stupid."

Irving was neither lazy nor stupid. But he was severely dyslexic: "I was an underdog. . . . If my classmates could read our history assignment in an hour, I allowed myself two or three. If I couldn't learn to spell, I would keep a list of my most frequently misspelled words." When his own son was diagnosed with dyslexia, Irving finally understood why he, himself, had been such a poor student. Irving's son read noticeably slower than his classmates, "with his finger following the sentence—as I read, as I *still* read. Unless I've written it, I read whatever 'it' is very slowly—and with my finger."

Since reading and writing didn't come easily, Irving learned that "to do anything really well, you have to overextend yourself. . . . In my case, I learned that I just had to pay twice as much attention. I came to appreciate that in doing something over and over again, something that was never natural becomes almost second nature. You learn that you have the capacity for that, and that it doesn't come overnight."

Do the precociously talented learn that lesson? Do they discover that the capacity to do something over and over again, to struggle, to have patience, can be mastered—but not overnight?

Some might. But those who struggle early may learn it better: "One reason I have confidence in writing the kind of novels I write," Irving said, "is that I have confidence in my stamina to go over something again and again no matter how difficult it is." After his tenth novel, Irving observed, "Rewriting is what I do best as a writer. I spend more time revising a novel or screenplay than I take to write the first draft."

"It's become an advantage," Irving has observed of his inability to read and spell as fluently as others. "In writing a novel, it doesn't hurt anybody to have to go slowly. It doesn't hurt anyone as a writer to have to go over something again and again."

With daily effort, Irving became one of the most masterful and prolific writers in history. With effort, he became a master, and with effort, his mastery produced stories that have touched millions of people, including me.

———

Grammy Award–winning musician and Oscar-nominated actor Will Smith has thought a lot about talent, effort, skill, and achievement. "I've never really viewed myself as particularly talented," he once observed. "Where I excel is ridiculous, sickening work ethic."

Accomplishment, in Will's eyes, is very much about going the distance. Asked to explain his ascendancy to the entertainment elite, Will said:

> The only thing that I see that is distinctly different about me is: I'm not afraid to die on a treadmill. I will not be outworked, period. You might have more talent than me, you might be smarter than me, you might be sexier than me. You might be all of those things. You got it on me in nine categories. But if we get on the treadmill together, there's two things: You're getting off first, or I'm going to die. It's really that simple.

In 1940, researchers at Harvard University had the same idea. In a study designed to understand the "characteristics of healthy young men" in order to "help people live happier, more successful lives," 130 sophomores were asked to run on a treadmill for up to five minutes. The treadmill was set at such a steep angle and cranked up to such a fast speed that the average man held on for only four minutes. Some lasted for only a minute and a half.

By design, the Treadmill Test was exhausting. Not just physically but mentally. By measuring and then adjusting for baseline physical fitness, the researchers designed the Treadmill Test to gauge "stamina and strength of will." In particular, Harvard researchers knew that running hard was not just a function of aerobic capacity and muscle strength but also the extent to which "a subject is willing to push himself or has a tendency to quit before the punishment becomes too severe."

Decades later, a psychiatrist named George Vaillant followed up on the young men in the original Treadmill Test. Then in their sixties, these men had been contacted by researchers every two years since graduating from college, and for each there was a corresponding file folder at Harvard literally bursting with questionnaires, correspondence, and notes from in-depth interviews. For instance, researchers noted for each man his income, career advancement, sick days, social activities, self-reported satisfaction with work and marriage, visits to psychiatrists, and use of mood-altering drugs like tranquilizers. All this information went into composite estimates of the men's overall psychological adjustment in adulthood.

It turns out that run time in the Treadmill Test at age twenty was a surprisingly reliable predictor of psychological adjustment throughout adulthood. George and his team considered that staying on the treadmill was also a function of how physically fit these men were in their youth, and that this finding merely indicated that physical health predicted later psychological well-being. However, they found that adjusting for baseline physical fitness "had little effect on the correlation of running time with mental health."

In other words, Will Smith is on to something. When it comes to how we fare in the marathon of life, effort counts tremendously.

"How long would *you* have stayed on the treadmill?" I asked George recently. I wanted to know because, in my eyes, George is himself a paragon of grit. Early in his career, not long after completing his residency in psychiatry, George discovered the treadmill data, along with all the other information on the men collected to that point. Like a baton, the study had been handed from one research team to another, with dwindling interest and energy. Until it got to him.

George revived the study. He reestablished contact with the men by mail and phone and, in addition, interviewed each in person, traveling to all corners of the world to do so. Now in his eighties, George has outlived most of the men in the original study. He is currently writing his fourth book on what is by now the longest continuous study of human development ever undertaken.

In answer to my question about his own treadmill perseverance, George replied, "Oh, I'm not all that persistent. When I do crossword puzzles on the airplane, I always look at the answers when I am a little bit frustrated."

So, not very gritty when it comes to crossword puzzles.

"And when something is broken in the house, I turn it over to my wife, and she fixes it."

"So you don't think you're gritty?" I asked.

"The reason why the Harvard study works is that I have been doing it constantly and persistently. It's the one ball I've kept my eye on. Because I'm totally fascinated by it. There is nothing more interesting than watching people grow."

And then, after a short pause, George recalled his days at prep school, where, as a varsity track athlete, he competed in pole vaulting. To improve, he and the other vaulters did pull-ups, which he calls "chins," because you start by hanging off a bar and then pull yourself up to where your chin hovers just above, then you drop down again, and repeat.

"I could do more chins than anyone. And it wasn't because I was very athletic—I wasn't. The reason is that I *did* a lot of chin-ups. I practiced."

The prolific writer and director Woody Allen, when asked about his advice for young artists, once said:

> My observation was that once a person actually completed a play or a novel he was well on his way to getting it produced or published, as opposed to a vast majority of people who tell me their ambition is to write, but who strike out on the very first level and indeed never write the play or book.

Or, in Allen's snappier formulation, "Eighty percent of success in life is showing up."

Back in the 1980s, both George H. W. Bush and Mario Cuomo frequently repeated this bit of wisdom in speech after speech, turning the saying into something of a meme. So, while these leaders of the Republican and Democratic parties must have disagreed on a great many things, they were in complete consensus on the importance of following through on what one has started.

I told George Vaillant that, if I'd been on the Harvard research team in 1940, I would have made a suggestion. I would have allowed the young men to come back the next day, if they wanted, and try the Treadmill Test again. I suspect that some would have come back to see if they could stay on longer, whereas others would have been content with their first timed effort. Maybe some would ask the researchers whether they knew of any strategies, physical or mental, in order to last longer. And maybe these fellows would even be interested in a third try, and a fourth. . . . Then I would create a grit score based on how many times men voluntarily returned to see if they could improve.

Staying on the treadmill is one thing, and I do think it's related to staying true to our commitments even when we're not comfortable. But getting back on the treadmill the next day, eager to try again, is in my view even more reflective of grit. Because when you don't come back the next day—when you permanently turn your back on a commitment—your effort plummets to zero. As a consequence, your skills stop improving, and at the same time, you stop producing anything with whatever skills you have.

The treadmill is, in fact, an appropriate metaphor. By some estimates, about 40 percent of people who buy home exercise equipment later say they ended up using it less than they'd expected. How hard we push ourselves in a given workout matters, of course, but I think the bigger impediment to progress is that sometimes we stop working out altogether. As any coach or athlete will tell you, consistency of effort over the long run is everything.

How often do people start down a path and then give up on it entirely? How many treadmills, exercise bikes, and weight sets are at this very moment gathering dust in basements across the country? How many kids go out for a sport and then quit even before the season is over? How many of us vow to knit sweaters for all of our friends but only manage half a sleeve before putting down the needles? Ditto for home vegetable gardens, compost bins, and diets. How many of us start something new, full of excitement and good intentions, and then give up—permanently—when we encounter the first real obstacle, the first long plateau in progress?

Many of us, it seems, quit what we start far too early and far too often. Even more than the effort a gritty person puts in on a single day, what matters is that they wake up the next day, and the next, ready to get on that treadmill and keep going.

———

If I have the math approximately right, then someone twice as talented but half as hardworking as another person might reach the same level of skill but still produce dramatically less over time. This is because as strivers are improving in skill, they are also *employing* that skill—to make pots, write books, direct movies, give concerts. If the quality and quantity of those pots, books, movies, and concerts are what count, then the striver who equals the person who is a natural in skill by working harder will, in the long run, accomplish more.

"The separation of talent and skill," Will Smith points out, "is one of the greatest misunderstood concepts for people who are trying to excel, who have dreams, who want to do things. Talent you have naturally. Skill is only developed by hours and hours and hours of beating on your craft."

I would add that skill is not the same thing as achievement, either. Without effort, your talent is nothing more than your unmet potential. Without effort, your skill is nothing more than what you could have done but didn't. With effort, talent becomes skill and, at the very same time, effort makes skill *productive*.

Chapter 4

HOW GRITTY ARE YOU?

I recently gave a lecture on grit to undergraduates at the Wharton School of Business. Even before I'd cleared my notes from the podium, an aspiring entrepreneur rushed to introduce himself.

He was charming—full of the energy and enthusiasm that makes teaching young people so rewarding. Breathlessly, he told me a story meant to illustrate his own prodigious grit. Earlier that year, he'd raised thousands of dollars for his start-up, going to heroic lengths to do so, and pulling several all-nighters in the process.

I was impressed and said so. But I hastened to add that grit is more about stamina than intensity. "So, if you're working on that project with the same energy in a year or two, email me. I can say more about your grit then."

He was puzzled. "Well, I might not be working on the same thing in a few years."

Good point. Lots of ventures that seem promising at the start turn out badly. Lots of optimistic business plans end up in the discard bin.

"Okay, so maybe this *particular* start-up won't be what you're working on. But if you're not working in the same industry, if you're on to some *totally unrelated* pursuit, then I'm not sure your story illustrates grit."

"You mean, stay in one company?" he asked.

"Not necessarily. But skipping around from one kind of pursuit to another—from one skill set to an entirely different one—that's not what gritty people do."

"But what if I move around a lot and, while I'm doing that, I'm working incredibly hard?"

"Grit isn't *just* working incredibly hard. That's only part of it."

Pause.

"Why?"

"Well, for one thing, there are no shortcuts to excellence. Developing real expertise, figuring out really hard problems, it all takes time— longer than most people imagine. And then, you know, you've got to apply those skills and produce goods or services that are valuable to people. Rome wasn't built in a day."

He was listening, so I continued.

"And here's the really important thing. Grit is about working on something you care about so much that you're willing to stay loyal to it."

"It's doing what you love. I get that."

"Right, it's doing what you love, but not just falling in love—*staying in love.*"

———

How gritty are you? Below is a version of the Grit Scale I developed for my study at West Point and which I used in other studies described in this book. Read each sentence and, on the right, check off the box that makes sense. Don't overthink the questions. Instead, just ask yourself how you compare—not just to your coworkers, friends, or family—but to "most people."

	Not at all like me	Not much like me	Some- what like me	Mostly like me	Very much like me
1. New ideas and projects sometimes distract me from previous ones.	5	4	3	2	1
2. Setbacks don't discourage me. I don't give up easily.	1	2	3	4	5
3. I often set a goal but later choose to pursue a different one.	5	4	3	2	1
4. I am a hard worker.	1	2	3	4	5
5. I have difficulty maintaining my focus on projects that take more than a few months to complete.	5	4	3	2	1
6. I finish whatever I begin.	1	2	3	4	5
7. My interests change from year to year.	5	4	3	2	1
8. I am diligent. I never give up.	1	2	3	4	5
9. I have been obsessed with a certain idea or project for a short time but later lost interest.	5	4	3	2	1
10. I have overcome setbacks to conquer an important challenge.	1	2	3	4	5

To calculate your total grit score, add up all the points for the boxes you checked and divide by 10. The maximum score on this scale is 5 (extremely gritty), and the lowest possible score is 1 (not at all gritty).

You can use the chart below to see how your scores compare to a large sample of American adults.*

Percentile	Grit Score
10%	2.5
20%	3.0
30%	3.3
40%	3.5
50%	3.8
60%	3.9
70%	4.1
80%	4.3
90%	4.5
95%	4.7
99%	4.9

Keep in mind that your score is a reflection of how you see yourself right now. How gritty you are at this point in your life might be different from how gritty you were when you were younger. And if you take the Grit Scale again later, you might get a different score. As this book will continue to show, there is every reason to believe that grit can change.

Grit has two components: passion and perseverance. If you want to dig a little deeper, you can calculate separate scores for each component: For your passion score, add up your points for the odd-numbered

---

* If, for example, you scored 4.1, you're grittier than about 70 percent of the adults in our sample.

items and divide by 5. For your perseverance score, add up your points for the even-numbered items and divide by 5.

If you scored high on passion, you probably scored high on perseverance, too. And vice versa. Still, I'll take a guess that your perseverance score is a wee bit higher than your passion score. This isn't true for all people, but it's true for most people I've studied. For instance, I took the scale while writing this chapter, and I scored 4.6 overall. My perseverance score was 5.0, and my passion score was only 4.2. Strange as it sounds, staying focused on consistent goals over time is more of a struggle for me than working hard and bouncing back from setbacks.

This consistent pattern—perseverance scores more often topping passion scores—is a clue that passion and perseverance aren't exactly the same thing. In the rest of this chapter, I'll explain how they differ and show how to understand them as two parts of a whole.

———

While taking the Grit Scale, you might have noticed that none of the passion questions asked how *intensely* you're committed to your goals. This may seem odd, because the word *passion* is often used to describe intense emotions. For a lot of people, passion is synonymous with infatuation or obsession. But in interviews about what it takes to succeed, high achievers often talk about commitment of a different kind. Rather than intensity, what comes up again and again in their remarks is the idea of *consistency over time*.

For instance, I've heard of chefs who grew up watching Julia Child on television and remained fascinated with cooking into adulthood. I've heard of investors whose curiosity about the financial markets is as keen in their fourth or fifth decade of investing as it was on their very first day of trading. I've heard of mathematicians who work on a problem—the *same* problem—day and night for years, without once deciding, "Oh, to heck with this theorem! I'm moving on to something else." And that's why the questions that generate your passion score ask you to reflect on how *steadily* you hold to goals over time. Is *passion* the right word to describe sustained, enduring devotion? Some might say I should find a better word. Maybe so. But the important thing is the idea itself: Enthusiasm is common. Endurance is rare.

Consider, for example, Jeffrey Gettleman. For about a decade, Jeff has been the East Africa bureau chief for the *New York Times*. In 2012, he won the Pulitzer Prize for International Reporting for his coverage of conflict in East Africa. He's a bit of a celebrity in the world of international journalism, widely admired for his courage to pursue stories that put his life at risk and, also, for his willingness to unflinchingly report events that are unthinkably horrific.

I met Jeff when we were in our early twenties. At the time, both of us were pursuing master's degrees at Oxford University. For me, this was before McKinsey, before teaching, and before becoming a psychologist. For Jeff, this was before he'd written his first news story. I think it's fair to say that, back then, neither of us knew quite what we wanted to be when we grew up—and we were both trying desperately to figure it out.

I caught up with Jeff on the phone recently. He was in Nairobi, his home base between trips to other parts of Africa. Every few minutes, we had to ask each other if we could still be heard. After reminiscing about our classmates and trading news about our children, I asked Jeff to reflect on the idea of passion and how it had played out in his life.

"For a very long time, I've had a very clear sense of where I wanted to be," Jeff told me. "And that passion is to live and work in East Africa."

"Oh, I didn't know—I assumed your passion was journalism, not a certain area of the world. If you could only be a journalist or only live in East Africa, which would you choose?"

I expected Jeff to pick journalism. He didn't.

"Look, journalism is a great fit for me. I've always gravitated towards writing. I've always been okay being in new situations. Even the confrontational side of journalism—that speaks to my personality. I like to challenge authority. But I think journalism has been, in a sense, a means to an end."

Jeff's passion emerged over a period of years. And it wasn't just a process of passive discovery—of unearthing a little gem hidden inside his psyche—but rather of active construction. Jeff didn't just go looking for his passion—he helped create it.

Moving to Ithaca, New York, from Evanston, Illinois, Jeff, at eighteen years old, could not have predicted his future career. At Cornell, he ended up majoring in philosophy, in part because "it was the easiest to fulfill the requirements." Then, the summer after freshman year, he visited East Africa. And that was the beginning of the beginning: "I don't know how to explain it. This place just blew my mind. There was a spirit here that I wanted to connect with, and I wanted to make it a part of my life."

As soon as he got back to Cornell, Jeff started taking courses in Swahili, and after sophomore year, he took a year off to backpack around the world. During that trip, he returned to East Africa, experiencing the same wonder he'd felt the first time he visited.

Still, it wasn't clear how he'd make a life there. How did he hit on journalism as a career path? A professor who admired Jeff's writing suggested as much, and Jeff remembers thinking, "That is the dumbest idea I had heard . . . who wants to work for a boring newspaper?" (I remember thinking the same thing once about becoming a professor: *Who wants to be a boring professor?*) Eventually, Jeff did work for the student paper, the *Cornell Daily Sun*—but as a photographer, not a writer.

"When I got to Oxford, I was pretty lost academically. It was shocking to the Oxford professors that I didn't really know what I wanted to do. They were like, 'Why are you here? This is a serious place. You should have a firm sense of what you want to study or you shouldn't be here.'"

My guess at the time was that Jeff would pursue photojournalism.

He reminded me of Robert Kincaid, the worldly, wise photographer played by Clint Eastwood in *The Bridges of Madison County*, which was released around the time we became friends. In fact, I can still remember the photographs Jeff showed me twenty years ago. I thought they were from *National Geographic*, but he'd actually taken them himself.

By his second year at Oxford, he figured out that journalism was an even better fit: "Once I learned more about being a journalist and how that could get me back to Africa, and how that actually would be fun, and I could write more creatively than I first imagined journalism was, then I was like, 'Screw it, this is what I'm going to do.' I set out a very deliberate path that was possible, because the journalism industry was very hierarchical, and it was clear how to get from A to B to C to D, et cetera."

Step A was writing for Oxford's student newspaper, *Cherwell*. Step B was a summer internship at a small paper in Wisconsin. Step C was the *St. Petersburg Times* in Florida on the Metro beat. Step D was the *Los Angeles Times*. Step E was the *New York Times* as a national correspondent in Atlanta. Step F was being sent overseas to cover war stories, and in 2006—just over a decade since he'd set himself the goal—he finally reached step G: becoming the *New York Times*' East Africa bureau chief.

"It was a really winding road that took me to all kinds of places. And it was difficult, and discouraging, and demoralizing, and scary, and all the rest. But eventually, I got here. I got exactly where I wanted to be."

As for so many other grit paragons, the common metaphor of passion as fireworks doesn't make sense when you think of what passion means to Jeff Gettleman. Fireworks erupt in a blaze of glory but quickly fizzle, leaving just wisps of smoke and a memory of what was once spectacular. What Jeff's journey suggests instead is passion as a *compass*—that thing that takes you some time to build, tinker with, and finally get right, and that then guides you on your long and winding road to where, ultimately, you want to be.

Seattle Seahawks coach Pete Carroll puts it this way: "Do you have a life philosophy?"

For some of us, the question makes no sense. We might say: *Well, I have a lot of things I'm pursuing. A lot of goals. A lot of projects. Which do you mean?*

But others have no problem answering with conviction: *This is what I want.*

Everything becomes a bit clearer when you understand the level of the goal Pete is asking about. He's not asking about what you want to get done today, specifically, or even this year. He's asking what you're trying to get out of life. In grit terms, he's asking about your passion.

Pete's philosophy is: *Do things better than they have ever been done before.* Like with Jeff, it took a while to figure out what, in the broader sense, he was aiming for. The pivotal moment came at a low point in his coaching career: just after getting fired as head coach of the New England Patriots. This was the first and only year in his life when Pete wasn't playing or coaching football. At that juncture, one of his good friends urged him to consider something more abstract than which job to take next: "You've got to have a philosophy."

Pete realized he didn't have one and needed to: "If I was ever going to get the chance to run an organization again, I would have to be prepared with a philosophy that would drive all my actions." Pete did a lot of thinking and reflecting: "My life in the next weeks and months was filled with writing notes and filling binders." At the same time, he was devouring the books of John Wooden, the legendary UCLA basketball coach who won a record-setting ten national championships.

Like a lot of coaches, Pete had already read Wooden. But this time, he was reading Wooden and understanding, at a much deeper level, what the coaching icon had to say. And the most important thing

Wooden said was that, though a team has to do a million things well, figuring out the overarching vision is of utmost importance.

Pete realized in that moment that particular goals—winning a particular game, or even a seasonal championship, or figuring out this element of the offensive lineup, or the way to talk to players—needed coordination, needed purpose: "A clear, well-defined philosophy gives you the guidelines and boundaries that keep you on track," he said.

———

One way to understand what Pete is talking about is to envision goals in a hierarchy.

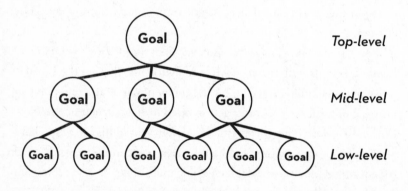

At the bottom of this hierarchy are our most concrete and specific goals—the tasks we have on our short-term to-do list: I want to get out the door today by eight a.m. I want to call my business partner back. I want to finish writing the email I started yesterday. These low-level goals exist merely as *means to ends*. We want to accomplish them only because they get us something *else* we want. In contrast, the higher the goal in this hierarchy, the more abstract, general, and important it is. The higher the goal, the more it's an end in itself, and the less it's merely a *means* to an end.

In the diagram I've sketched out here, there are just three levels.

That's an oversimplification. Between the lowest and the highest level might be several layers of mid-level goals. For instance, getting out the door by eight a.m. is a low-level goal. It only matters because of a mid-level goal: arriving at work on time. Why do you care about that? Because you want to be punctual. Why do you care about that? Because being punctual shows respect for the people with whom you work. Why is that important? Because you strive to be a good leader.

If in the course of asking yourself these "Why?" questions your answer is simply "Just because!" then you know you've gotten to the top of a goal hierarchy. The top-level goal is not a means to any other end. It is, instead, an *end in itself*. Some psychologists like to call this an "ultimate concern." Myself, I think of this top-level goal as a compass that gives direction and meaning to all the goals below it.

Consider Hall of Fame pitcher Tom Seaver. When he retired in 1987 at the age of forty-two, he'd compiled 311 wins; 3,640 strikeouts; 61 shutouts; and a 2.86 earned run average. In 1992, when Seaver was elected to the Hall of Fame, he received the highest-ever percentage of votes: 98.8 percent. During his twenty-year professional baseball career, Seaver aimed to pitch "the best I possibly can day after day, year after year." Here is how that intention gave meaning and structure to all his lower-order goals:

> Pitching . . . determines what I eat, when I go to bed, what I do when I'm awake. It determines how I spend my life when I'm not pitching. If it means I have to come to Florida and can't get tanned because I might get a burn that would keep me from throwing for a few days, then I never go shirtless in the sun. . . . If it means I have to remind myself to pet dogs with my left hand or throw logs on the fire with my left hand, then I do that, too. If it means in the winter I eat cottage cheese instead of chocolate chip cookies in order to keep my weight down, then I eat cottage cheese.

The life Seaver described sounds grim. But that's not how Seaver saw things: "Pitching is what makes me happy. I've devoted my life to it. . . . I've made up my mind what I want to do. I'm happy when I pitch well so I only do things that help me be happy."

What I mean by passion is not just that you have something you care about. What I mean is that you care about that *same* ultimate goal in an abiding, loyal, steady way. You are not capricious. Each day, you wake up thinking of the questions you fell asleep thinking about. You are, in a sense, pointing in the same direction, ever eager to take even the smallest step forward than to take a step to the side, toward some other destination. At the extreme, one might call your focus obsessive. Most of your actions derive their significance from their allegiance to your ultimate concern, your life philosophy.

You have your priorities in order.

Grit is about holding the same top-level goal for a very long time. Furthermore, this "life philosophy," as Pete Carroll might put it, is so interesting and important that it organizes a great deal of your waking activity. In very gritty people, most mid-level and low-level goals are, in some way or another, related to that ultimate goal. In contrast, a lack of grit can come from having less coherent goal structures.

Here are a few ways a lack of grit can show itself. I've met many young people who can articulate a dream—for example, to be a doctor or to play basketball in the NBA—and can vividly imagine how wonderful that would be, but they can't point to the mid-level and lower-level goals that will get them there. Their goal hierarchy has a top-level goal but no supporting mid-level or low-level goals:

This is what my good friend and fellow psychologist Gabriele Oettingen calls "positive fantasizing." Gabriele's research suggests that indulging in visions of a positive future without figuring out how to get there, chiefly by considering what obstacles stand in the way, has short-term payoffs but long-term costs. In the short-term, you feel pretty great about your aspiration to be a doctor. In the long-term, you live with the disappointment of not having achieved your goal.

Even more common, I think, is having a bunch of mid-level goals that don't correspond to any unifying, top-level goal:

Or having a few competing goal hierarchies that aren't in any way connected with each other:

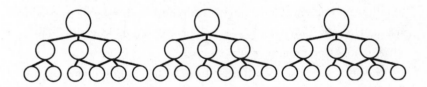

To some extent, goal conflict is a necessary feature of human existence. For instance, I have one goal hierarchy as a professional and another as a mother. Even Tom Seaver admits that the travel and practice schedule of a professional baseball player made it hard to spend as much time with his wife and children as he would have liked. So, though pitching was his professional passion, there were other goal hierarchies that obviously mattered to him.

Like Seaver, I have one goal hierarchy for work: *Use psychological science to help kids thrive.* But I have a separate goal hierarchy that involves being the best mother I can be to my two daughters. As any working parent knows, having two "ultimate concerns" isn't easy. There seems never to be enough time, energy, or attention to go around. I've decided to live with that tension. As a young woman, I considered alternatives—not having my career or not raising a family—and decided that, morally, there was no "right decision," only a decision that was right for me.

So, the idea that every waking moment in our lives should be guided by one top-level goal is an idealized extreme that may not be desirable even for the grittiest of us. Still, I would argue that it's possible to pare down long lists of mid-level and low-level work goals according to how they serve a goal of supreme importance. And I think *one* top-level *professional* goal, rather than any other number, is ideal.

In sum, the more unified, aligned, and coordinated our goal hierarchies, the better.

————

Warren Buffett—the self-made multibillionaire whose personal wealth, acquired entirely within his own lifetime, is roughly twice the size of Harvard University's endowment—reportedly gave his pilot a simple three-step process for prioritizing.

The story goes like this: Buffett turns to his faithful pilot and says that he must have dreams greater than flying Buffett around to where he needs to go. The pilot confesses that, yes, he does. And then Buffett takes him through three steps.

First, you write down a list of twenty-five career goals.

Second, you do some soul-searching and circle the five highest-priority goals. Just five.

Third, you take a good hard look at the twenty goals you didn't circle. These you avoid at all costs. They're what distract you; they eat away time and energy, taking your eye from the goals that matter more.

When I first heard this story, I thought, *Who could have as many as twenty-five different career goals? That's kind of ridiculous, isn't it?* Then

I started writing down on a piece of lined paper all of the projects I'm currently working on. When I got to line thirty-two, I realized that I could benefit from this exercise.

Interestingly, most of the goals I spontaneously thought of were mid-level goals. People generally default to that level of goal when they're asked to write down a number of goals, not just one.

To help me prioritize, I added columns that allowed me to sort out how interesting and important these projects were. I rated each goal on a scale from 1 to 10, from least to most interesting and then again from least to most important. I multiplied these numbers together to get a number from 1 to 100. None of my goals had an "interest x importance" rating as high as 100, but none were as low as 1, either.

Then I tried to take Buffett's advice and circle just a few of the most interesting and important goals, relegating the rest to the avoid-at-all-cost category.

I tried, but I just couldn't do it.

After a day or so of wondering who was right—me or Warren Buffett—I realized that a lot of my goals were, in fact, related to one another. The majority, in fact, were means to ends, setting me up to make progress toward one ultimate goal: helping kids achieve and thrive. There were only a few professional goals for which this wasn't true. Reluctantly, I decided to put those on the avoid-at-all-cost list.

Now, if I could ever sit down with Buffett and go through my list with him (which is unlikely, since I doubt my needs rate a place in his goal hierarchy), he would surely tell me that the point of this exercise is to face the fact that time and energy are limited. Any successful person has to decide what to do in part by deciding what *not* to do. I get that. And I still have a ways to go on that count.

But I would also say that conventional prioritizing isn't enough. When you have to divide your actions among a number of very different high-level career goals, you're extremely conflicted. You need *one* internal compass—not two, three, four, or five.

Frank Modell, the *New Yorker*, July 7, 1962, The New Yorker Collection/The Cartoon Bank.

So, to Buffett's three-step exercise in prioritizing, I would add an additional step: Ask yourself, *To what extent do these goals serve a common purpose?* The more they're part of the same goal hierarchy— important because they then serve the same ultimate concern—the more focused your passion.

If you follow this method of prioritization, will you become a Hall of Fame pitcher or earn more money than anyone else in history? Probably not. But you'll stand a better chance of getting somewhere you care about—a better chance of moving closer to where you *want* to be.

———

When you see your goals organized in a hierarchy, you realize that grit is not at all about stubbornly pursuing—at all costs and ad infinitum— *every* single low-level goal on your list. In fact, you can expect to aban- don a few of the things you're working very hard on at this moment.

Not all of them will work out. Sure, you should try hard—even a little longer than you might think necessary. But don't beat your head against the wall attempting to follow through on something that is, merely, a means to a more important end.

I thought about how important it is to know how low-level goals fit into one's overall hierarchy when I listened to Roz Chast, the celebrated *New Yorker* cartoonist, give a talk at the local library. She told us her rejection rate is, at this stage in her career, about 90 percent. She claimed that it used to be much, much higher.

I called Bob Mankoff, the cartoon editor for the *New Yorker*, to ask how typical that number is. To me, it seemed shockingly high. Bob told me that Roz was indeed an anomaly. *Phew!* I thought. I didn't want to think about all the cartoonists in the world getting rejected nine times out of ten. But then Bob told me that most cartoonists live with *even more* rejection. At his magazine, "contract cartoonists," who have dramatically better odds of getting published than anyone else, collectively submit about five hundred cartoons every week. In a given issue, there is only room, on average, for about seventeen of them. I did the math: that's a rejection rate of more than 96 percent.

"Holy smokes! Who would keep going when the odds are that grim?"

Well, for one: Bob himself.

Bob's story reveals a lot about how dogged perseverance toward a top-level goal requires, paradoxically perhaps, some flexibility at lower levels in the goal hierarchy. It's as if the highest-level goal gets written in ink, once you've done enough living and reflecting to know what that goal is, and the lower-level goals get written in pencil, so you can revise them and sometimes erase them altogether, and then figure out new ones to take their place.

Here's my not-at-all-*New Yorker*–quality drawing to show what I mean:

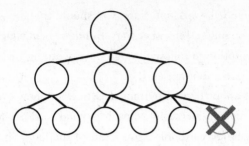

The low-level goal with the angry-looking X through it has been blocked. It's a rejection slip, a setback, a dead end, a failure. The gritty person will be disappointed, or even heartbroken, but not for long.

Soon enough, the gritty person identifies a new low-level goal—draws another cartoon, for example—that serves the same purpose.

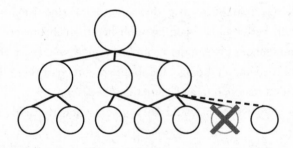

One of the mottos of the Green Berets is: "Improvise, adapt, over-come." A lot of us were told as children, "If at first you don't succeed, try, try again." Sound advice, but as they say "try, try again, then try something different." At lower levels of a goal hierarchy, that's exactly what's needed.

Here's Bob Mankoff's story:

Like Jeff Gettleman, the *New York Times* East Africa bureau chief, Bob didn't always have a clearly defined passion. As a child, Bob liked to draw, and instead of attending his local high school in the Bronx, he went to the LaGuardia High School of Music and Art, later fictionalized in the movie *Fame*. Once there, though, he got a look at the competition and was intimidated.

"Being exposed to real drawing talent," Bob recalls, "made mine wither. I didn't touch a pen, pencil, or paintbrush for three years after graduating." Instead, he enrolled at Syracuse University, where he studied philosophy and psychology.

In his senior year, he bought a book called *Learning to Cartoon* by the legendary Syd Hoff, an exemplar of the "effort counts twice" maxim. Over his lifetime, Hoff contributed 571 cartoons to the *New Yorker*, wrote and illustrated more than sixty children's books, drew two syndicated comic strips, and contributed literally thousands of drawings and cartoons to other publications. Hoff's book opens cheerily with "Is it hard becoming a cartoonist? No, it isn't. And to prove it, I've written this book. . . ." It ends with a chapter called "How to Survive Rejection Slips." In between are lessons on composition, perspective, the human figure, facial expressions, and so on.

Bob used Hoff's advice to create twenty-seven cartoons. He walked from one magazine to another, trying to make a sale—but not the *New Yorker*, which didn't see cartoonists in person. And he was, of course, summarily rejected by every editor he saw. Most asked him to try again, with more cartoons, the next week. "More?" Bob wondered. "How could anyone do more than twenty-seven cartoons?"

Before he could reread Hoff's last chapter on rejection slips, Bob received notice that he was eligible to be drafted for combat in Vietnam. He had no great desire to go; in fact, he had a great desire *not* to. So he repurposed himself—quickly—as a graduate student in experimental psychology. Over the next few years, while running rats in mazes, he found time, when he could, to draw. Then, just before earning his doctorate, he had the realization that research psychology wasn't his calling: "I remember thinking that my defining personality characteristic was something else. I'm the funniest guy you ever met—that's the way I thought of myself—I'm *funny*."

For a while, Bob considered two ways of making humor his career: "I said, okay, I'm going to do stand-up, or I'm going to be a cartoonist." He threw himself into both with gusto: "All day I would write routines and then, at night, I would draw cartoons." But over time, one of these two mid-level goals became more attractive than the other: "Stand-up was different back then. There weren't really comedy clubs. I'd have to go to the Borscht Belt, and I didn't really want to. . . . I knew my humor was not going to work like I wanted it to for these people."

So Bob dropped stand-up comedy and devoted his entire energy to cartoons. "After two years of submitting, all I had to show for it were enough *New Yorker* rejection slips to wallpaper my bathroom." There were small victories—cartoons sold to other magazines—but by that time Bob's top-level goal had become a whole lot more specific and ambitious: He didn't just want to be funny for a living, he wanted to be among the best cartoonists in the world. "The *New Yorker* was to cartooning what the New York Yankees were to baseball—the Best Team," Bob explains. "If you could make that team, you too were one of the best."

The piles of rejection slips suggested to Bob that "try, try again" was not working. He decided to do something different. "I went to the New York Public Library and I looked up all the cartoons back to 1925 that had ever been printed in the *New Yorker*." At first, he thought maybe he didn't draw well enough, but it was plain to see that some very successful *New Yorker* cartoonists were third-rate draftsmen. Then Bob thought that something might be awry with the length of his captions—too short or too long—but that possibility wasn't supported, either. Captions were generally brief, but not always, and anyway, Bob's didn't seem unusual in that respect. Then Bob thought maybe he was missing the mark with his *type* of humor. No again: some successful cartoons were whimsical, some satirical, some philosophical, and some just interesting.

The one thing all the cartoons had in common was this: they made the reader *think*.

And here was another common thread: every cartoonist had a personal style that was distinctively their own. There was no single "best" style. On the contrary, what mattered was that style was, in some very deep and idiosyncratic way, an expression of the individual cartoonist.

Paging through, literally, every cartoon the *New Yorker* had ever published, Bob knew he could do as well. Or better. "I thought, 'I can do this, I can do this.' I had complete confidence." He knew he could draw cartoons that would make people think, and he knew he could develop his own style: "I worked through various styles. Eventually I did my dot style." The now-famous dot style of Bob's cartoons is called stippling, and Bob had originally tried it out back in high school, when he discovered the French impressionist Georges Seurat.

After getting rejected from the *New Yorker* about two thousand times between 1974 and 1977, Bob sent in the cartoon, below. It was accepted.

Robert Mankoff, the *New Yorker*, June 20, 1977, The *New Yorker* Collection/The Cartoon Bank.

The next year, he sold thirteen cartoons to the *New Yorker*, then twenty-five the following year, then twenty-seven. In 1981, Bob received a letter from the magazine asking if he'd consider becoming a contract cartoonist. He said yes.

———

In his role as editor and mentor, Bob advises aspiring cartoonists to submit their drawings in batches of ten, "because in cartooning, as in life, nine out of ten things never work out."

Indeed, giving up on lower-level goals is not only forgivable, it's sometimes absolutely necessary. You should give up when one lower-level goal can be swapped for another that is more feasible. It also makes sense to switch your path when a different lower-level goal—a different means to the same end—is just more efficient, or more fun, or for whatever reason makes more sense than your original plan.

On any long journey, detours are to be expected.

However, the higher-level the goal, the more it makes sense to be stubborn. Personally, I try not to get too hung up on a particular rejected grant application, academic paper, or failed experiment. The pain of those failures is real, but I don't dwell on them for long before moving on. In contrast, I don't give up as easily on mid-level goals, and frankly, I can't imagine anything that would change my ultimate aim, my life philosophy, as Pete might say. My compass, once I found all the parts and put it together, keeps pointing me in the same direction, week after month after year.

———

Long before I conducted the first interviews that put me on the trail of grit, a Stanford psychologist named Catharine Cox was, herself, cataloging the characteristics of high achievers.

In 1926, Cox published her findings, based on the biographical details of 301 exceptionally accomplished historical figures. These eminent individuals included poets, political and religious leaders, scientists, soldiers, philosophers, artists, and musicians. All lived and died in the four centuries prior to Cox's investigation, and all left behind records of accomplishment worthy of documentation in six popular encyclopedias.

Cox's initial goal was to estimate how smart each of these individuals were, both relative to one another and also compared to the rest of humanity. In pursuit of those estimates, she combed through the available evidence, searching for signs of intellectual precocity—and from the age and superiority of these accomplishments she reckoned each person's childhood IQ. The published summary of this study—if you can call a book of more than eight hundred pages a summary— includes a case history for each of Cox's 301, arranged in order from least to most intelligent.

According to Cox, the very smartest in the bunch was the philosopher John Stuart Mill, who earned an estimated childhood IQ score of 190 by learning Greek at age three, writing a history of Rome at age six, and assisting his father in correcting the proofs of a history of India at age twelve. The least intelligent in Cox's ranking—whose estimated childhood IQs of 100 to 110 are just a hair above average for humanity—included the founder of modern astronomy, Nicolaus Copernicus; the chemist and physicist Michael Faraday; and the Spanish poet and novelist Miguel de Cervantes. Isaac Newton ranks squarely in the middle, with an IQ of 130—the bare minimum that a child needs in order to qualify for many of today's gifted and talented programs.

From these IQ estimates, Cox concluded that, as a group, accomplished historical figures are smarter than most of us. No surprise there.

A more unexpected observation was how little IQ mattered in distinguishing the most from the least accomplished. The average childhood IQ of the most eminent geniuses, whom Cox dubbed the First Ten, was 146. The average IQ of the least eminent, dubbed the Last Ten, was 143. The spread was trivial. In other words, the relationship between intelligence and eminence in Cox's sample was *exceedingly slight*.

Cox's First Ten (Most Eminent Geniuses)

Sir Francis Bacon

Napoleon Bonaparte

Edmund Burke

Johann Wolfgang von Goethe

Martin Luther

John Milton

Isaac Newton

William Pitt

Voltaire

George Washington

Cox's Last Ten (Least Eminent Geniuses)

Christian K. J. von Bunsen

Thomas Chalmers

Thomas Chatterton

Richard Cobden

Samuel Taylor Coleridge

Georges J. Danton

Joseph Haydn

Hugues-Félicité-Robert de Lamennais

Giuseppe Mazzini

Joachim Murat

If intellectual talent wasn't the determinant of whether a person ascended to the First Ten or was relegated to the Last Ten, then what was? While poring over thousands of pages of biographical data, Cox and her assistant also evaluated sixty-seven different personality traits for a subset of one hundred geniuses. Cox deliberately chose a rainbow of traits—in fact, she covered the full range of what modern psychologists consider to be important—to allow for the fullest possible exploration of the differences that set apart the eminent from the rest of humanity and, further, the First Ten from the Last Ten.

For most of the sixty-seven indicators, Cox found only trivial differences between the eminent and the general population. For instance, eminence had little to do with extroversion, cheerfulness, or sense of humor. And not all the high achievers had earned high marks in school. Rather, what definitively set apart the eminent from the rest of humanity were a cluster of four indicators. Notably, these also distinguished the First Ten from the Last Ten—the super-eminent from the merely eminent. Cox grouped these together and called them "persistence of motive."

Two indicators could easily be rephrased as passion items for the Grit Scale.

Degree to which he works with distant objects in view (as opposed to living from hand to mouth). Active preparation for later life. Working toward a definite goal.

Tendency not to abandon tasks from mere changeability. Not seeking something fresh because of novelty. Not "looking for a change."

And the other two could easily be rewritten as perseverance items for the Grit Scale.

Degree of strength of will or perseverance. Quiet determination to stick to a course once decided upon.

Tendency not to abandon tasks in the face of obstacles. Perseverance, tenacity, doggedness.

In her summary comments, Cox concluded that "high but not the highest intelligence, combined with the greatest degree of persistence, will achieve greater eminence than the highest degree of intelligence with somewhat less persistence."

———

However *you* scored on the Grit Scale, I hope it prompted self-reflection. It's progress just clarifying your goals, and the extent to which they are—or aren't—aligned toward a single passion of supreme importance. It's also progress to better understand how well you're currently able to persevere in the face of life's rejection slips.

It's a start. Let's continue, in the next chapter, to see how grit can and does change. And, then, in the rest of the book, let's learn how to accelerate that growth.

Chapter 5

GRIT GROWS

"How much of our grit is in our genes?"

I'm asked some version of this question pretty much anytime I give a talk on grit. The nature-nurture question is a very basic one. We have an intuitive sense that some things about us—like our height—are pretty much determined in the genetic lottery, while other things—like whether we speak English or French—are a result of our upbringing and experience. "You can't train height" is a popular expression in basketball coaching, and many people who learn about grit want to know if it's more like height or more like language.

To the question of whether we get grit from our DNA, there is a short answer and a long one. The short answer is "in part." The long answer is, well, more complicated. In my view, the longer answer is worth our attention. Science has made huge strides in figuring out how genes, experience, and their interplay make us who we are. From what I can tell, the inherent complexity of these scientific facts has led, unfortunately, to their continually being misunderstood.

To begin, I can tell you with complete conviction that every human trait is influenced by *both* genes and experience.

Consider height. Height is indeed heritable: genetic differences are a big reason why some people are really tall, some really short, and a bunch of people are of varying heights in between.

But it's also true that the *average* height of men and women has increased dramatically in just a few generations. For instance, military records show that the average British man was five feet five inches tall about 150 years ago, but today that average is five feet ten inches. Height gains have been even more dramatic in other countries; in the Netherlands, the average man now stands almost six foot one—a gain of more than six inches over the last 150 years. I am reminded of these dramatic generational gains in height whenever I get together with my Dutch collaborators. They bend down solicitously, but it still feels like standing in a forest of redwoods.

It's unlikely that the gene pool has changed all that dramatically in just a few generations. Instead, the most powerful height boosters have been nutrition, clean air and water, and modern medicine. (Incidentally, generational gains in weight have been even more dramatic, and again, that seems to be the consequence of eating more and moving around less rather than changes in our DNA.) Even within a generation, you can see the influence of environment on height. Children who are provided healthy food in abundance will grow up taller, whereas malnourishment stunts growth.

Likewise, traits like honesty and generosity and, yes, grit, are genetically influenced and, in addition, influenced by experience. Ditto for IQ, extroversion, enjoying the great outdoors, having a sweet tooth, the likelihood that you'll end up a chain-smoker, your risk of getting skin cancer, and really any other trait you can think of. Nature matters, and so does nurture.

———

Talents, in all their varieties, are also genetically influenced. Some of us are born with genes that make it easier to learn to carry a tune, or dunk a basketball, or solve a quadratic equation. But against intuition, talents are *not* entirely genetic: the rate at which we develop any skill is also, crucially, a function of experience.

For instance, sociologist Dan Chambliss swam competitively in high school but stopped when it seemed clear he wasn't going to make it as a nationally ranked swimmer.

"I'm small," he explained, "and my ankles won't plantar flex." Come again? "I can't point my toes. I can only flex them. It's an anatomical limitation. Which means, basically, at the elite level, I could only swim breaststroke." After our exchange, I did a little research on plantar flexion. Stretching exercises can improve your range of motion, but the length of certain bones does make a difference in how flexible your feet and ankles are.

Still, the biggest impediment to improving wasn't anatomy; it was how he was coached: "In retrospect, I look back now and can see I had horribly bad coaches in a couple of crucial places. One of my high school coaches—I had him for four years—literally taught me zero. Nothing. He taught me how to do a breaststroke turn, and he taught me incorrectly."

What happened when Dan did, finally, experience good coaching, in part from hanging around the national and Olympic coaches he was studying?

"Years later, I got back into the pool, got in shape again, and swam a two-hundred-yard individual medley as fast as I did in high school."

Again, same story. Not just nature, and not just nurture. Both.

———

How do scientists know, with unwavering conviction, that both nature and nurture play a role in determining things like talent and grit? Over the past few decades, researchers have been studying identical and fraternal twins, raised in the same family or raised in different families. Identical twins have all the same DNA, while fraternal twins, on average, only share about half. That fact, and a whole lot of fancy statistics (well, not *that* fancy—more mundane, really, once a good teacher explains them to you), allows researchers to infer, from how similar the twins grow up to be, the heritability of a trait.

Very recently, researchers in London let me know they'd administered the Grit Scale to more than two thousand pairs of teenage twins living in the United Kingdom. This study estimated the heritability of the perseverance subscale to be 37 percent and the passion subscale to be 20 percent. These estimates are on par for heritability estimates for other personality traits, and in the simplest terms, this means that some of the variation in grit in the population can be attributed to genetic factors, and the rest can be attributed to experience.

I hasten to add that there isn't just *one* gene that explains the heritability of grit. On the contrary, dozens of research studies have shown that almost all human traits are polygenic, meaning that traits are influenced by more than one gene. Many more, in fact. Height, for example, is influenced by, at last count, at least 697 different genes. And some of the genes that influence height influence other traits as well. In total, the human genome contains as many as twenty-five thousand different genes, and they tend to interact with one another and with environmental influences in complicated, still poorly understood, ways.

In sum, what have we learned? First: grit, talent, and all other psychological traits relevant to success in life are influenced by genes and also by experience. Second: there's no single gene for grit, or indeed any other psychological trait.

———

I'd like to make a third, important point: heritability estimates explain why people differ from the average, but they say nothing about the average itself.

While the heritability of height says something about variability— why in a given population some people are taller and some shorter—it says nothing about how average height has changed. This is important because it provides evidence that the environment we grow up in really does matter, and it matters a lot.

Here's another striking example, and one more relevant to the science of success: the Flynn effect. Named after Jim Flynn, the New Zealand social scientist who discovered it, the Flynn effect refers to startling gains in IQ scores over the past century. How big are the gains? On the most widely used IQ tests today—the Wechsler Intelligence Scale for Children and the Wechsler Adult Intelligence Scale—gains have averaged more than fifteen points in the last fifty years in the more than thirty countries that have been studied. Put another way, if you scored people a century ago against modern norms, they would have an average IQ score of 70—borderline for having an intellectual disability. If you scored people today against the norms of a century ago, we would have an average IQ score of 130—the typical cut score for mentally gifted programs.

When I first learned about the Flynn effect, I didn't believe it. How could it be that we're all getting that much smarter so quickly?

I called Jim to share my incredulity—and my desire to learn more—and, globe-trotter that he is, he actually flew all the way to Philadelphia to meet with me and give a talk on his work. At our first encounter, I remember thinking that Jim looked like a caricature of an academic: tall, a little bony, wire-rimmed glasses, and a rather unruly head of curly steel-gray hair.

Flynn began his talk with the basic facts on IQ change. Digging through the raw scores of IQ tests taken over the years, he found that the improvements on some tests were much bigger than others. He went to the chalkboard and sketched out a steep line indicating that scores had climbed most sharply for IQ tests assessing abstract reasoning. For instance, many young children today can answer the question "Dogs and rabbits: How are they alike?" They might tell you that both dogs and rabbits are alive, or that they're both animals. In the scoring manual, these answers only earn a half credit. Some children might go so far as to say that they're both mammals, and for that insight, they'd earn a full credit. In contrast, young children a century ago might look at you quizzically and say, "Dogs chase rabbits." Zero points.

As a species, we're getting better and better at abstract reasoning.

By way of explaining massive gains in certain IQ subtests but not in others, Flynn told a story about basketball and television. Basketball, at all levels of competition, has gotten more competitive over the last century. Flynn played a little ball himself as a student and remembers the game changing even within a few years. What happened?

According to Flynn, what happened was television. Basketball was a great game to watch on the small screen and the exposure fueled the game's popularity. Once television became a household fixture, more kids started playing the game, trying left-handed layups, cross-over dribbles, graceful hook shots, and other skills that seemed routine among star players. And by getting better, each kid inadvertently enriched the learning environment for the kids he or she was playing against. Because one thing that makes you better at basketball is playing with kids who are just a little more skilled.

Flynn called this virtuous cycle of skill improvement the social multiplier effect, and he used the same logic to explain generational changes in abstract reasoning. More and more, over the past century, our jobs and daily lives ask us to think analytically, logically. We go to school for longer, and in school, we're asked, more and more, to reason rather than rely on rote memorization.

Either small environmental differences, or genetic ones, can trigger a virtuous cycle. Either way, the effects are multiplied socially, through culture, because each of us enriches the environment of all of us.

———

Here is a graph showing how Grit Scale scores vary by age. These are data from a large sample of American adults, and you can see from the horizontal axis that the grittiest adults in my sample were in their late sixties or older; the least gritty were in their twenties.

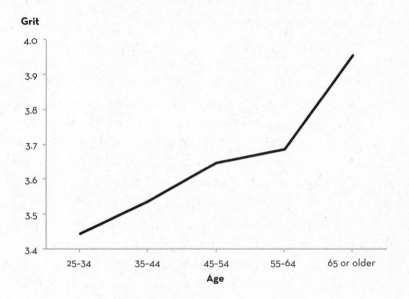

One explanation for this data is that there's a sort of "reverse Flynn effect" for grit. For instance, it's possible that adults in their seventh decade of life are grittier because they grew up in a very different cultural era, perhaps one whose values and norms emphasized sustained passion and perseverance more than has been the case recently. In other words, it could be that the Greatest Generation is grittier than the millennials because cultural forces are different today than yesterday.

This explanation for why grit and age go hand in hand was suggested to me by an older colleague who, looking over my shoulder at the same graph, shook his head and said, "I knew it! I've been teaching the same undergraduates the same course at the same university for decades. And I'll tell you, they just don't work as hard these days as they used to!" My dad, who gave his entire professional life as a chemist to DuPont and quite literally retired with the gold watch, might say the same of the Wharton entrepreneur who approached me after my lecture. Even while pulling all-nighters for his present venture, the young man half expected to be on to something entirely new within a few years.

———

Alternatively, it's possible these age trends have nothing to do with generational changes in grit. Instead, what the data may be showing is how people *mature* over time. My own experience, and the stories of grit paragons like Jeff Gettleman and Bob Mankoff suggest that, indeed, grit grows as we figure out our life philosophy, learn to dust ourselves off after rejection and disappointment, and learn to tell the difference between low-level goals that should be abandoned quickly and higher-level goals that demand more tenacity. The maturation story is that we *develop* the capacity for long-term passion and perseverance as we get older.

To distinguish between these rival explanations, we need a different kind of study. To generate the data I just showed you, I asked people of different ages about their current level of grit. What I got was a snapshot of grit in younger and older adults. Ideally, I'd follow these people for the rest of their lives, the way psychologist George Vaillant followed the Harvard men. Since the Grit Scale hasn't been around very long, I can't play you a time-lapse movie of grit over the life course. What I want is that movie. What I have is a snapshot.

Fortunately, many other aspects of personality have been examined longitudinally. In dozens of studies that have followed people over years and decades, the trends are clear. Most of us become more conscientious, confident, caring, and calm with life experience. A lot of that change happens between the ages of twenty and forty, but, in fact, there's no epoch in the human life span where personality stops evolving. Collectively, these data demonstrate what personality psychologists now call "the maturity principle."

We grow up. Or at least, most of us do.

To some extent, these changes are preprogrammed and biological. Puberty and menopause are things that change our personalities, for example. But on the whole, personality change is more a function of life experience.

Exactly how do life experiences change personality?

One reason we change is that we learn something we simply didn't know before. For instance, we might learn through trial and error that repeatedly swapping out one career ambition for another is unfulfilling. That's certainly what happened to me in my twenties. After running a nonprofit, then pursuing neuroscience research, then management consulting, then teaching, I learned that being a "promising beginner" is fun, but being an actual expert is infinitely more gratifying. I also learned that years of hard work are often mistaken for innate talent, and that passion is as necessary as perseverance to world-class excellence.

Likewise, we learn, as novelist John Irving did, that "to do anything really well, you have to overextend yourself," to appreciate that, "in doing something over and over again, something that was never natural becomes almost second nature," and finally, that the capacity to do work that diligently "doesn't come overnight."

Other than insights about the human condition, what else is there that changes with age?

What changes, I think, are our circumstances. As we grow older, we're thrust into new situations. We get our first job. We may get married. Our parents get older, and we find ourselves their caretakers. Often, these new situations call on us to act differently than we used to. And, because there's no species on the planet more adaptable than ours, we change. We rise to the occasion.

In other words, we change when we *need* to. Necessity is the mother of adaptation.

Here's a trivial example. Somehow, my youngest daughter, Lucy, reached the age of three without learning to use the potty. My husband

and I had done our best to bribe, cajole, and trick her into leaving diapers behind. We'd read all the books about all the right things to do, and we'd tried to do all those things—or at least we tried as energetically as is possible for working parents with other things on their to-do lists. To no avail. Lucy's will proved stronger than ours.

Soon after her third birthday, Lucy changed preschool classrooms: from the toddler classroom, where almost all the children were still in diapers, to the "big kid" classroom, which didn't even have a changing table. The first day I dropped her off in the new room, her eyes widened to saucers, scanning this new environment—a little bit afraid, I think, and more likely than not wishing she could stay in her old room, where she'd grown comfortable.

I'll never forget picking Lucy up that afternoon. She smiled at me proudly and announced she'd used the potty. And then, in so many words, she told me she was done with diapers. And she was. Potty training happened in a single moment in time. How? Because when a child lines up for the potty with all the other children and sees that she's expected to take her turn, she does exactly that. She learns to do what she needs to do.

Bernie Noe, the headmaster of the Lakeside School in Seattle, recently shared the following story about his own daughter. It illustrates the maturity principle to a T. Noe's family lives on campus, and as a teenager, his daughter was late to school almost every day. One summer, his daughter got a job folding clothes at the local American Eagle. On her first day, the store manager said, "Oh, by the way, the first time you're late, you're fired." She was stunned. No second chances? All her life, there'd been patience, understanding, and second chances.

So then what happened?

"It was amazing," Noe remembered. "Quite literally, it was the most immediate behavior change I've ever seen her make." Suddenly, his daughter was setting two alarms to make sure she was on time, or early, to a job where being late was simply not tolerated. As a headmaster tasked with shepherding young people along toward maturity, Noe considers his power to do so somewhat limited. "If you're a business, you don't care whether a kid thinks they're special. What you care about is 'Can you deliver? If you can't deliver, hey, we don't have any use for you.'"

Lectures don't have half the effect of consequences.

What the maturity principle comes down to, I think, is this. Over time, we learn life lessons we don't forget, and we adapt in response to the growing demands of our circumstances. Eventually, new ways of thinking and acting become habitual. There comes a day when we can hardly remember our immature former selves. We've adapted, those adaptations have become durable, and, finally, our identity—the sort of person we see ourselves to be—has evolved. We've matured.

Taken together, the data I've collected on grit and age are consistent with two different stories. One story says that our grit changes as a function of the cultural era in which we grow up. The other story says that we get grittier as we get older. Both could be true, and I have a suspicion that both *are*, at least to an extent. Either way, this snapshot reveals that grit is not entirely fixed. Like every aspect of your psychological character, grit is more plastic than you might think.

———

If grit can grow, how does that happen?

I get emails and letters almost every day from people who wish they had more grit. They lament that they never stuck with anything in order to get really good at it. They feel they've squandered their talents. They desperately want a long-term goal, and they want to pursue that goal with passion and perseverance.

But they don't know where to begin.

A good place to start is to understand where you are today. If you're not as gritty as you want to be, ask yourself *why*.

The most obvious answer people come up with goes something like this: "I guess I'm just lazy."

Here's another: "I'm just a flake."

Or: "I'm congenitally incapable of sticking with things."

All of these answers, I think, are wrong.

In fact, when people drop out of things, they do so for a reason. Actually, they do so for *different* reasons. Any of the following four thoughts might go through your head right before you quit what you're doing:

"I'm bored."

"The effort isn't worth it."

"This isn't important to me."

"I can't do this, so I might as well give up."

There's nothing wrong—morally or otherwise—with thoughts like these. As I tried to show in this chapter, paragons of grit quit goals, too. But the higher the level of the goal in question, the more stubborn they are about seeing it through. Most important, paragons of grit don't swap compasses: when it comes to the one, singularly important aim that guides almost everything else they do, the very gritty tend *not* to utter the statements above.

––––––

A lot of what I've learned about how grit grows comes from interviewing men and women who epitomize the qualities of passion and perseverance. I've included snippets of those conversations throughout this book so that you, too, can peer inside the mind and heart of a grit paragon and see whether there's a belief, attitude, or habit worth emulating.

These stories of grit are one kind of data, and they complement the more systematic, quantitative studies I've done in places like West

Point and the National Spelling Bee. Together, the research reveals the psychological assets that mature paragons of grit have in common. There are four. They counter each of the buzz-killers listed above, and they tend to develop, over the years, in a particular order.

First comes *interest*. Passion begins with intrinsically enjoying what you do. Every gritty person I've studied can point to aspects of their work they enjoy less than others, and most have to put up with at least one or two chores they don't enjoy at all. Nevertheless, they're captivated by the endeavor as a whole. With enduring fascination and childlike curiosity, they practically shout out, "I love what I do!"

Next comes the capacity to *practice*. One form of perseverance is the daily discipline of trying to do things better than we did yesterday. So, after you've discovered and developed interest in a particular area, you must devote yourself to the sort of focused, full-hearted, challenge-exceeding-skill practice that leads to mastery. You must zero in on your weaknesses, and you must do so over and over again, for hours a day, week after month after year. To be gritty is to resist complacency. "Whatever it takes, I want to improve!" is a refrain of all paragons of grit, no matter their particular interest, and no matter how excellent they already are.

Third is *purpose*. What ripens passion is the conviction that your work matters. For most people, interest without purpose is nearly impossible to sustain for a lifetime. It is therefore imperative that you identify your work as both personally interesting and, at the same time, integrally connected to the well-being of others. For a few, a sense of purpose dawns early, but for many, the motivation to serve others heightens *after* the development of interest and years of disciplined practice. Regardless, fully mature exemplars of grit invariably tell me, "My work is important—both to me and to others."

And, finally, *hope*. Hope is a rising-to-the-occasion kind of perseverance. In this book, I discuss it after interest, practice, and purpose—

but hope does *not* define the last stage of grit. It defines *every* stage. From the very beginning to the very end, it is inestimably important to learn to keep going even when things are difficult, even when we have doubts. At various points, in big ways and small, we get knocked down. If we stay down, grit loses. If we get up, grit prevails.

————

Without the meddling of a psychologist like me, you may have figured grit out all on your own. You may already have a deep and abiding interest, a ready appetite for constant challenge, an evolved sense of purpose, and buoyant confidence in your ability to keep going that no adversity could sink. If so, you're probably close to 5 out of 5 on the Grit Scale. I applaud you!

If, on the other hand, you're not as gritty as you wish you were, then there's something for you in the chapters that follow. Like calculus and piano, you can learn the psychology of grit on your own, but a little guidance can be a tremendous help.

The four psychological assets of interest, practice, purpose, and hope are not *You have it or you don't* commodities. You can learn to discover, develop, and deepen your interests. You can acquire the habit of discipline. You can cultivate a sense of purpose and meaning. And you can teach yourself to hope.

You can grow your grit from the inside out. If you'd like to know how, read on.

Part II

GROWING GRIT FROM THE INSIDE OUT

Chapter 6

INTEREST

Follow your passion is a popular theme of commencement speeches. I've sat through my fair share, both as a student and professor. I'd wager that at least half of all speakers, maybe more, underscore the importance of doing something you love.

For instance, Will Shortz, long-time editor of the *New York Times* crossword puzzle, told students at Indiana University: "My advice for you is, figure out what you enjoy doing most in life, and then try to do it full-time. Life is short. Follow your passion."

Jeff Bezos told Princeton graduates the story of leaving a high-salary, high-status Manhattan finance job to start Amazon: "After much consideration, I took the less safe path to follow my passion." He has also said, "Whatever it is that you want to do, you'll find in life that if you're not passionate about what it is you're working on, you won't be able to stick with it."

And it's not just on hot June days in our cap and gown that we get this advice. I hear the same thing—over and over again, nearly verbatim—from the grit paragons I interview.

So does Hester Lacey.

Hester is a British journalist who has been interviewing achievers of the caliber of Shortz and Bezos—one per week—since 2011. Her column appears weekly in the *Financial Times*. Whether they're fashion designers (Nicole Farhi), authors (Salman Rushdie), musicians (Lang Lang), comedians (Michael Palin), chocolatiers (Chantal Coady), or bartenders (Colin Field), Hester asks the same questions, including: "What drives you on?" and "If you lost everything tomorrow, what would you do?"

I asked Hester what she's learned from talking to more than two hundred "mega successful" people, as she described them during our conversation.

"One thing that comes up time and time again is: 'I love what I do.' People couch it differently. Quite often, they say just that: 'I love what I do.' But they also say things like 'I'm so lucky, I get up every morning looking forward to work, I can't wait to get into the studio, I can't wait to get on with the next project.' These people are doing things not because they have to or because it's financially lucrative. . . ."

———

Follow your passion was not the message I heard growing up.

Instead, I was told that the practical realities of surviving "in the real world" were far more important than any young person living a "sheltered life" such as my own could imagine. I was warned that overly idealistic dreams of "finding something I loved" could in fact be a breadcrumb trail into poverty and disappointment. I was reminded that certain jobs, like being a doctor, were both high-income and high-status, and that these things would matter more to me in the long run than I might appreciate in the moment.

As you might have guessed, the individual proffering this advice was my dad.

"So, why'd you become a chemist?" I once asked.

"Because my father told me to," he answered without a hint of resentment. "When I was a boy, history was my favorite subject." He then explained that he'd enjoyed math and science, too, but there was really no choice when it came to what he'd study in college. The family business was textiles, and my grandfather dispatched each of his sons to study trades relevant to one stage or another of textile production. "Our business needed a chemist, not a historian."

As it turned out, the Communist Revolution in China brought a premature end to the family textile business. Not long after he settled here in the United States, my dad went to work for DuPont. Thirty-five years later, he retired as the highest-ranking scientist in the company.

Given how absorbed my dad was in his work—often lost in reverie about some scientific or management problem—and how successful he was over the arc of his career, it seems worth considering the possibility that it's best to choose practicality over passion.

Just how ridiculous *is* it to advise young people to go out and do what they love? Within the last decade or so, scientists who study interests have arrived at a definitive answer.

First, research shows that people are enormously more satisfied with their jobs when they do something that fits their personal interests. This is the conclusion of a meta-analysis that aggregated data from almost a hundred different studies that collectively included working adults in just about every conceivable profession. For instance, people who enjoy thinking about abstract ideas are *not* happy managing the minutiae of logistically complicated projects; they'd rather be solving math problems. And people who really enjoy interacting with people are *not* happy when their job is to work alone at a computer all day; they're much better off in jobs like sales or teaching. What's more, people whose jobs match their personal interests are, in general, happier with their lives as a whole.

Second, people *perform* better at work when what they do interests them. This is the conclusion of another meta-analysis of sixty studies conducted over the past sixty years. Employees whose intrinsic personal interests fit with their occupations do their jobs better, are more helpful to their coworkers, and stay at their jobs longer. College students whose personal interests align with their major earn higher grades and are less likely to drop out.

It's certainly true that you can't get a job just doing *anything* you enjoy. It's tough to make a living playing Minecraft, no matter how good you get at it. And there are a lot of people in the world whose circumstances preclude the luxury of choosing among a broad array of occupational options. Like it or not, there are very real constraints in the choices we can make about how we earn a living.

Nevertheless, as William James foretold a century ago, these new scientific findings affirm commencement speech wisdom: the "casting vote" for how well we can expect to do in any endeavor is "desire and passion, the strength of [our] interest. . . ."

———

In a 2014 Gallup poll, more than two-thirds of adults said they were not engaged at work, a good portion of whom were "actively disengaged."

The picture is even bleaker abroad. In a survey of 141 nations, Gallup found that every country but Canada has even higher numbers of "not engaged" and "actively disengaged" workers than the United States. Worldwide, only 13 percent of adults call themselves "engaged" at work.

So it seems that very few people end up loving what they do for a living.

It's difficult to reconcile the straightforward directives offered in inspirational speeches with epidemic levels of indifference toward work. When it comes to lining up our occupations with what we enjoy, how come so many of us miss the mark? And does my dad's success offer a counterexample to the passion argument? What should we make of the fact that, by the time I came along, my father's work really was his passion? Should we stop telling people to *follow your passion* and, instead, tell them to *follow our orders*?

I don't think so.

In fact, I see Will Shortz and Jeff Bezos as terrific inspirations for what work can be. While it's naive to think that any of us could love every minute of what we do, I believe the thousands of data points in those meta-analyses, which confirm the commonsense intuition that interest matters. Nobody is interested in everything, and everyone is interested in something. So matching your job to what captures your attention and imagination is a good idea. It may not guarantee happiness and success, but it sure helps the odds.

That said, I don't think most young people need encouragement to follow their passion. Most *would* do exactly that—in a heartbeat—if only they had a passion in the first place. If I'm ever invited to give a commencement speech, I'll begin with the advice to *foster a passion*. And then I'll spend the rest of my time trying to change young minds about how that actually happens.

———

When I first started interviewing grit paragons, I assumed they'd all have stories about the singular moment when, suddenly, they'd discovered their God-given passion. In my mind's eye, this was a filmable event, with dramatic lighting and a soundtrack of rousing orchestral music commensurate with its monumental, life-changing import.

In the opening scene of *Julie & Julia*, a younger Julia Child than any of us watched on television is dining in a fancy French restaurant with her husband, Paul. Julia takes one bite of her *sole meunière*— beautifully seared and perfectly deboned by the waiter moments before and now napped in a sauce of Normandy butter, lemon, and parsley. She swoons. She's never experienced anything like this before. She always liked to eat, but she never knew food could be *this* good.

"The whole experience was an opening up of the soul and spirit for me," Julia said many years later. "I was hooked, and for life, as it turned out."

Such cinematic moments were what I expected from my grit paragons. And I think this is also what young graduates—roasting in their caps and gowns, the hard edge of the folding chair biting into their thighs—imagine it must be like to discover your life's passion. One moment, you have no idea what to do with your time on earth. And the next, it's all clear—you know exactly who you were meant to be.

But, in fact, most grit paragons I've interviewed told me they spent years exploring several different interests, and the one that eventually came to occupy all of their waking (and some sleeping) thoughts wasn't recognizably their life's destiny on first acquaintance.

Olympic gold medalist swimmer Rowdy Gaines, for example, told me: "When I was a kid, I loved sports. When I got to high school, I went out for football, baseball, basketball, golf, and tennis, in that order, before I went for swimming. I kept plugging away. I figured I'd just keep going from one sport to the next until I found something that I could really fall in love with." Swimming stuck, but it wasn't exactly love at first sight. "The day I tried out for the swim team, I went to the school library to check out track and field because I kind of had a feeling I was going to get cut. I figured I'd try out for track and field next."

As a teenager, James Beard Award–winning chef Marc Vetri was as interested in music as he was in cooking. After college, he moved to Los Angeles. "I went to a music school out there for a year, and I worked nights in restaurants to make money. Later, when I was in a band, I worked mornings in restaurants so I could do the music thing at night. Then it was like, 'Well, I'm making money in the restaurants, and I'm really starting to like it, and I'm not making anything in music.' And then I had an opportunity to go to Italy, and that was it." It's hard for me to picture my favorite chef playing the guitar instead of making pasta, but when I asked what he thought about the road not taken, he said, "Well, music and cooking—they're both creative industries. I'm glad I went this way, but I think I could have been a musician instead."

As for Julia Child, that ethereal morsel of *sole meunière* was indeed a revelation. But her epiphany was that classical French cuisine was divine, *not* that she would become a chef, cookbook author, and, eventually, the woman who would teach America to make coq au vin in their very own kitchens. Indeed, Julia's autobiography reveals that this memorable meal was followed by a *succession* of interest-stimulating experiences. An incomplete list would include countless delicious meals in the bistros of Paris; conversations and friendships with friendly fishmongers, butchers, and produce vendors in the city's open-air markets; encounters with two encyclopedic French cookbooks—the first loaned to her by her French tutor and the second a gift from her ever-supportive husband, Paul; hours of cooking classes at Le Cordon Bleu under the tutelage of the marvelously enthusiastic yet demanding Chef Bugnard; and the acquaintance of two Parisian women who had the idea of writing a cookbook for Americans.

What would have happened if Julia—who once dreamed of becoming a novelist and, as a child, possessed, as she put it, "zero interest in the stove"—had returned home to California after that fateful bite of perfectly cooked fish? We can't know for sure, but clearly in Julia's romance with French food, that first bite of sole was just the first kiss. "Really, the more I cook, the more I like to cook," she later told her sister-in-law. "To think it has taken me forty years to find my true passion (cat and husband excepted)."

So, while we might envy those who love what they do for a living, we shouldn't assume that they started from a different place than the rest of us. Chances are, they took quite some time figuring out exactly what they wanted to do with their lives. Commencement speakers may say about their vocation, "I can't imagine doing anything else," but, in fact, there was a time earlier in life when they could.

———

A few months ago, I read a post on Reddit titled "Fleeting Interest in Everything, No Career Direction":

I'm in my early thirties and have no idea what to do with myself, career-wise. All my life I've been one of those people who has been told how smart I am/how much potential I have. I'm interested in so much stuff that I'm paralyzed to try anything. It seems like every job requires a specialized certificate or designation that requires long-term time and financial investment—before you can even try the job, which is a bit of a drag.

I have a lot of sympathy for the thirty-something who wrote this post. As a college professor, I also have a lot of sympathy for the twenty-somethings who come to me for career advice.

My colleague Barry Schwartz has been dispensing counsel to anxious young adults for much longer than I have. He's been teaching psychology at Swarthmore College for forty-five years.

Barry thinks that what prevents a lot of young people from developing a serious career interest is unrealistic expectations. "It's really the same problem a lot of young people have finding a romantic partner," he said. "They want somebody who's really attractive and smart and kind and empathetic and thoughtful and funny. Try telling a twenty-one-year-old that you can't find a person who is absolutely the best in *every* way. They don't listen. They're holding out for perfection."

"What about your wonderful wife, Myrna?" I asked.

"Oh, she *is* wonderful. More wonderful than I am, certainly. But is she perfect? Is she the *only* person I could have made a happy life with? Am I the *only* man in the world with whom she could have made a wonderful marriage? I don't think so."

A related problem, Barry says, is the mythology that falling in love with a career should be sudden and swift: "There are a lot of things where the subtleties and exhilarations come with sticking with it for a while, getting elbow-deep into something. A lot of things seem uninteresting and superficial until you start doing them and, after a while, you realize that there are so many facets you didn't know at the start, and you never can fully solve the problem, or fully understand it, or what have you. Well, that requires that you stick with it."

After a pause, Barry said, "Actually, finding a mate is the perfect analogy. Meeting a potential match—not the one-and-only perfect match, but a promising one—is only the very beginning."

———

There's a lot we don't know about the psychology of interest. I wish we knew, for example, why some of us (including me) find cooking a fascinating subject, while many others couldn't care less. Why is Marc Vetri attracted to creative endeavors, and why does Rowdy Gaines like sports? Aside from the rather vague explanation that interests are, like everything else about us, partly heritable and partly a function of life experience, I can't tell you. But scientific research on the evolution of interests has yielded some important insights. My sense is that, unfortunately, these basic facts aren't commonly understood.

What most of us think of when we think of passion is a sudden, all-at-once discovery—that first bite of *sole meunière* bringing with it the certainty of the years you'll spend in the kitchen . . . slipping into the water at your first swim meet and getting out with the foreknowledge that you'll one day be an Olympian . . . getting to the end of *The Catcher in the Rye* and realizing you're destined to be a writer. But a first encounter with what might *eventually* lead to a lifelong passion is exactly that—just the opening scene in a much longer, less dramatic narrative.

To the thirty-something on Reddit with a "fleeting interest in everything" and "no career direction," here's what science has to say: passion for your work is a little bit of *discovery*, followed by a lot of *development*, and then a lifetime of *deepening*.

Let me explain.

First of all, childhood is generally far too early to know what we want to be when we grow up. Longitudinal studies following thousands of people across time have shown that most people only *begin* to gravitate toward certain vocational interests, and away from others, around middle school. This is certainly the pattern I've seen in my interview research, and it's also what journalist Hester Lacey has found in her interviews with the "mega successful." Keep in mind, however, that a seventh grader—even a future paragon of grit—is unlikely to have a fully articulated passion at that age. A seventh grader is just beginning to figure out her general likes and dislikes.

Second, interests are *not* discovered through introspection. Instead, interests are triggered by interactions with the outside world. The process of interest discovery can be messy, serendipitous, and inefficient. This is because you can't really predict with certainty what will capture your attention and what won't. You can't simply *will* yourself to like things, either. As Jeff Bezos has observed, "One of the huge mistakes people make is that they try to *force* an interest on themselves." Without experimenting, you can't figure out which interests will stick, and which won't.

Paradoxically, the initial discovery of an interest often goes unnoticed by the discoverer. In other words, when you just start to get interested in something, you may not even realize that's what's happening. The emotion of boredom is always self-conscious—you know it when you feel it—but when your attention is attracted to a new activity or experience, you may have very little reflective appreciation of what's happening to you. This means that, at the start of a new endeavor, asking yourself nervously every few days whether you've found your passion is premature.

Third, what follows the initial discovery of an interest is a much lengthier and increasingly proactive period of interest development. Crucially, the initial triggering of a new interest must be followed by subsequent encounters that retrigger your attention—again and again and again.

For instance, NASA astronaut Mike Hopkins told me that it was watching space shuttle launches on television in high school that ini-tially inspired his lifelong interest in space travel. But it wasn't just *one* launch that hooked him. It was several shown in succession over a period of years. Soon enough, he started digging for more information on NASA, and "one piece of information led to another and another."

For master potter Warren MacKenzie, ceramics class in college—which he only took, initially, because all the painting classes were full—was followed by the discovery of *A Potter's Book* by the great Bernard Leach, and then a year-long internship with Leach himself.

Finally, interests thrive when there is a crew of encouraging sup-porters, including parents, teachers, coaches, and peers. Why are other people so important? For one thing, they provide the ongoing stimu-lation and information that is essential to actually liking something more and more. Also—more obviously—positive feedback makes us feel happy, competent, and secure.

Take Marc Vetri as an example. There are few things I enjoy reading more than his cookbooks and essays about food, but he was a solid-C student throughout school. "I never worked hard at academics," he told me. "I was always just like, 'This is kind of boring.'" In contrast, Marc spent delightful Sunday afternoons at his Sicilian grandmother's house in South Philly. "She'd make meatballs and lasagna and all that stuff, and I always liked to head down early to help her out. By the time I was eleven or so, I started wanting to make that stuff at home, too."

As a teenager, Marc had a part-time job washing dishes in a local restaurant. "And I loved that. I worked hard." Why? Making money was one motivation, but another was the camaraderie of the kitchen. "Around that time I was sort of a social outcast. I was kind of awk-ward. I had a stutter. Everyone at school thought I was weird. I was like, 'Oh, here I can wash dishes, and I can watch the guys on the line [cooking] while I'm washing, and I can eat. Everyone is nice, and they like me.'"

If you read Marc's cookbooks, you'll be struck by how many friends and mentors he's made in the world of food. Page through and look for pictures of Marc alone, and you'll be hard-pressed to find many. And read the acknowledgments of *Il Viaggio Di Vetri*. It runs to two pages with the names of people who made his journey possible, including this note: "Mom and Dad, you've always let me find my own way and helped guide me through it. You'll never know how much I appreciate it. I'll always need you."

Is it "a drag" that passions don't come to us all at once, as epiphanies, without the need to actively develop them? Maybe. But the reality is that our early interests are fragile, vaguely defined, and in need of energetic, years-long cultivation and refinement.

Sometimes, when I talk to anxious parents, I get the impression they've misunderstood what I mean by grit. I tell them that half of grit is perseverance—in response, I get appreciative head nods—but I *also* tell them that nobody works doggedly on something they don't find intrinsically interesting. Here, heads often stop nodding and, instead, cock to the side.

"Just because you love something doesn't mean you'll be great," says self-proclaimed Tiger Mom Amy Chua. "Not if you don't work. Most people stink at the things they love." I couldn't agree more. Even in the development of your interests, there is work—practicing, studying, learning—to be done. Still, my point is that most people stink even *more* at what they *don't* love.

So, parents, parents-to-be, and non-parents of all ages, I have a message for you: *Before hard work comes play.* Before those who've yet to fix on a passion are ready to spend hours a day diligently honing skills, they must goof around, triggering and retriggering interest. Of course, developing an interest requires time and energy, and yes, some discipline and sacrifice. But at this earliest stage, novices *aren't* obsessed with getting better. They're *not* thinking years and years into the future. They *don't* know what their top-level, life-orienting goal will be. More than anything else, they're having fun.

In other words, even the most accomplished of experts start out as unserious beginners.

This is also the conclusion of psychologist Benjamin Bloom, who interviewed 120 people who achieved world-class skills in sports, arts, or science—plus their parents, coaches, and teachers. Among Bloom's important findings is that the development of skill progresses through three different stages, each lasting several years. Interests are discovered and developed in what Bloom called "the early years."

Encouragement during the early years is crucial because beginners are still figuring out whether they want to commit or cut bait. Accordingly, Bloom and his research team found that the best mentors at this stage were especially warm and supportive: "Perhaps the major quality of these teachers was that they made the initial learning very pleasant and rewarding. Much of the introduction to the field was as playful activity, and the learning at the beginning of this stage was much like a game."

A degree of autonomy during the early years is also important. Longitudinal studies tracking learners confirm that overbearing parents and teachers erode intrinsic motivation. Kids whose parents let them make their own choices about what they like are more likely to develop interests later identified as a passion. So, while my dad in Shanghai in 1950 didn't think twice about his father assigning him a career path, most young people today would find it difficult to fully "own" interests decided without their input.

Sports psychologist Jean Côté finds that shortcutting this stage of relaxed, playful interest, discovery, and development has dire consequences. In his research, professional athletes like Rowdy Gaines who, as children, sampled a variety of different sports before committing to one, generally fare much better in the long run. This early breadth of experience helps the young athlete figure out which sport fits better than others. Sampling also provides an opportunity to "cross-train" muscles and skills that will eventually complement more focused training. While athletes who skip this stage often enjoy an early advantage in competition against less specialized peers, Côté finds that they're more likely to become injured physically and to burn out.

We'll discuss what Bloom calls "the middle years" in the next chapter, on practice. Finally, we'll plumb "the later years" in chapter 8 when we discuss purpose.

For now, what I hope to convey is that experts and beginners have different motivational needs. At the start of an endeavor, we need encouragement and freedom to figure out what we enjoy. We need small wins. We need applause. Yes, we can handle a tincture of criticism and corrective feedback. Yes, we need to practice. But not too much and not too soon. Rush a beginner and you'll bludgeon their budding interest. It's very, very hard to get that back once you do.

———

Let's return to our commencement speakers. They're case studies in passion, so there's something to be learned from how they spent their early years.

New York Times puzzle editor Will Shortz told me that his mother was "a writer and a lover of words," and that her mother, in turn, had been a crossword fan. An inclination toward language, Shortz speculated, could very well be in his genes.

But the unique path he walked was not just a matter of genetic destiny. Not very long after he learned to read and write, Shortz came across a puzzle book. "I was just entranced by it," he recalls. "I just wanted to make my own."

Predictably, that first puzzle book—the initial trigger for his curiosity—was followed by a slew of others. "Word puzzles, math puzzles, you name it. . . ." Soon enough, Shortz knew all of the major puzzle makers by name, acquiring the complete Dover Books collection of his hero Sam Loyd, as well as the works of a half-dozen other puzzle makers whose names are as familiar to Shortz as they are foreign to me.

Who bought all those books?

His mother.

What else did she do?

"I remember when I was very young my mom had a bridge club over, and to keep me quiet for the afternoon she took a piece of paper, ruled it into squares, and showed me how to enter long words across and up and down. And I was happy all afternoon making my little puzzles. When the bridge club left, my mother came in and numbered the grid for me and showed me how to write clues. So that was my first crossword."

And then Shortz's mother did what few mothers—including me—would have the initiative or know-how to do: "My mom encouraged me to sell my puzzles once I started making them, because as a writer, she submitted articles for publication to magazines and newspapers. Once she saw this interest that I had, she showed me how to submit my work.

"I sold my first puzzle when I was fourteen, and I became a regular contributor to Dell puzzle magazines when I was sixteen."

Shortz's mother was clearly on the lookout for what might pique her son's interest: "My mom did a lot of great things," he told me. "For instance, I loved listening to radio and pop music and rock music when I was a kid. When she saw this interest, she got a guitar from a neighbor and set it on the bunk bed above my bed. I had the opportunity, if I wanted it, to pick up the guitar and start playing."

But the desire to make music was nothing compared to the desire to make puzzles. "After nine months, when I had never touched the guitar, she took it back. I guess I liked listening to music, but I had no interest in playing it."

When Shortz enrolled at Indiana University, it was his mom who found the individualized program that enabled Shortz to invent his own major: to this day, Shortz remains the only person in the world to hold a college degree in enigmatology—the study of puzzles.

———

What about Jeff Bezos?

Jeff's unusually interest-filled childhood has a lot to do with his unusually curious mother, Jackie.

Jeff came into the world two weeks after Jackie turned seventeen years old. "So," she told me, "I didn't have a lot of preconceived notions about what I was supposed to do."

She remembers being deeply intrigued by Jeff and his younger brother and sister: "I was just so curious about these little creatures and who they were and what they were going to do. I paid attention to what interested each one—they were all different—and followed their lead. I felt it was my responsibility to let them do deep dives into what they enjoyed."

For instance, at three, Jeff asked multiple times to sleep in a "big bed." Jackie explained that *eventually* he would sleep in a "big bed," but not yet. She walked into his room the next day and found him, screwdriver in hand, disassembling his crib. Jackie didn't scold him. Instead, she sat on the floor and helped. Jeff slept in a "big bed" that night.

By middle school, he was inventing all sorts of mechanical contraptions, including an alarm on his bedroom door that made a loud buzzing sound whenever one of his siblings trespassed across the threshold. "We made so many trips to RadioShack," Jackie said, laughing. "Sometimes we'd go back four times in a day because we needed another component."

"Once, he took string and tied all the handles of the kitchen cupboards together, and then, when you opened one, all of them would pop open."

I tried to picture myself in these situations. I tried to picture *not* freaking out. I tried to imagine doing what Jackie did, which was to notice that her oldest son was blooming into a world-class problem solver, and then merrily nurture that interest.

"My moniker at the house was 'Captain of Chaos,' " Jackie told me, "and that's because just about anything that you wanted to do would be acceptable in some fashion."

Jackie remembers that when Jeff decided to build an infinity cube, essentially a motorized set of mirrors that reflect one another's images back and forth ad infinitum, she was sitting on the sidewalk with a friend. "Jeff comes up to us and is telling us all the science behind it, and I listen and nod my head and ask a question every once in a while. After he walked away, my friend asked if I understood everything. And I said, 'It's not important that I understand everything. It's important that I listen.' "

By high school, Jeff had turned the family garage into a laboratory for inventing and experimentation. One day, Jackie got a call from Jeff's high school saying he was skipping classes after lunch. When he got home, she asked him where he'd been going in the afternoons. Jeff told her he'd found a local professor who was letting him experiment with airplane wings and friction and drag, and—"Okay," Jackie said. "I got it. Now, let's see if we can negotiate a legal way to do that."

In college, Jeff majored in computer science and electrical engineering, and after graduating, applied his programming skills to the management of investment funds. Several years later, Jeff built an Internet bookstore named after the longest river in the world: Amazon .com. (He also registered the URL www.relentless.com; type it into your browser and see where it takes you. . . .)

———

"I'm always learning," Will Shortz told me. "I'm always stretching my brain in a new way, trying to find a new clue for a word, search out a new theme. I read once—a writer said that if you're bored with writing, that means you're bored with life. I think the same is true of puzzles.

If you're bored with puzzles, you're bored with life, because they're so diverse."

Pretty much every grit paragon I've talked to, including my own dad, says the same thing. And in examining one large-scale study after another, I find that the grittier an individual is, the fewer career changes they're likely to make.

In contrast, we all know people who habitually throw themselves headlong into a new project, developing a fierce interest, only to move on after three or four or five years to something entirely different. There seems no harm in pursuing a variety of different hobbies, but endlessly dating new occupations, and never settling down with just one, is a more serious matter.

"I call them short-termers," Jane Golden told me.

Jane has been promoting public art in my home city of Philadelphia for more than thirty years as the director of the revered Mural Arts Program. At last count, she's helped convert the walls of more than 3,600 buildings into murals; hers is the single largest public art program in the country. Most people who know her would describe her commitment to mural arts as "relentless," and Jane would agree.

"Short-termers come work here for a little while and then they move on, and then they go somewhere else, and then somewhere else again, and so on. I'm always sort of looking at them like they're from another planet because I'm like, 'How's that? How do you not lock in to something?' "

Of course, it's Jane's unwavering focus that needs explaining, not the limited attention spans of the short-termers who come and go. Fundamentally, the emotion of boredom, after doing something for a while, is a very natural reaction. All human beings, even from infancy, tend to look away from things they've already seen and, instead, turn their gaze to things that are new and surprising. In fact, the word *interest* comes from the Latin *interesse*, which means "to differ." To be interesting is, literally, to be different. We are, by our natures, neophiles.

Even though getting tired of things after a while is common, it's not inevitable. If you revisit the Grit Scale, you'll see that half the items ask about how consistent your interests are over long stretches of time. This links back to the fact that grit paragons don't just discover something they enjoy and develop that interest—they also learn to *deepen* it.

As a young woman, Jane thought she'd become a painter. Now she battles bureaucratic red tape and raises money and deals with neighborhood politics. I wondered whether she'd sacrificed her life to a cause she felt was more meaningful but less interesting. I wondered if she'd given up novelty.

"When I stopped painting, it was very difficult," Jane told me. "But then I discovered that growing the Mural Arts Program could be a creative endeavor. And that was great, because I'm a very curious person.

"From the outside, you might see my life as mundane: 'Jane, you're just running the Mural Arts Program and you've been doing that forever.' I would say, 'No, listen, today I went to a maximum security prison. I was in North Philly. I went to church. I was in a boardroom. I met with a deputy commissioner. I met with a city council person. I worked at an artists' residency program. I saw kids graduating.'"

Then Jane used a painter's analogy: "I'm like an artist who looks at the sky every morning and sees a variety of really brilliant colors where other people would just see blue or gray. I'm seeing in the course of a single day this tremendous complexity and nuance. I see something that is ever evolving and rich."

For help understanding the ever-deepening interests of experts, I turned to the psychologist Paul Silvia.

Paul is a leading authority on the emotion of interest. He began our conversation by pointing out that babies know just about zilch when they're born. Unlike other animals, which have strong instincts to act in certain ways, babies need to learn almost everything from experience. If babies *didn't* have a strong drive for novelty, they wouldn't learn as much, and that would make it less likely they'd survive. "So, interest—the desire to learn new things, to explore the world, to seek novelty, to be on the lookout for change and variety—it's a basic drive."

How, then, do we explain the enduring interests of grit paragons?

Like me, Paul has found that experts often say things like "The more I know, the less I understand." Sir John Templeton, for example, who pioneered the idea of diversified mutual funds, made the motto of his philanthropic foundation "How little we know, how eager to learn."

The key, Paul explained, is that novelty for the beginner comes in one form, and novelty for the expert in another. For the beginner, novelty is anything that hasn't been encountered before. *For the expert, novelty is nuance.*

"Take modern art," Paul said. "A lot of pieces could seem very similar to a novice that seem very different to an expert. Novices don't have the necessary background knowledge. They just see colors and shapes. They're not sure what it's all about." But the art expert has comparatively enormous understanding. He or she has developed a sensitivity to details that the rest of us can't even see.

Here's another example. Ever watch the Olympics? Ever listen to the commentators say things, in real time, like "Oh! That triple lutz was just a little short!" "That push-off was perfectly timed"? You sit there and wonder how these commentators can perceive such microscopic differences in the performance of one athlete versus another without watching the video playback in slow motion. I need that video playback. I am insensitive to those nuances. But an expert has the accumulated knowledge and skill to see what I, a beginner, cannot.

If you'd like to follow your passion but haven't yet fostered one, you must begin at the beginning: discovery.

Ask yourself a few simple questions: *What do I like to think about?*

Where does my mind wander? What do I really care about? What matters most to me? How do I enjoy spending my time? And, in contrast, what do I find absolutely unbearable? If you find it hard to answer these questions, try recalling your teen years, the stage of life at which vocational interests commonly sprout.

As soon as you have even a general direction in mind, you must trigger your nascent interests. Do this by going out into the world and *doing* something. To young graduates wringing their hands over what to do, I say, *Experiment! Try! You'll certainly learn more than if you don't!*

At this early stage of exploration, here are a few relevant rules of thumb taken from Will Shortz's essay "How to Solve the *New York Times* Crossword Puzzle":

Begin with the answers you're surest of and build from there. However ill-defined your interests, there are some things you know you'd hate doing for a living, and some things that seem more promising than others. That's a start.

Don't be afraid to guess. Like it or not, there's a certain amount of trial and error inherent in the process of interest discovery. Unlike the answers to crossword puzzles, there isn't just *one* thing you can do that might develop into a passion. There are many. You don't have to find the "right" one, or even the "best" one—just a direction that feels good. It can also be difficult to know if something will be a good fit until you try it for a while.

Don't be afraid to erase an answer that isn't working out. At some point, you may choose to write your top-level goal in indelible ink, but until you know for sure, work in pencil.

If, on the other hand, you already have a good sense of what you enjoy spending your time doing, it's time to develop your interest. After discovery comes development.

Remember that interests must be triggered again and again and again. Find ways to make that happen. And have patience. The development of interests takes time. Keep asking questions, and let the answers to those questions lead you to more questions. Continue to dig. Seek out other people who share your interests. Sidle up to an encouraging mentor. Whatever your age, over time your role as a learner will become a more active and informed one. Over a period of years, your knowledge and expertise will grow, and along with it your confidence and curiosity to know more.

Finally, if you've been doing something you like for a few years and still wouldn't quite call it a passion, see if you can deepen your interests. Since novelty is what your brain craves, you'll be tempted to move on to something new, and that could be what makes the most sense. However, if you want to stay engaged for more than a few years in *any* endeavor, you'll need to find a way to enjoy the nuances that only a true aficionado can appreciate. "The old in the new is what claims the attention," said William James. "The old with a slightly new turn."

In sum, the directive to *follow your passion* is not bad advice. But what may be even more useful is to understand how passions are fostered in the first place.

Chapter 7

PRACTICE

In one of my earliest research studies, I found that grittier kids at the National Spelling Bee practiced more than their less gritty competitors. These extra hours of practice, in turn, explained their superior performance in final competition.

This finding made a lot of sense. As a math teacher, I'd observed a huge range in effort among my students. Some kids spent, quite literally, zero minutes a week on their homework; others studied for hours a day. Considering all the studies showing that gritty people typically stick with their commitments longer than others, it seemed like the major advantage of grit was, simply, *more time on task*.

At the same time, I could think of a lot of people who'd racked up decades of experience in their jobs but nevertheless seemed to stagnate at a middling level of competence. I'm sure you can, too. Think about it. Do you know anyone who's been doing something for a long, long time—maybe their entire professional lives—and yet the best you can say of their skill is that they're pretty much okay and not bad enough to fire? As a colleague of mine likes to joke: some people get twenty years of experience, while others get *one* year of experience . . . twenty times in a row.

Kaizen is Japanese for resisting the plateau of arrested development. Its literal translation is: "continuous improvement." A while back, the idea got some traction in American business culture when it was touted as the core principle behind Japan's spectacularly efficient manufacturing economy. After interviewing dozens and dozens of grit paragons, I can tell you that they all exude kaizen. There are no exceptions.

Likewise, in her interviews with "mega successful" people, journalist Hester Lacey has noticed that all of them demonstrate a striking desire to excel beyond their already remarkable level of expertise: "An actor might say, 'I may never play a role perfectly, but I want to do it as well as I possibly can. And in every role, I want to bring something new. I want to develop.' A writer might say, 'I want every book I do to be better than the last.'

"It's a persistent desire to do better," Hester explained. "It's the opposite of being complacent. But it's a *positive* state of mind, not a negative one. It's not looking backward with dissatisfaction. It's looking *forward* and wanting to grow."

My interview research made me wonder whether grit is not just about *quantity* of time devoted to interests, but also *quality* of time. Not just *more time on task*, but also *better time on task*.

I started reading everything I could about how skills develop.

Soon enough, this led me to the doorstep of cognitive psychologist Anders Ericsson. Ericsson has spent his career studying how experts acquire world-class skills. He's studied Olympic athletes, chess grandmasters, renowned concert pianists, prima ballerinas, PGA golfers, Scrabble champions, and expert radiologists. The list goes on.

Put it this way: Ericsson is the world expert on world experts.

Below, I've drawn a graph that summarizes what Ericsson's learned. If you track the development of internationally renowned performers, you invariably find that their skill improves gradually over years. As they get better, their rate of improvement slows. This turns out to be true for all of us. The more you know about your field, the slighter will be your improvement from one day to the next.

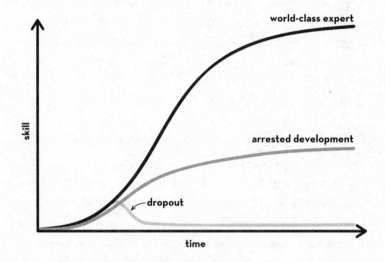

That there's a learning curve for skill development isn't surprising. But the timescale on which that development happens is. In one of Ericsson's studies, the very best violinists at a German music academy accumulated about ten thousand hours of practice over ten years before achieving elite levels of expertise. By comparison, less accomplished students accumulated about half as much practice over the same period.

Perhaps not so coincidentally, the dancer Martha Graham declared, "It takes about ten years to make a mature dancer." More than a century ago, psychologists studying telegraph operators observed that reaching complete fluency in Morse code was rare because of the "many years of hard apprenticeship" required. How many years? "Our evidence," the researchers concluded, "is that it requires ten years to make a thoroughly seasoned press dispatcher."

If you've read Ericsson's original research, you know that ten thousand hours of practice spread over ten years is just a rough average. Some of the musicians he studied reached the high-water mark of expertise before that, and some after. But there's a good reason why "the ten-thousand-hour rule" and "the ten-year-rule" have gone viral. They give you a visceral sense of the scale of the required investment. Not a few hours, not dozens, not scores, not hundreds. Thousands and thousands of hours of practice over years and years and years.

———

The really crucial insight of Ericsson's research, though, is *not* that experts log more hours of practice. Rather, it's that experts practice *differently*. Unlike most of us, experts are logging thousands upon thousands of hours of what Ericsson calls *deliberate practice*.

I suspected Ericsson could provide answers as to why, if practice is so important, experience doesn't always lead to excellence. So I decided to ask him about it, using myself as a prime example.

"Look, Professor Ericsson, I've been jogging about an hour a day, several days a week, since I was eighteen. And I'm not a second faster than I ever was. I've run for thousands of hours, and it doesn't look like I'm anywhere close to making the Olympics."

"That's interesting," he replied. "May I ask you a few questions?"

"Sure."

"Do you have a specific goal for your training?"

"To be healthy? To fit into my jeans?"

"Ah, yes. But when you go for a run, do you have a target in terms of the pace you'd like to keep? Or a distance goal? In other words, is there a *specific* aspect of your running you're trying to improve?"

"Um, no. I guess not."

Then he asked what I thought about while I was running.

"Oh, you know, I listen to NPR. Sometimes I think about the things I need to get done that day. I might plan what to make for dinner."

Then he verified that I wasn't keeping track of my runs in any systematic way. No diary of my pace, or my distance, or the routes I took, my ending heart rate, or how many intervals I'd sprinted instead of jogged. Why would I need to do that? There was no variety to my routine. Every run was like the last.

"I assume you don't have a coach?"

I laughed.

"Ah," he purred. "I think I understand. You aren't improving because you're *not* doing deliberate practice."

———

This is how experts practice:

First, they set a stretch goal, zeroing in on just one narrow aspect of their overall performance. Rather than focus on what they already do well, experts strive to improve specific weaknesses. They intentionally seek out challenges they can't yet meet. Olympic gold medal swimmer Rowdy Gaines, for example, said, "At every practice, I would try to beat myself. If my coach gave me ten 100s one day and asked me to hold 1:15, then the next day when he gave me ten 100s, I'd try to hold 1:14." * Virtuoso violist Roberto Díaz describes "working to find your Achilles' heel—the specific aspect of the music that needs problem solving."

Then, with undivided attention and great effort, experts strive to reach their stretch goal. Interestingly, many choose to do so while nobody's watching. Basketball great Kevin Durant has said, "I probably spend 70 percent of my time by myself, working on my game,

———

* This means swimming one hundred meters in one minute and fifteen seconds, and then trying to do the same in one minute and fourteen seconds, and so on.

just trying to fine-tune every single piece of my game." Likewise, the amount of time musicians devote to practicing alone is a much better predictor of how quickly they develop than time spent practicing with other musicians.

As soon as possible, experts hungrily seek feedback on how they did. Necessarily, much of that feedback is negative. This means that experts are more interested in what they did *wrong*—so they can fix it—than what they did *right*. The active processing of this feedback is as essential as its immediacy.

Here's how Ulrik Christensen learned this lesson. Christensen is a physician-turned-entrepreneur whose adaptive learning software is designed around the principles of deliberate practice. One of his early projects was a virtual reality game that teaches doctors the proper handling of urgent, complex cardiac conditions such as strokes and heart attacks. During one training session, he found himself alone with a physician who seemed unable to finish.

"I couldn't figure it out," Christensen told me. "This guy wasn't stupid, but after hours of detailed feedback on what he'd done wrong, he still wasn't getting the right answers. Everyone else had gone home, and there we were, stuck." Exasperated, Christensen stopped him just before he got the next round of feedback. "Time-out," Christensen said. "What you just did, treating this patient, is there anything you did just now where you were in doubt? Anything where you weren't sure it met the new guidelines?"

The doctor thought a moment and then listed decisions he'd been certain about; then he named a few choices about which he was less sure. In other words, he *reflected* for a moment on what he knew and what he didn't.

Christensen nodded, listening, and when the doctor was finished, he let him see the computer screen with the same feedback that had been displayed a dozen times before. On the next trial, the doctor executed the procedure correctly.

And after feedback, then what?

Then experts do it all over again, and again, and again. Until they have finally mastered what they set out to do. Until what was a struggle before is now fluent and flawless. Until conscious incompetence becomes unconscious competence.

In the story of the doctor who finally took a moment to think about what he was doing, Christensen kept the practice going until the doctor was doing the procedure without any errors at all. After four consecutive, perfectly correct repetitions, Christensen said, "Good job. We're done with this for the day."

And . . . then what? What follows mastery of a stretch goal?

Then experts start all over again with a *new* stretch goal.

One by one, these subtle refinements add up to dazzling mastery.

———

Deliberate practice was first studied in chess players and then in musicians and athletes. If you're not a chess player, musician, or athlete, you might be wondering whether the general principles of deliberate practice apply to you.

Without hesitation, I can tell you the answer: *YES.* Even the most complex and creative of human abilities can be broken down into its component skills, each of which can be practiced, practiced, practiced.

For example, deliberate practice is how Benjamin Franklin described improving his writing. In his autobiography, Franklin describes collecting the very best essays in his favorite magazine, the *Spectator.* He read and reread them, taking notes, and then he hid the originals in a drawer. Next, Franklin rewrote the essays. "Then I compared my *Spectator* with the original, discovered some of my faults, and corrected them." Like the modern-day experts Ericsson studies, Franklin zeroed in on specific weaknesses and drilled them relentlessly. For instance, to improve his ability to make logical arguments, Franklin would jumble his notes on essays and then attempt to put them in a sensible order: "This was to teach me method in the arrangement of the thoughts." Likewise, to enhance his command of language, Franklin practiced, over and over again, the translation of prose into poetry and poetry into prose.

Franklin's witty aphorisms make it hard to believe he wasn't a "natural" writer from the very start. But perhaps we should let Franklin himself have the last word on the matter: *There are no gains without pains.*

But what if you're not a writer, either?

If you're in business, listen to what management guru Peter Drucker said after a lifetime of advising CEOs. Effective management "demands doing certain—and fairly simple—things. It consists of a small number of practices. . . ."

If you're a surgeon, consider what Atul Gawande has said: "People often assume that you have to have great hands to become a surgeon, but it's not true." What's most important, Gawande said, is "practicing this one difficult thing day and night for years on end."

If you want to break a world record, as magician David Blaine did when he held his breath underwater for seventeen minutes, watch his TED talk. At the very end, the man who can control every aspect of his physiology breaks down, sobbing: "As a magician, I try to show things to people that seem impossible. And I think magic, whether I'm holding my breath or shuffling a deck of cards, is pretty simple. It's practice, it's training, and it's"—he sobs—"experimenting"—he sobs again—"while pushing through the pain to be the best that I can be. And that's what magic is to me. . . ."

———

After getting to know each other a little better, Ericsson and I designed a study to discover how, exactly, gritty kids triumph at the National Spelling Bee.

I already knew that grittier spellers accumulated more practice and performed better than their less gritty competitors. What I didn't know was whether deliberate practice was driving these skill improvements, and whether it was grit that enabled spellers to do more of it.

With the help of Ericsson's students, we began by interviewing spelling bee finalists to learn what sorts of things they did to prepare for competition. In parallel, we pored through published books on the topic, including *How to Spell Like a Champ* by the bee's own national director, Paige Kimble.

We learned that there are basically three types of activities recommended by experienced spellers, their parents, and coaches: First, reading for pleasure and playing word games like Scrabble. Second, getting quizzed by another person or a computer program. Third, unassisted and solitary spelling practice, including memorizing new words from the dictionary, reviewing words in a spelling notebook, and committing to memory Latin, Greek, and other word origins. Only this third category of activity met the criteria for deliberate practice.

Several months before the final competition, spellers were mailed questionnaires. In addition to the Grit Scale, we asked them to complete a log in which they estimated the hours per week they spent on various spelling activities. We also asked them to rate how it felt to do these activities—in terms of enjoyment and effort—in the moment they were doing them.

That May, when the finals aired on ESPN, Anders Ericsson and I were watching.

Who took home the trophy? A thirteen-year-old girl named Kerry Close. It was her fifth consecutive year of competition, and from the log she completed in our study, I estimate she'd accumulated at least three thousand hours of spelling practice. Kerry's triumphant last words at the microphone, articulated with confidence and a smile, were: "Ursprache. U-R-S-P-R-A-C-H-E. Ursprache."

"I'm studying as hard as I can for my last year—to go for it," Kerry told a journalist who'd been tracking her preparations. "I'm trying to learn words off the regular list, to learn more obscure words that have a chance of coming up." The year before, the same journalist made the observation that Kerry "does more word study by herself. She works with numerous spelling study guides, makes lists of interesting words from her reading, and labors her way through the dictionary."

When we analyzed our data, we first confirmed what I'd found the year before: grittier spellers practiced more than less gritty spellers. But the most important finding was that the *type* of practice mattered tremendously. *Deliberate practice predicted advancing to further rounds in final competition far better than any other kind of preparation.*

When I share these findings with parents and students, I hasten to add that there are many, many learning benefits to being quizzed. Shining a light on what you *think* you know but *actually* haven't yet mastered is one. Indeed, winner Kerry Close later told me that she used quizzing to diagnose her weaknesses—to identify certain words or types of words she consistently misspelled so that she could focus her efforts on mastering them. In a sense, quizzing may have been a necessary prelude to doing more targeted, more efficient, deliberate practice.

What about reading for fun? *Nada.* Pretty much all of the kids in the National Spelling Bee are interested in language, but there wasn't even a *hint* of a relationship between reading for fun, which they all enjoyed, and spelling prowess.

———

If you judge practice by how much it improves your skill, then deliberate practice has no rival. This lesson seemed to become increasingly clear to spellers as they spent more time competing. With each successive year of experience, they spent more time practicing deliberately. The same trend was even more pronounced in the month before the actual finals, when the average speller was devoting ten hours per week to deliberate practice.

If, however, you judge practice by what it *feels* like, you might come to a different conclusion. On average, spellers rated deliberate practice as significantly *more effortful*, and significantly *less enjoyable*, than anything else they did to prepare for competition. In contrast, spellers experienced reading books for pleasure and playing word games like Scrabble as effortless and as enjoyable as "eating your favorite food."

A vivid—if somewhat melodramatic—firsthand description of what deliberate practice can feel like comes from dancer Martha Graham: "Dancing appears glamorous, easy, delightful. But the path to the paradise of that achievement is not easier than any other. There is fatigue so great that the body cries even in its sleep. There are times of complete frustration. There are daily small deaths."

Not everyone would describe working outside their comfort zone in such extreme terms, but Ericsson generally finds that deliberate practice is experienced as supremely effortful. As evidence that working at the far edge of our skills with complete concentration is exhausting, he points out that even world-class performers at the *peak* of their careers can only handle a maximum of one hour of deliberate practice before needing a break, and in total, can only do about three to five hours of deliberate practice per day.

It's also relevant that many athletes and musicians take naps after their most intensive training sessions. Why? Rest and recovery may seem an obvious necessity for athletes. But nonathletes say much the same about their most intense exertions, suggesting that it is the mental work, as much as the physical stresses, that makes deliberate practice so strenuous. For instance, here's how director Judd Apatow describes making a film: "Every day is an experiment. Every scene might not work and so you're concentrating—*Is it working? Should I get an extra line for editing? What would I change if I had to, if I hated this in three months, why would I hate it?* And you're concentrating and you're exhausted. . . . It's pretty intense."

And, finally, world-class performers who retire tend not to keep up nearly the same deliberate practice schedule. If practice was intrinsically pleasurable—enjoyable for its own sake—you'd expect them to keep doing it.

———

The year after Ericsson and I began working together, Mihaly Csikszentmihalyi* spent his summer at my university as a scholar in residence. Csikszentmihalyi is as eminent a psychologist as Ericsson, and both have devoted their careers to studying experts. But their accounts of world-class expertise couldn't be more different.

For Csikszentmihalyi, the signature experience of experts is *flow*, a state of complete concentration "that leads to a feeling of spontaneity." Flow is performing at high levels of challenge and yet feeling "effortless," like "you don't have to think about it, you're just doing it."

For example, an orchestra conductor told Csikszentmihalyi:

You are in an ecstatic state to such a point that you feel as though you almost don't exist. . . . My hand seems devoid of myself, and I have nothing to do with what's happening. I just sit there watching in a state of awe and wonderment. And [the music] just flows out by itself.

And a competitive figure skater gave this description of the flow state:

It was just one of those programs that clicked. I mean everything went right, everything felt good . . . it's just such a rush, like you

———
* Pronounced *cheeks-sent-me-high*. And for years, Mihaly has gone by "Mike."

could feel it could go on and on and on, like you don't want it to stop because it's going so well. It's almost as though you don't have to think, everything goes automatically without thinking. . . .

Csikszentmihalyi has gathered similar first-person reports from hundreds of experts. In every field studied, optimal experience is described in similar terms.

Ericsson is skeptical that deliberate practice could ever feel as enjoyable as flow. In his view, "skilled people can sometimes experience highly enjoyable states ('flow' as described by Mihaly Csikszentmihalyi, 1990) during their performance. These states are, however, incompatible with deliberate practice. . . ." Why? Because deliberate practice is carefully planned, and flow is spontaneous. Because deliberate practice requires working where challenges exceed skill, and flow is most commonly experienced when challenge and skill are in balance. And, most important, because deliberate practice is exceptionally effortful, and flow is, by definition, effortless.

Csikszentmihalyi has published a contrary opinion: "Researchers who study the development of talents have concluded that to learn any complex skill well takes about 10,000 hours of practice. . . . And the practice can be very boring and unpleasant. While this state of affairs is all too often true, the consequences are by no means self-evident." Csikszentmihalyi goes on to share a personal story that helps explain his perspective. In Hungary, where he grew up, on the tall wooden gate at the entrance to the local elementary school, hung a sign that read: *The roots of knowledge are bitter, but its fruits are sweet.* This always struck him as deeply untrue: "Even when the learning is hard," he writes, "it is not bitter when you feel that it is worth having, that you can master it, that practicing what you learned will express who you are and help you achieve what you desire."

So who's right?

As fate would have it, the same summer Csikszentmihalyi was visiting, Ericsson was also in town. I arranged for them to debate the topic of "passion and world-class performance" before an audience of about eighty educators.

When they sat down at the table in the front of the lecture hall, I realized that the two men are near-perfect doppelgängers. Both are tall and solidly built. Both are European by birth, with slight accents that somehow make them seem even more eminent and scholarly. Both sport close-cropped beards, and though only Csikszentmihalyi's has gone all white, either man would be a good choice if you were looking for someone to play Santa Claus.

On the day of the panel, I was a little anxious. I don't like conflict—even when it's not mine.

It turns out I had nothing to worry about. The proponents of deliberate practice versus flow behaved as perfect gentlemen. No insults were exchanged. There wasn't even a hint of disrespect.

Instead, Ericsson and Csikszentmihalyi sat shoulder to shoulder, each taking the microphone when it was their turn, each methodically summarizing decades of research supporting starkly contrasting perspectives. When one was speaking, the other appeared to listen intently. And then the microphone would change hands. So it went for ninety minutes.

Do experts suffer, I wanted to know. *Or are they ecstatic?*

Somehow, the dialogue I hoped would resolve this conundrum played out as two separate presentations—one on deliberate practice and the other on flow—spliced together.

When it was all over, I found myself a little disappointed. It wasn't the drama that I missed, it was the resolution. I still didn't have an answer to my question: Is expert performance a matter of arduous and not-so-fun-in-the-moment exertion, or can it be effortless and joyous?

———

For years after that anticlimactic summit, I read and thought about the issue. Finally, because I never developed the conviction that might prompt me to reject one side and take the other, I decided to collect some data. I asked thousands of adults who'd taken the Grit Scale online to take a second questionnaire assessing flow. The participants in this study included men and women of all ages representing all manner of professions: actors, bakers, bank tellers, barbers, dentists, doctors, police officers, secretaries, teachers, waiters, and welders . . . to name just a few.

Across these diverse occupations, grittier adults reported experiencing *more* flow, not less. In other words, flow and grit go hand in hand.

Putting together what I learned from this survey, the findings on National Spelling Bee finalists, and a decadelong inspection of the relevant research literature, I've come to the following conclusion: *Gritty people do more deliberate practice and experience more flow.* There's no contradiction here, for two reasons. First, deliberate practice is a behavior, and flow is an experience. Anders Ericsson is talking about what experts *do*; Mihaly Csikszentmihalyi is talking about how experts *feel*. Second, you don't have to be doing deliberate practice and experiencing flow at the same time. And, in fact, I think that for most experts, they rarely go together.

More research is needed to settle the question, and in the next few years, I'm hoping that Ericsson, Csikszentmihalyi, and I can collaborate to do exactly that.

Currently, my view is that the primary motivation for doing effortful deliberate practice is to improve your skill. You're concentrating one hundred percent, and you've deliberately set the level of challenge to exceed your current level of skill. You're in "problem solving" mode, analyzing everything you do to bring it closer to the ideal—the goal you set at the beginning of the practice session. You're getting feedback, and a lot of that feedback is about what you're doing wrong, and you're using that feedback to make adjustments and try again.

The motivation that predominates during flow, in contrast, is entirely different. The flow state is intrinsically pleasurable. You don't care whether you're improving some narrow aspect of your skill set. And though you're concentrating one hundred percent, you're not at all in "problem solving" mode. You're not analyzing what you're doing; you're just doing. You're getting feedback, but because the level of challenge *just meets* your current level of skill, that feedback is telling you that you're doing a lot right. You feel like you're in complete control, because you are. You're floating. You lose track of time. No matter how fast you're running or how intensely you're thinking, when you're in flow, everything *feels* effortless.

In other words, deliberate practice is for preparation, and flow is for performance.

Let's return to swimmer Rowdy Gaines.

Gaines told me he once tabulated how much practice it took to develop the stamina, technique, confidence, and judgment to win an Olympic gold medal. In the eight-year period leading up to the 1984 games, he swam, in increments of fifty-yard laps, at least twenty thousand miles. Of course, if you add in the years before and after, the odometer goes even higher.

"I swam around the world," he told me with a soft laugh, "for a race that lasted forty-nine seconds."

"Did you enjoy those miles?" I asked. "I mean, did you love practicing?"

"I'm not going to lie," he replied. "I never really enjoyed going to practice, and I certainly didn't enjoy it while I was there. In fact, there were brief moments, walking to the pool at four or four-thirty in the morning, or sometimes when I couldn't take the pain, when I'd think, 'God, is this worth it?'"

"So why didn't you quit?"

"It's very simple," Rowdy said. "It's because I loved swimming. . . . I had a passion for competing, for the *result* of training, for the feeling of being in shape, for winning, for traveling, for meeting friends. I hated practice, but I had an overall passion for swimming."

Olympic gold medalist rower Mads Rasmussen offered a similar account of his motivation: "It's about hard work. When it's not fun, you do what you need to do anyway. Because when you achieve results, it's incredibly fun. You get to enjoy the 'Aha' at the end, and that is what drags you along a lot of the way."

The idea of years of challenge-exceeding-skill practice leading to moments of challenge-meeting-skill flow explains why elite performance can *look* so effortless: in a sense, it *is*. Here's an example. Eighteen-year-old swimmer Katie Ledecky recently broke her own world record in the 1,500-meter freestyle. Improbably, history was made during a preliminary round at a competition in Kazan, Russia. "To be honest, it felt pretty easy," she said afterward. "I was so relaxed." But it's not flow to which Ledecky credits her speed: "Breaking that record is testament to the work I have put in and the shape I am in right now."

Indeed, Ledecky has been swimming since she was six. She's developed a reputation for working fiercely hard at every single practice, sometimes training with male swimmers for added challenge. Three years ago, Ledecky described blanking out a little bit in the race that won her the gold medal in the eight-hundred-meter freestyle. "One thing in terms of swimming that people don't really know," she later said, "is that the work you put in [during] practice shows off in the meet."

———

Here's my own story of hours of effortful deliberate practice leading to moments of effortless flow. A few years ago, a producer named Juliet Blake called to ask if I'd be interested in giving a six-minute TED talk. "Sure," I said. "Sounds fun!"

"Wonderful! After you have your talk ready, we'll have a video conference where we watch you give it, and we'll give you some feedback. You know, something like a rehearsal."

Hmmm, "feedback" you say? Something other than applause? More slowly, I said, "Sure . . . that sounds fine."

I prepared a talk and on the appointed day connected with Juliet and her boss, the leader of TED, Chris Anderson. Staring into the webcam, I delivered my talk in the allotted time. Then I waited for my effusive praise.

If there was any, I missed it.

Instead, what I got was Chris telling me he'd gotten lost in all my scientific jargon. Too many syllables. Too many slides. And not enough clear, understandable examples. Further, how I'd come to this whole line of research—my road from teacher to psychologist—was unclear and unsatisfying. Juliet agreed. She added that I'd managed to tell a story with absolutely zero suspense. The way I'd designed my talk was like telling the punch line of a joke at the very beginning.

Ouch! That bad, huh? Juliet and Chris are busy people, and I knew I wouldn't get a second chance at getting coached. So I forced myself to listen. Afterward, I pondered who knew better how to give a great talk on grit: them or me?

It didn't take long to realize that *they* were the experienced storytellers, and I was the scientist who needed feedback to make her talk better.

So I rewrote the talk, practiced in front of my family, and got more negative feedback. "Why do you say 'Um' all the time?" my older daughter, Amanda, asked. "Yeah, why do you do that, Mom?" my younger daughter, Lucy, chimed in. "And you bite your lip when you're nervous. Don't do that. It's distracting."

More practice. More refinements.

Then the fateful day arrived. I gave a talk that bore only a weak resemblance to the one I'd originally proposed. It was better. A *lot* better. Watch that talk and you'll see me in flow. Search YouTube for the many rehearsals that preceded it—or, for that matter, footage of *anyone* doing effortful, mistake-ridden, repetitive deliberate practice—and my guess is you'll come up empty.

Nobody wants to show you the hours and hours of becoming. They'd rather show the highlight of what they've become.

After it was all over, I rushed to meet my husband and mother-in-law, who'd been in the audience that day to cheer me on. As soon as they were within earshot, I called out preemptively: "Just the effusive praise, please!" And they delivered.

———

Lately, I've been asking gritty performers and their coaches in diverse fields to elaborate on how it feels to do deliberate practice. Many agree with dancer Martha Graham that attempting to do what you cannot yet do is frustrating, uncomfortable, and even painful.

However, some have suggested that, in fact, the experience of deliberate practice can be extremely positive—not just in the long-term but in the moment. *Fun* isn't quite the word they use to describe deliberate practice, but neither is *bitter*. And, too, top performers point out that the alternative to deliberate practice—mindlessly "going through the motions" without improvement—can be its own form of suffering.

I puzzled over these observations for a while, and then I decided to look back at the diary data that Ericsson and I had collected from the National Spelling Bee finalists. While I knew that spellers rated deliberate practice as especially effortful and unenjoyable, I also recalled that there was quite a spread around these averages. In other words, not all spellers had the same exact experience.

I looked to see how grittier competitors experienced deliberate practice. Compared to their less passionate, less persevering competitors, grittier spellers not only logged more hours of deliberate practice, they rated it as both *more enjoyable* and *more effortful*. That's right. Grittier kids reported working harder than other kids when doing deliberate practice but, at the same time, said they enjoyed it more than other kids, too.

It's hard to know for sure what to make of this finding. One possibility is that grittier kids spend more time doing deliberate practice, and that, over the years, they develop a taste for hard work as they experience the rewards of their labor. This is the "learn to love the burn" story. Alternatively, it could be that grittier kids enjoy the hard work more, and that gets them to do more of it. This is the "some people enjoy a challenge" story.

I can't tell you which of these accounts is accurate, and if I had to guess, I'd say there's some truth to both. As we'll learn in chapter 11, there's solid scientific evidence that the subjective experience of effort—what it *feels* like to work hard—can and does change when, for example, effort is rewarded in some way. I've watched my own daughters learn to enjoy working hard more than they used to, and I can say the same for myself.

On the other hand, Katie Ledecky's coach, Bruce Gemmell, says she's *always* relished a tough challenge.

"There's a little video clip that Katie's parents have of one of her first swim meets," Bruce told me. "It's just one lap. She's six years old. She swims a few strokes and then grabs on to the lane line. She swims a few more strokes and grabs on to the lane line again. Finally, she gets to the end of the pool and gets out of the water. Dad's filming it, and he asks, 'Tell me about your first race. How was it?' She goes, 'Great!' A few seconds later, she adds, 'That was hard!' And she's beaming— a smile from ear to ear. That says it all right there. She has that attitude with everything we do."

In the same conversation, Bruce told me that Katie willingly does more deliberate practice than anyone he's ever met. "We'll try a drill that she's horrible at—something where she'll start off in the poorest third of the group doing it. Then I'll catch her sneaking practice time to get better at it, so within some period of time, she's one of the best in the group. Some other swimmers, well, they try and they fail at it, and I have to cajole and beg them to try it again."

If deliberate practice can be "awesome," can it ever feel like effortless flow?

When I asked spelling champ Kerry Close if she'd ever experienced the state of flow during deliberate practice, she said, "No, the only time I could say that I was in flow was when I wasn't being challenged." At the same time, she described deliberate practice as gratifying in its own way: "Some of my most *rewarding* studying," she told me, "was on my own, forcing myself to break down a big task into multiple parts and getting it done."

As of now, there isn't enough research to say whether deliberate practice can be experienced as effortless flow. My guess is that deliberate practice can be deeply gratifying, but in a different way than flow. In other words, there are *different kinds* of positive experience: the thrill of getting better is one, and the ecstasy of performing at your best is another.

———

Other than getting yourself a terrific coach, mentor, or teacher, how can you get the most out of deliberate practice and—because you've earned it—experience more flow?

First, *know the science.*

Each of the basic requirements of deliberate practice is unremarkable:

- A clearly defined stretch goal
- Full concentration and effort
- Immediate and informative feedback
- Repetition with reflection and refinement

But how many hours of practice do most people accomplish that checks all *four* of these boxes? My guess is that many people are cruising through life doing precisely *zero* hours of daily deliberate practice.

Even supermotivated people who're working to exhaustion may not be doing deliberate practice. For instance, when a Japanese rowing team invited Olympic gold medalist Mads Rasmussen to come visit, he was shocked at how many hours of practice their athletes were logging. It's not hours of brute-force exhaustion you're after, he told them. It's high-quality, thoughtful training goals pursued, just as Ericsson's research has shown, for just a few hours a day, tops.

Noa Kageyama, a performance psychologist on the faculty of the Juilliard School of Music, says he's been playing the violin since he was two but didn't really start practicing deliberately until he was twenty-two. Why not? There was no lack of motivation—at one point, young Noa was taking lessons with four different teachers and, literally, commuting to three different cities to work with them all. Really, the problem was just that Noa didn't know better. Once he discovered there was an actual science of practice—an approach that would improve his skills more efficiently—both the quality of his practice and his satisfaction with his progress skyrocketed. He's now devoted himself to sharing that knowledge with other musicians.

A few years ago, my graduate student Lauren Eskreis-Winkler and I decided to teach kids about deliberate practice. We put together self-guided lessons, complete with cartoons and stories, illustrating key differences between deliberate practice and less effective ways of studying. We explained that no matter their initial talent, great performers in every domain improve through deliberate practice. We let students know that hidden behind every effortless performance on YouTube are hours and hours of unrecorded, invisible-to-outsiders, challenging, effortful, mistake-ridden practice. We told them that trying to do things they can't yet do, failing, and learning what they need to do differently is *exactly* the way experts practice. We helped them understand that feelings of frustration aren't necessarily a sign they're on the wrong track. On the contrary, we told them that wishing they did things better is extremely common during learning. We then tested this intervention against different kinds of placebo control activities.

What we found is that students can change the way they think about practice and achievement. For instance, asked what advice they'd give to another student on how to succeed in school, students who learned about deliberate practice were more likely to recommend "focus on your weaknesses" and "concentrate one hundred percent." Given the choice between doing deliberate practice in math versus entertaining themselves with social media and gaming websites, they elected to do more deliberate practice. And, finally, in the case of those who'd been performing at a below-average level in class, learning about deliberate practice increased their report card grades.

Which leads to my *second* suggestion for getting the most out of deliberate practice: *Make it a habit.*

By this I mean, figure out when and where you're most comfortable doing deliberate practice. Once you've made your selection, do deliberate practice then and there every day. Why? Because routines are a godsend when it comes to doing something hard. A mountain of research studies, including a few of my own, show that when you have a habit of practicing at the same time and in the same place every day, you hardly have to think about getting started. You just do.

The book *Daily Rituals* by Mason Currey describes a day in the life of one hundred sixty-one artists, scientists, and other creators. If you look for a particular rule, like *Always drink coffee*, or *Never drink coffee*, or *Only work in your bedroom*, or *Never work in your bedroom*, you won't find it. But if instead you ask, "What do these creators have in common?" you'll find the answer right in the title: daily rituals. In their own particular way, all the experts in this book consistently put in hours and hours of solitary deliberate practice. They follow routines. They're creatures of habit.

For instance, cartoonist Charles Schulz, who drew almost eighteen thousand *Peanuts* comic strips in his career, rose at dawn, showered, shaved, and had breakfast with his children. He then drove his kids to school and went to his studio, where he worked through lunch (a ham sandwich and a glass of milk) until his children returned from school. Writer Maya Angelou's routine was to get up and have coffee with her husband, and then, by seven in the morning, deliver herself to a "tiny mean" hotel room with no distractions until two in the afternoon.

Eventually, if you keep practicing in the same time and place, what once took conscious thought to initiate becomes automatic. "There is no more miserable human being," observed William James, than the one for whom "the beginning of every bit of work" must be decided anew each day.

I myself learned that lesson quickly. I now know what Joyce Carol Oates meant when she likened completing the first draft of a book to "pushing a peanut across a very dirty kitchen floor with your nose." So what'd I do? Here's the simple daily plan that helped me get going: *When it's eight in the morning and I'm in my home office, I will reread yesterday's draft.* This habit didn't make the writing easier, per se, but it sure made it easier to get started.

My third suggestion for getting the most out of deliberate practice is to *change the way you experience it.*

Around the time I was revisiting my National Spelling Bee data and discovering how much more enjoyable the experience of deliberate practice is for grittier competitors, I called up a swimming coach named Terry Laughlin. Terry has coached every level of swimmer, from complete newbie to Olympic champion, and broken records himself in open-water Masters swimming. I was particularly interested in his perspective because he's long advocated what he calls a "total immersion" approach to swimming—essentially a relaxed, mindful approach to gliding through the water.

"Deliberate practice can feel wonderful," Terry told me. "If you try, you can learn to embrace challenge rather than fear it. You can do all the things you're supposed to do during deliberate practice—a clear goal, feedback, all of it—and still feel great while you're doing it.

"It's all about in-the-moment self-awareness *without judgment*," he continued. "It's about relieving yourself of the judgment that gets in the way of enjoying the challenge."

After hanging up with Terry, I began to think about the fact that infants and toddlers spend most of their time trying to do things they can't, again and again—and yet they don't seem especially embarrassed or anxious. *No pain, no gain* is a rule that doesn't seem to apply to the preschool set.

Elena Bodrova and Deborah Leong, psychologists who've devoted their careers to studying how children learn, agree that learning from mistakes is something babies and toddlers don't mind at all. Watch a baby struggle to sit up, or a toddler learn to walk: you'll see one error after another, failure after failure, a lot of challenge exceeding skill, a lot of concentration, a lot of feedback, a lot of learning. Emotionally? Well, they're too young to ask, but very young children don't seem tortured while they're trying to do things they can't yet do.

And then . . . something changes. According to Elena and Deborah, around the time children enter kindergarten, they begin to notice that their mistakes inspire certain reactions in grown-ups. What do we do? We frown. Our cheeks flush a bit. We rush over to our little ones to point out that they've done something *wrong*. And what's the lesson we're teaching? Embarrassment. Fear. Shame. Coach Bruce Gemmell says that's exactly what happens to many of his swimmers: "Between coaches and parents and friends and the media, they've learned that failing is *bad*, so they protect themselves and won't stick their neck out and give their best effort."

"Shame doesn't help you fix anything," Deborah told me.

So what's to be done?

Elena and Deborah ask teachers to *model* emotion-free mistake making. They actually instruct teachers to commit an error on purpose and then let students see them say, with a smile, "Oh, gosh, I thought there were *five* blocks in this pile! Let me count again! One . . . two . . . three . . . four . . . five . . . *six*! There are *six* blocks! Great! I learned I need to touch each block as I count!"

Whether you can make deliberate practice as ecstatic as flow, I don't know, but I do think you can try saying to yourself, and to others, "That was hard! It was great!"

Chapter 8

PURPOSE

Interest is one source of passion. Purpose—the intention to contribute to the well-being of others—is another. The mature passions of gritty people depend on both.

For some, purpose comes first. This is the only way I can understand a paragon of grit like Alex Scott. Ever since Alex could remember, she'd been sick. Her neuroblastoma had been diagnosed when she was a year old. Shortly after her fourth birthday, Alex told her mother, "When I get out of the hospital, I want to have a lemonade stand." And she did. She operated her first lemonade stand before she turned five, raising two thousand dollars for her doctors to "help other kids, like they helped me." When Alex passed away four years later, she'd inspired so many people to create their own lemonade stands that she'd raised more than a million dollars. Alex's family has continued her legacy, and to date, Alex's Lemonade Stand Foundation has raised more than one hundred million dollars for cancer research.

Alex was extraordinary. But most people first become attracted to things they enjoy and only later appreciate how these personal interests might also benefit others. In other words, the more common sequence is to start out with a relatively self-oriented interest, then learn self-disciplined practice, and, finally, integrate that work with an other-centered purpose.

The psychologist Benjamin Bloom was among the first to notice this three-phase progression.

Thirty years ago, when Bloom set out to interview world-class athletes, artists, mathematicians, and scientists, he knew he'd learn something about how people reach the top of their fields. What he didn't foresee was that he'd discover a general model of learning that applied to all the fields he studied. Despite superficial differences in their upbringing and training, all the extraordinary people in Bloom's study had progressed through three distinct periods of development. We discussed what Bloom called the "early years" in chapter 6 on interest and "the middle years" in chapter 7 on practice. We've now come to the third, final, and longest phase in Bloom's model—the "later years"—when, as he put it, "the larger purpose and meaning" of work finally becomes apparent.

———

When I talk to grit paragons, and they tell me that what they're pursuing has *purpose*, they mean something much deeper than mere intention. They're not just goal-oriented; the nature of their goals is special.

When I probe, asking, "Can you tell me more? What do you mean?" there sometimes follows an earnest, stumbling struggle to put how they feel into words. But always—always—those next sentences mention other people. Sometimes it's very particular ("my children," "my clients," "my students") and sometimes quite abstract ("this country," "the sport," "science," "society"). However they say it, the message is the same: the long days and evenings of toil, the setbacks and disappointments and struggle, the sacrifice—all this is worth it because, ultimately, their efforts pay dividends to *other people*.

At its core, the idea of purpose is the idea that what we do matters to people other than ourselves.

A precocious altruist like Alex Scott is an easy-to-fathom example of other-centered purpose.

So is art activist Jane Golden, the grit paragon we met in chapter 6. Interest in art led Jane to become a muralist in Los Angeles after graduating from college. In her late twenties, Jane was diagnosed with lupus and told she didn't have long to live. "The news came as such a shock," she told me. "It gave me a new perspective on life." When Jane recovered from the disease's most acute symptoms, she realized she would outlive the doctors' initial predictions, but with chronic pain.

Moving back to her hometown of Philadelphia, she took over a small anti-graffiti program in the mayor's office and, over the next three decades, grew it into one of the largest public art programs in the world.

Now in her late fifties, Jane continues to work from early morning to late in the evening, six or seven days a week. One colleague likens working with her to running a campaign office the night before an election—except Election Day never comes. For Jane, those hours translate into more murals and programs, and that means more opportunities for people in the community to create and experience art.

When I asked Jane about her lupus, she admitted, matter-of-factly, that pain is a constant companion. She once told a journalist: "There are moments when I cry. I think I just can't do it anymore, push that boulder up the hill. But feeling sorry for myself is pointless, so I find ways to get energized." Why? Because her work is interesting? That's only the beginning of Jane's motivation. "Everything I do is in a spirit of service," she told me. "I feel driven by it. It's a moral imperative." Putting it more succinctly, she said: "Art saves lives."

Other grit paragons have top-level goals that are purposeful in less obvious ways.

Renowned wine critic Antonio Galloni, for instance, told me: "An appreciation for wine is something I'm passionate about sharing with other people. When I walk into a restaurant, I want to see a beautiful bottle of wine on every table."

Antonio says his mission is "to help people understand their own palates." When that happens, he says, it's like a lightbulb goes off, and he wants "to make a million lightbulbs go off."

So, while interest for Antonio came first—his parents owned a food and wine shop while he was growing up, and he "was always fascinated by wine, even at a young age"—his passion is very much enhanced by the idea of helping other people: "I'm not a brain surgeon, I'm not curing cancer. But in this one small way, I think I'm going to make the world better. I wake up every morning with a sense of purpose."

In my "grit lexicon," therefore, *purpose* means "the intention to contribute to the well-being of others."

———

After hearing, repeatedly, from grit paragons how deeply connected they felt their work was to other people, I decided to analyze that connection more closely. Sure, purpose might matter, but how *much* does it matter, relative to other priorities? It seemed possible that single-minded focus on a top-level goal is, in fact, typically more *selfish* than *selfless*.

Aristotle was among the first to recognize that there are at least two ways to pursue happiness. He called one "eudaimonic"—in harmony with one's good (*eu*) inner spirit (*daemon*)—and the other "hedonic"—aimed at positive, in-the-moment, inherently self-centered experiences. Aristotle clearly took a side on the issue, deeming the hedonic life primitive and vulgar, and upholding the eudaimonic life as noble and pure.

But, in fact, both of these two approaches to happiness have very deep evolutionary roots.

On one hand, human beings seek pleasure because, by and large, the things that bring us pleasure are those that increase our chances of survival. If our ancestors hadn't craved food and sex, for example, they wouldn't have lived very long or had many offspring. To some extent, all of us are, as Freud put it, driven by the "pleasure principle."

On the other hand, human beings have evolved to seek meaning and purpose. In the most profound way, we're social creatures. Why? Because the drive to connect with and serve others *also* promotes survival. How? Because people who cooperate are more likely to survive than loners. Society depends on stable interpersonal relationships, and society in so many ways keeps us fed, shelters us from the elements, and protects us from enemies. The desire to connect is as basic a human need as our appetite for pleasure.

To some extent, we're *all* hardwired to pursue both hedonic and eudaimonic happiness. But the *relative* weight we give these two kinds of pursuits can vary. Some of us care about purpose much more than we care about pleasure, and vice versa.

To probe the motivations that underlie grit, I recruited sixteen thousand American adults and asked them to complete the Grit Scale. As part of a long supplementary questionnaire, study participants read statements about *purpose*—for instance, "What I do matters to society"—and indicated the extent to which each applied to them. They did the same for six statements about the importance of *pleasure*—for instance, "For me, the good life is the pleasurable life." From these responses, we generated scores ranging from 1 to 5 for their orientations to purpose and pleasure, respectively.

Below, I've plotted the data from this large-scale study. As you can see, gritty people aren't monks, nor are they hedonists. In terms of pleasure-seeking, they're just like anyone else; pleasure is moderately important no matter how gritty you are. In sharp contrast, you can see that grittier people are *dramatically* more motivated than others to seek a meaningful, other-centered life. Higher scores on purpose correlate with *higher* scores on the Grit Scale.

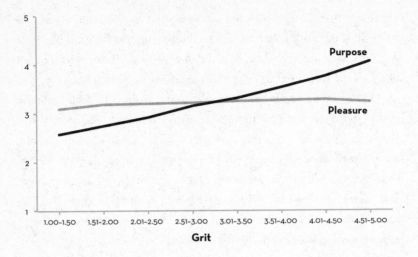

This is not to say that all grit paragons are saints, but rather, that most gritty people see their ultimate aims as deeply connected to the world beyond themselves.

My claim here is that, for most people, purpose is a tremendously powerful source of motivation. There may be exceptions, but the rarity of these exceptions proves the rule.

—————

What am I missing?

Well, it's unlikely that my sample included many terrorists or serial killers. And it's true that I haven't interviewed political despots or Mafia bosses. I guess you could argue that I'm overlooking a whole population of grit paragons whose goals are purely selfish or, worse, directed at harming others.

On this point, I concede. Partly. In theory, you can be a misanthropic, misguided paragon of grit. Joseph Stalin and Adolf Hitler, for instance, were most certainly gritty. They also prove that the idea of purpose can be perverted. How many millions of innocent people have perished at the hands of demagogues whose *stated* intention was to contribute to the well-being of others?

In other words, a genuinely positive, altruistic purpose is not an absolute requirement of grit. And I have to admit that, yes, it is possible to be a gritty villain.

But, on the whole, I take the survey data I've gathered, and what paragons of grit tell me in person, at face value. So, while interest is crucial to sustaining passion over the long-term, so, too, is the desire to connect with and help others.

My guess is that, if you take a moment to reflect on the times in your life when you've really been at your best—when you've risen to the challenges before you, finding strength to do what might have seemed impossible—you'll realize that the goals you achieved were connected in some way, shape, or form to the *benefit of other people*.

In sum, there may be gritty villains in the world, but my research suggests there are many more gritty heroes.

———

Fortunate indeed are those who have a top-level goal so consequential to the world that it imbues everything they do, no matter how small or tedious, with significance. Consider the parable of the bricklayers:

Three bricklayers are asked: "What are you doing?"

The first says, "I am laying bricks."

The second says, "I am building a church."

And the third says, "I am building the house of God."

The first bricklayer has a job. The second has a career. The third has a calling.

Many of us would like to be like the third bricklayer, but instead identify with the first or second.

Yale management professor Amy Wrzesniewski has found that people have no trouble at all telling her which of the three bricklayers

they identify with. In about equal numbers, workers identify themselves as having:

a job ("I view my job as just a necessity of life, much like breathing or sleeping"),
a career ("I view my job primarily as a stepping-stone to other
  jobs"), or
a calling ("My work is one of the most important things in my
  life").

Using Amy's measures, I, too, have found that only a minority of
workers consider their occupations a calling. Not surprisingly, those
who do are significantly grittier than those who feel that "job" or
"career" more aptly describes their work.

Those fortunate people who do see their work as a calling—as
opposed to a job or a career—reliably say "my work makes the world a
better place." And it's these people who seem most satisfied with their
jobs and their lives overall. In one study, adults who felt their work was
a calling missed at least a third fewer days of work than those with a
job or a career.

Likewise, a recent survey of 982 zookeepers—who belong to a profession in which 80 percent of workers have college degrees and yet
on average earn a salary of $25,000—found that those who identified
their work as a calling ("Working with animals feels like my calling
in life") also expressed a deep sense of purpose ("The work that I
do makes the world a better place"). Zookeepers with a calling were
also more willing to sacrifice unpaid time, after hours, to care for sick
animals. And it was zookeepers with a calling who expressed a sense
of moral duty ("I have a moral obligation to give my animals the best
possible care").

———

I'll point out the obvious: there's nothing "wrong" with having no professional ambition other than to make an honest living. But most of us yearn for much more. This was the conclusion of journalist Studs Terkel, who in the 1970s interviewed more than a hundred working adults in all sorts of professions.

Not surprisingly, Terkel found that only a small minority of workers identified their work as a calling. But it wasn't for lack of wanting. All of us, Terkel concluded, are looking for "daily meaning as well as daily bread . . . for a sort of life rather than a Monday through Friday sort of dying."

The despair of spending the majority of our waking hours doing something that lacks purpose is vividly embodied in the story of Nora Watson, a twenty-eight-year-old staff writer for an institution publishing health-care information: "Most of us are looking for a calling, not a job," she told Terkel. "There's nothing I would enjoy more than a job that was so meaningful to me that I brought it home." And yet, she admitted to doing about two hours of real work a day and spending the rest of the time pretending to work. "I'm the only person in the whole damn building with a desk facing the window instead of the door. I just turn myself around from all that I can.

"I don't think I have a calling—at this moment—except to be me," Nora said toward the end of her interview. "But nobody pays you for being you, so I'm at the Institution—for the moment. . . ."

In the course of his research, Terkel did meet a "happy few who find a savor in their daily job." From an outsider's point of view, those with a calling didn't always labor in professions more conducive to purpose than Nora. One was a stonemason, another a bookbinder. A fifty-eight-year-old garbage collector named Roy Schmidt told Terkel that his job was exhausting, dirty, and dangerous. He knew most other occupations, including his previous office job, would be considered more attractive to most people. And yet, he said: "I don't look down on my job in any way. . . . It's meaningful to society."

Contrast Nora's closing words with the ending of Roy's interview: "I was told a story one time by a doctor. Years ago, in France . . . if you didn't stand in favor with the king, they'd give you the lowest job, of cleaning the streets of Paris—which must have been a mess in those days. One lord goofed up somewhere along the line, so they put him in charge of it. And he did such a wonderful job that he was commended for it. The worst job in the French kingdom and he was patted on the back for what he did. That was the first story I ever heard about garbage where it really *meant* something."

———

In the parable of the bricklayers, everyone has the same occupation, but their subjective experience—how they themselves *viewed* their work—couldn't be more different.

Likewise, Amy's research suggests that callings have little to do with formal job descriptions. In fact, she believes that just about *any* occupation can be a job, career, or calling. For instance, when she studied secretaries, she initially expected very few to identify their work as a calling. When her data came back, she found that secretaries identified themselves as having a job, career, or calling in equal numbers—just about the same proportion she'd identified in other samples.

Amy's conclusion is that it's not that some kinds of occupations are necessarily jobs and others are careers and still others are callings. Instead, what matters is whether the person doing the work *believes* that laying down the next brick is just something that has to be done, or instead something that will lead to further personal success, or, finally, work that connects the individual to something far greater than the self.

I agree. How you *see* your work is more important than your job title.

And this means that you can go from job to career to calling—all without changing your occupation.

"What do you tell people," I recently asked Amy, "when they ask you for advice?"

"A lot of people assume that what they need to do is *find* their calling," she said. "I think a lot of anxiety comes from the assumption that your calling is like a magical entity that exists in the world, waiting to be discovered."

That's also how people mistakenly think about interests, I pointed out. They don't realize they need to play an active role in *developing and deepening* their interests.

"A calling is not some fully formed thing that you find," she tells advice seekers. "It's much more dynamic. Whatever you do—whether you're a janitor or the CEO—you can continually look at what you do and ask how it connects to other people, how it connects to the bigger picture, how it can be an expression of your deepest values."

In other words, a bricklayer who one day says, "I am laying bricks" might at some point *become* the bricklayer who recognizes "I am building the house of God."

———

Amy's observation that the same individual in the same occupation can at different times think of it as a job, career, or calling brought to mind Joe Leader.

Joe is a senior vice president at NYC Transit. Basically, he's the New York City subway's lead engineer. It's a task of almost unimaginable proportions. Annually, more than 1.7 billion trips are taken on the city's subways, making it the busiest subway system in the United States. There are 469 stations. Laid end to end, the tracks for the subway system would reach all the way to Chicago.

As a young man, Leader wasn't looking for a calling. He was looking to pay back student loans.

"When I was coming out of college," he told me, "my biggest concern was just getting a job. Any job. Transit came to our campus to recruit engineers, and I got hired."

As an intern, Leader was assigned to work on the tracks. "I threw in rails, I was pulling ties, I was doing cable work for the third rail."

Not everyone would find that work interesting, but Joe did. "It was fun. When I was first on the job, and all my buddies were business or computer guys, we used to go out, and on the way home from the bars in the evening, they used to run up and down a platform and say, 'Joe, what's this, what's this?' I used to tell them: that's a third-rail insulator, that's an insulated joint. To me, it was fun."

So, interest was the seed of his passion.

Joe soon ended up doing a lot of planning work, which he also enjoyed. As his interests and expertise deepened, and he started to distinguish himself, he began to see transit engineering as a long-term career. "On my days off, I went down to the laundromat to do the laundry. You know those big tables for folding your clothes? Well, all the women used to laugh because I'd bring my engineering drawings and lay them out and work on them. I really fell in love with that part of the job."

Within a year, Joe said he began to look at his work differently. Sometimes, he'd look at a bolt or rivet and realize that some fellow had put that in decades ago, and here it was, still in the same place, still making the trains run, still helping people to get where they needed to be.

"I began to feel like I was making a contribution to society," he told me. "I understood I was responsible for moving people every single day. And when I became a project manager, I would walk away from these big installation jobs—you know, a hundred panels or a whole interlocking [of signals]—and I knew that what we'd done was going to last for thirty years. That was when I felt I had a vocation, or I would say, a calling."

To hear Joe Leader talk about his work might make you wonder if, after a year of not finding your work to be a calling, you should give up hope. Among her MBA students, Amy Wrzesniewski finds that many give their job only a couple of years before concluding that it couldn't possibly be their life's passion.

It may comfort you to know that it took Michael Baime much longer.

Baime is a professor of internal medicine at the University of Pennsylvania. You might think his calling is to heal and to teach. That's only partly right. Michael's passion is well-being through mindfulness. It took him years to integrate his personal interest in mindfulness with the other-centered purpose of helping people lead healthier, happier lives. Only when interest and purpose melded did he feel like he was doing what he'd been put on this planet to do.

I asked Michael how he got interested in mindfulness, and he took me all the way back to his boyhood. "I was looking up at the sky," he told me. "And the strangest thing happened. I felt like I was actually getting lost in the sky. I felt it as a sort of opening, like I was becoming much larger. It was the most wonderful experience I've ever had."

Later, Michael found that he could make the same thing happen just by paying attention to his own thoughts. "I became obsessed," he told me. "I didn't know what to call it, but I would do it all the time."

Several years later, Michael was browsing in a bookstore with his mother when he came upon a book that described his experience exactly. The book was by Alan Watts, a British philosopher who wrote about meditation for Western audiences long before it became fashionable.

With his parents' encouragement, Michael took classes in meditation throughout high school and college. As graduation approached, he had to decide what to do next. *Professional meditator* was not an actual full-time occupation. He decided to become a doctor.

Several years into medical school, Michael confessed to one of his meditation teachers, "This isn't really what I want to do. This isn't right for me." Medicine was important, but it didn't match up with his deepest personal interests. "Stay," said the teacher. "You'll help more people if you become a doctor."

Michael stayed.

After finishing his coursework, Michael says, "I didn't really know what I wanted to do. To kind of tread water, I just signed up for the first year of internship."

To his surprise, he enjoyed practicing medicine. "It was a fine way to be helpful to people. It wasn't like medical school, which isn't so much about helping people as cutting apart cadavers and memorizing the Krebs cycle." Rapidly, he progressed from intern to fellow to running the medical clinic to becoming the assistant director of residency and, finally, chief of general internal medicine.

Still, medicine wasn't quite what Michael would consider a calling.

"As I practiced, I realized that the thing many of my patients really needed wasn't another prescription or X-ray, but actually what I'd been doing for myself since I was a kid. What many patients needed was to stop and breathe and fully connect with their lived experience."

That realization led Michael to create a meditation class for patients with serious health conditions. That was in 1992. Since then, he's expanded the program and, just this year, taken it on as a full-time occupation. To date, about fifteen thousand patients, nurses, and physicians have been trained.

Recently, I asked Michael to give a lecture on mindfulness for local schoolteachers. On the day of his talk, he stepped up to the podium and looked intently at his audience. One by one, he made eye contact with each of the seventy educators who'd given up their Sunday afternoon to hear what he had to say. There was a long pause.

And then, with a smile I can only describe as radiant, he began: "I have a calling."

———

I was twenty-one when I first experienced the power of a *purposeful* top-level goal.

In the spring of my junior year in college, I went to the career services center to find something to do that summer. Turning the pages of an enormous three-ring binder labeled SUMMER PUBLIC SERVICE, I came across a program called Summerbridge. The program was looking for college students to design and teach summer enrichment classes for middle school students from disadvantaged backgrounds.

Teaching kids for a summer sounds like a good idea, I thought. *I could teach biology and ecology. I'll show them how to make a solar oven out of tinfoil and cardboard. We'll roast hot dogs. It'll be fun.*

I didn't think, *This experience is going to change everything.*

I didn't think, *Sure, you're premed now, but not for long.*

I didn't think, *Hold on tight—you're about to discover the power of purpose.*

To be honest, I can't tell you much about that summer. The details escape me. I do know I woke long before dawn each day, including weekends, to prepare for my classes. I do know I worked long into the night. I remember specific kids, and certain moments. But it wasn't until I returned home and had a moment to reflect that I realized what had happened. I'd glimpsed the possibility that a child's connection with a teacher can be life-changing—for both.

When I returned to campus that fall, I sought out other students who'd taught at Summerbridge programs. One of these students, Philip King, happened to live in the same dorm. Like me, he felt a palpable urgency to start another Summerbridge program. The idea was too compelling. We *couldn't not* try.

We had no money, no idea how to start a nonprofit, no connections, and, in my case, nothing but skepticism and worry from parents convinced this was a catastrophically stupid way to use a Harvard education.

Philip and I had nothing and, yet, we had exactly what we needed. We had purpose.

As anyone who has started an organization from scratch can tell you, there are a million tasks, big and small, and no instruction manual for any of them. If Philip and I were doing something that was merely interesting, we couldn't have done it at all. But because creating this program was in our minds—and in our *hearts*—so overwhelmingly important for kids, it gave us a courage and energy neither of us had ever known before.

Because we weren't asking for ourselves, Philip and I found the gumption to knock on the doors of just about every small business and restaurant in Cambridge, asking for donations. We found the patience to sit in countless waiting rooms of powers-that-be. We waited and waited, sometimes hours on end, until these authority figures had time to see us. Then we found the stubbornness to keep asking and asking until we secured what we needed.

And so it went for everything we had to do—because we weren't doing it for ourselves, we were doing it for a greater cause.

Two weeks after Philip and I graduated, we opened the doors to the program. That summer, seven high school and college students discovered what it was like to be a teacher. Thirty fifth-grade boys and girls discovered what it was like to spend their summer vacation learning, studying, working hard, and—though it may have seemed impossible before they actually did it—having fun at the same time.

That was more than twenty years ago. Now called Breakthrough Greater Boston, the program has grown far beyond what Philip and I could have imagined, providing tuition-free, year-round academic enrichment for hundreds of students every year. To date, more than a thousand young men and women have taught in the program, many of whom have gone on to pursue full-time careers in education.

Summerbridge led me to pursue teaching. Teaching led me to an enduring interest in helping children do so much more with their lives than they might ever dream possible.

And yet . . .

For me, teaching wasn't enough. Still unfulfilled was the little girl in me who loved science, who was fascinated by human nature, who, when she was sixteen and had a chance to take a summer enrichment class, picked—of all the courses in the catalog—psychology.

Writing this book made me realize that I'm someone who had an inkling about my interests in adolescence, then some clarity about purpose in my twenties, and finally, in my thirties, the experience and expertise to say that my top-level, life-organizing goal is, and will be until my last breath: *Use psychological science to help kids thrive.*

One reason my dad was so upset about Summerbridge is that he loves me. He thought I would sacrifice my welfare for the well-being of other people who, frankly, he didn't love as much as his own daughter.

Indeed, the concepts of grit and purpose might, in principle, seem to conflict. How is it possible to stay narrowly focused on your own top-level goal while also having the peripheral vision to worry about anyone else? If grit is about having a pyramid of goals that all serve a single personal objective, how do *other people* fit into the picture?

"Most people think self-oriented and other-oriented motivations are opposite ends of a continuum," says my colleague and Wharton professor Adam Grant. "Yet, I've consistently found that they're completely independent. You can have neither, and you can have both." In other words, you can want to be a top dog and, at the same time, be driven to help others.

Adam's research demonstrates that leaders and employees who keep both personal *and* prosocial interests in mind do better in the long run than those who are 100 percent selfishly motivated.

For instance, Adam once asked municipal firefighters, "Why are you motivated to do your work?" He then tracked their overtime hours over the next two months, expecting firefighters who were more motivated to help others to demonstrate the greatest grit. But many of those who were driven to help others worked *fewer* overtime hours. Why?

A second motivation was missing: interest in the work itself. Only when they enjoyed the work did the desire to help others result in more effort. In fact, firefighters who expressed prosocial motives ("Because I want to help others through my work") *and* intrinsic interest in their work ("Because I enjoy it") averaged more than 50 percent more overtime per week than others.

When Adam asked the same question—"Why are you motivated to do your work?"—of 140 fund-raisers at a call center for a public university, he found nearly identical results. Only the fund-raisers who expressed stronger prosocial motives *and* who found the work intrinsically engaging made more calls and, in turn, raised more money for the university.

Developmental psychologists David Yeager and Matt Bundick find the same pattern of results in adolescents. For example, in one study, David interviewed about a hundred adolescents, asking them to tell him, in their own words, what they wanted to be when they grew up, and why.

Some talked about their future in purely self-oriented terms ("I want to be a fashion designer because it's a fun thing to do. . . . What's important . . . is that you really enjoy [your career]").

Others only mentioned other-oriented motives ("I want to be a doctor. I want to help people out . . .").

And, finally, some adolescents mentioned both self- *and* other-oriented motives: "If I was a marine biologist, I would push [to] keep everything clean. . . . I would pick a certain place and go help that place out, like the fish and everything. . . . I've always loved having fish tanks and fish because they get to swim and it's, like, free. It's like flying underwater or something."

Two years later, young people who'd mentioned *both* self- and other-oriented motives rated their schoolwork as more personally meaningful than classmates who'd named either motive alone.

———

For many of the grit paragons I've interviewed, the road to a purposeful, interesting passion was unpredictable.

Aurora and Franco Fonte are Australian entrepreneurs whose facilities services company has 2,500 employees and generates more than $130 million in annual revenue.

Twenty-seven years ago, Aurora and Franco were newly married and dead broke. They got the idea to start a restaurant but didn't have enough money to launch one. Instead, they began cleaning shopping malls and small office buildings—not out of any sense of calling, but because it paid the bills.

Soon enough, their career ambitions took a turn. They could see a brighter future in building maintenance than in hospitality. They both worked ferociously hard, putting in eighty-hour weeks, sometimes with their infant children in carriers strapped across their chests, scrubbing the bathroom tiles in their customers' buildings as if they were their own.

Through all the ups and downs—and there were many—Franco told me: "We always persevered. We didn't give in to obstacles. There was no way were going to let ourselves fail."

I confessed to Aurora and Franco that it was hard for me to imagine how cleaning bathrooms—or even building a multimillion-dollar corporation that cleans bathrooms—could feel like a calling.

"It's not about the cleaning," Aurora explained, her voice tightening with emotion. "It's about building something. It's about our clients and solving their problems. Most of all, it's about the incredible people we employ—they have the biggest souls, and we feel a huge responsibility toward them."

———

According to Stanford developmental psychologist Bill Damon, such a beyond-the-self orientation can and should be deliberately cultivated. Now in the fifth decade of his distinguished career, Bill studies how adolescents learn to lead lives that are personally gratifying and, at the same time, beneficial to the larger community. The study of purpose, he says, is his calling.

In Bill's words, purpose is a final answer to the question "*Why? Why are you doing this?*"

What has Bill learned about the origins of purpose?

"In data set after data set," he told me, "there's a pattern. Everyone has a spark. And that's the very beginning of purpose. That spark is something you're interested in."

Next, you need to observe someone who is purposeful. The purposeful role model could be a family member, a historical figure, a political figure. It doesn't really matter who it is, and it doesn't even matter whether that purpose is related to what the child will end up doing. "What matters," Bill explained, "is that *someone* demonstrates that it's possible to accomplish something on behalf of others."

In fact, he can't remember a single case in which the development of purpose unfolded without the earlier observation of a purposeful role model. "Ideally," he said, "the child really gets to see how difficult a life of purpose is—all the frustrations and the obstacles—but also how gratifying, ultimately, it can be."

What follows is a revelation, as Bill put it. The person discovers a problem in the world that needs solving. This discovery can come in many ways. Sometimes from personal loss or adversity. Sometimes from learning about the loss and adversity confronting others.

But seeing that someone needs our help isn't enough, Bill hastened to add. Purpose requires a second revelation: "I *personally* can make a difference." This conviction, this intention to take action, he says, is why it's so important to have observed a role model enact purpose in their own life. "You have to believe that your efforts will not be in vain."

––––

Kat Cole is someone who had a role model for purpose-driven grit.

I met Kat when she was the thirty-five-year-old president of the Cinnabon bakery chain. If you listen to her story without reflecting much on it, you might dub it "rags to riches," but if you lean in and pay attention you'll hear a different theme: "from poverty to purpose."

Kat grew up in Jacksonville, Florida. Her mother, Jo, worked up the courage to leave Kat's alcoholic father when Kat was nine. Jo worked three jobs to make enough money to support Kat and her two sisters, and yet still found time to be a giver. "She'd be baking for someone, running an errand for someone—she intuitively saw every small opportunity to do something for others. Everyone she got to know, whether they were coworkers or just people in the community, became family to her."

Kat emulated both her mother's work ethic and her profound desire to be helpful.

Before we get to Kat's motivation, though, let's consider her unlikely ascent up the corporate ladder. Kat's résumé begins with a stint, at age fifteen, selling clothes at the local mall. At eighteen, she was old enough to waitress. She got a job as a "Hooters girl" and one year later was asked to help open the first Hooters restaurant in Australia. Ditto for Mexico City, the Bahamas, and then Argentina. By twenty-two, she was running a department of ten. By twenty-six, she was vice president. As a member of the executive team, Kat helped expand the Hooters franchise to more than four hundred sites in twenty-eight countries. When the company was bought by a private equity firm, Kat, at age thirty-two, had such an impressive track record that Cinnabon recruited her to be its president. Under Kat's watch, Cinnabon sales grew faster than they had in more than a decade, and within four years exceeded one billion dollars.

Now let's consider what makes Kat tick.

One time early in Kat's waitressing days at Hooters, the cooks quit in the middle of their shift. "So," she told me matter-of-factly, "I went back with the manager and helped cook the food so all the tables got served."

Why?

"First of all, I was surviving off tips. That's how I paid my bills. If people didn't get their food, they wouldn't pay their check, and they certainly wouldn't leave a tip. Second, I was so curious to see if I could do it. And third, I wanted to be helpful."

Tips and curiosity are pretty self-oriented motivations, but wanting to be helpful is, quite literally, other-oriented. Here was an example of how a single action—jumping behind the stove to make food for all those waiting customers—benefited the individual *and* the people around her.

The next thing Kat knew, she was training kitchen employees and helping out with the back-office operations. "Then one day, the bartender needed to leave early, and the same thing happened. Another day, the manager quit, and I learned how to run a shift. In the course of six months, I'd worked every job in the building. Not only did I work those jobs, I became the trainer to help teach all those roles to other people."

Jumping into the breach and being especially helpful wasn't a calculated move to get ahead in the corporation. Nevertheless, that beyond-the-call-of-duty performance led to an invitation to help open international locations, which led to a corporate executive position, and so on.

Not so coincidentally, it's the sort of thing her mother, Jo, would have done. "My passion is to help people," Jo told me. "No matter at business, or away from business, if you need somebody to come over and build something, or help out in some way, I'm that person who wants to be there for you. To me, any success I've had, it's because I love to share. There's no reserve in me—whatever I have, I'm willing to give to you or anyone else."

Kat attributes her philosophy to her mother, who raised her "to work hard and give back." And that ethic still guides her today.

"Gradually, I became more and more aware that I was very good at going into new environments and helping people realize they're capable of more than they know. I was discovering that this was my thing. And I started to realize that if I could help people—individuals—do that, then I could help teams. If I could help teams, I could help companies. If I could help companies, I could help brands. If I could help brands, I could help communities and countries."

Not long ago, Kat posted an essay on her blog, titled "See What's Possible, and Help Others Do the Same." "When I am around people," Kat wrote, "my heart and soul radiate with the awareness that I am in the presence of greatness. Maybe greatness unfound, or greatness underdeveloped, but the potential or existence of greatness nevertheless. You never know who will go on to do good or even great things or become the next great influencer in the world—so treat everyone like they are that person."

———

Whatever your age, it's never too early or late to begin cultivating a sense of purpose. I have three recommendations, each borrowed from one of the purpose researchers mentioned in this chapter.

David Yeager recommends *reflecting on how the work you're already doing can make a positive contribution to society*.

In several longitudinal experiments, David Yeager and his colleague Dave Paunesku asked high school students, "How could the world be a better place?" and then asked them to draw connections to what they were learning in school. In response, one ninth grader wrote, "I would like to get a job as some sort of genetic researcher. I would use this job to help improve the world by possibly engineering crops to produce more food. . . ." Another said, "I think that having an education allows you to understand the world around you. . . . I will not be able to help anyone without first going to school."

This simple exercise, which took less than a class period to complete, dramatically energized student engagement. Compared to a placebo control exercise, reflecting on purpose led students to double the amount of time they spent studying for an upcoming exam, work harder on tedious math problems when given the option to watch entertaining videos instead, and, in math and science classes, bring home better report card grades.

Amy Wrzesniewski recommends *thinking about how, in small but meaningful ways, you can change your current work to enhance its connection to your core values*.

Amy calls this idea "job crafting," and it's an intervention she's been studying with fellow psychologists Jane Dutton, Justin Berg, and Adam Grant. This is not a Pollyanna, every-job-can-be-nirvana idea. It is, simply, the notion that whatever your occupation, you can maneuver within your job description—adding, delegating, and customizing what you do to match your interests and values.

Amy and her collaborators recently tested this idea at Google. Employees working in positions that don't immediately bring the word *purpose* to mind—in sales, marketing, finance, operations, and accounting, for example—were randomly assigned to a job-crafting workshop. They came up with their own ideas for tweaking their daily routines, each employee making a personalized "map" for what would constitute more meaningful and enjoyable work. Six weeks later, managers and coworkers rated the employees who attended this workshop as significantly happier and more effective.

Finally, Bill Damon recommends *finding inspiration in a purposeful role model*. He'd like you to respond in writing to some of the questions he uses in his interview research, including, "Imagine yourself fifteen years from now. What do you think will be most important to you then?" and "Can you think of someone whose life inspires you to be a better person? Who? Why?"

When I carried out Bill's exercise, I realized that the person in my life who, more than anyone, has shown me the beauty of other-centered purpose is my mom. She is, without exaggeration, the kindest person I've ever met.

Growing up, I didn't always appreciate Mom's generous spirit. I resented the strangers who shared our table every Thanksgiving—not just distant relatives who'd recently emigrated from China, but their roommates, and their roommates' friends. Pretty much anyone who didn't have a place to go who happened to run into my mom in the month of November was warmly welcomed into our home.

One year, Mom gave away my birthday presents a month after I'd unwrapped them, and another, she gave away my sister's entire stuffed animal collection. We threw tantrums and wept and accused her of not loving us. "But there are children who need them more," she said, genuinely surprised at our reaction. "You have so much. They have so little."

When I told my father I wouldn't be taking the MCAT exam for medical school and, instead, would devote myself to creating the Summerbridge program, he was apoplectic. "Why do you care about poor kids? They're not family! You don't even know them!" I now realize why. All my life, I'd seen what one person—my mother—could do to help many others. I'd witnessed the power of purpose.

Chapter 9

HOPE

There's an old Japanese saying: *Fall seven, rise eight.* If I were ever to get a tattoo, I'd get these four simple words indelibly inked.

What is hope?

One kind of hope is the expectation that tomorrow will be better than today. It's the kind of hope that has us yearning for sunnier weather, or a smoother path ahead. It comes without the burden of responsibility. The onus is on the universe to make things better.

Grit depends on a different kind of hope. It rests on the expectation that our own efforts can improve our future. *I have a feeling tomorrow will be better* is different from *I resolve to make tomorrow better.* The hope that gritty people have has nothing to do with luck and everything to do with getting up again.

———

In the spring semester of my first year of college, I enrolled in neurobiology.

I would come to each class early and sit in the front row, where I'd copy every equation and diagram into my notebook. Outside of lecture, I did all the assigned readings and required problem sets. Going into the first quiz, I was a little shaky in a few areas—it was a tough course, and my high school biology coursework left a lot to be desired—but on the whole I felt pretty confident.

The quiz started out fine but quickly became more difficult. I began to panic, thinking over and over: *I'm not going to finish! I have no idea what I'm doing! I'm going to fail!* This, of course, was a self-fulfilling prophecy. The more my mind was crowded by those heart-palpitating thoughts, the less I could concentrate. Time ran out before I'd even read the last problem.

A few days later, the professor handed back the quiz. I looked down disconsolately at my miserable grade and, shortly thereafter, shuffled into the office of my assigned teaching assistant. "You should really consider dropping this course," he advised. "You're just a freshman. You have three more years. You can always take the class later."

"I took AP Bio in high school," I countered.

"How did you do?"

"I got an A, but my teacher didn't teach us much, which is probably why I didn't take the actual AP exam." This confirmed his intuition that I should drop the course.

Virtually the same scenario repeated itself with the midterm, for which I'd studied madly, and after which, I found myself in the teaching assistant's office once again. This time his tone was more urgent. "You do *not* want a failing grade on your transcript. It's not too late to withdraw from the course. If you do, nothing will get factored into your GPA."

I thanked him for his time and closed the door behind me. In the hallway, I surprised myself by not crying. Instead, I reviewed the facts of the situation: two failures and only one more exam—the final—before the end of the semester. I realized I should have started out in a lower-level course, and now, more than halfway through the semester, it was obvious my energetic studying wasn't proving sufficient. If I stayed, there was a good chance I'd choke on the final and end up with an F on my transcript. If I dropped the course, I'd cut my losses.

I curled my hands into fists, clenched my jaw, and marched directly to the registrar's office. At that moment, I'd resolved to stay enrolled in—and, in fact, *major in*—neurobiology.

Looking back on that pivotal day, I can see that I'd been knocked down—or, more accurately, tripped on my own two feet and fell flat on my face. Regardless, it was a moment when I could have stayed down. I could have said to myself: *I'm an idiot! Nothing I do is good enough!* And I could have dropped the class.

Instead, my self-talk was defiantly hopeful: *I won't quit! I can figure this out!*

For the rest of the semester, I not only tried harder, I tried things I hadn't done before. I went to every teaching assistants' office hours. I asked for extra work. I practiced doing the most difficult problems under time pressure—mimicking the conditions under which I needed to produce a flawless performance. I knew my nerves were going to be a problem at exam time, so I resolved to attain a level of mastery where nothing could surprise me. By the time the final exam came around, I felt like I could have written it myself.

I aced the final. My overall grade in the course was a B—the lowest grade I'd get in four years, but, ultimately, the one that made me the proudest.

———

Little did I know when I was foundering in my neurobiology class that I was re-creating the conditions of a famous psychology experiment.

Let me wind back the clock to 1964. Two first-year psychology doctoral students named Marty Seligman and Steve Maier are in a windowless laboratory, watching a caged dog receive electric shocks to its back paws. The shocks come randomly and without warning. If the dog does nothing, the shock lasts five seconds, but if the dog pushes its nose against a panel at the front of the cage, the shock ends early. In a separate cage, another dog is receiving the same shocks at exactly the same intervals, but there's no panel to push on. In other words, both dogs get the exact same dosage of shock at the exact same times, but only the first dog is in control of how long each shock lasts. After sixty-four shocks, both dogs go back to their home cages, and new dogs are brought in for the same procedure.

The next day, one by one, all the dogs are placed in a different cage called a shuttle box. In the middle, there's a low wall, just high enough that the dogs can leap the barrier if they try. A high-pitched tone plays, heralding an impending shock, which comes through the floor of the half of the shuttle box where the dog is standing. Nearly all the dogs who had control over the shocks the previous day learn to leap the barrier. They hear the tone and jump over the wall to safety. In contrast, two-thirds of the dogs who had *no* control over the shocks the previous day just lie down whimpering, passively waiting for the punishments to stop.

This seminal experiment proved for the first time that it isn't suffering that leads to hopelessness. It's suffering you think you can't control.

Many years after deciding to major in the subject I was failing, I sat in a graduate student cubicle a few doors down from Marty's office, reading about this experiment on learned helplessness. I quickly saw the parallels to my earlier experience. The first neurobiology quiz brought unexpected pain. I struggled to improve my situation, but when the midterm came, I got shocked again. The shuttle box was the rest of the semester. Would I conclude from my earlier experience that I was helpless to change my situation? After all, my immediate experience suggested that two disastrous outcomes would be followed by a third.

Or would I be like the few dogs who, despite recent memories of uncontrollable pain, held fast to hope? Would I consider my earlier suffering to be the result of particular mistakes I could avoid in the future? Would I expand my focus beyond the recent past, remembering the many times I'd shrugged off failure and eventually prevailed?

As it turns out, I behaved like the one-third of dogs in Marty and Steve's study that persevered. I got up again and kept fighting.

———

In the decade following that 1964 experiment, additional experiments revealed that suffering without control reliably produces symptoms of clinical depression, including changes in appetite and physical activity, sleep problems, and poor concentration.

When Marty and Steve first proposed that animals and people can *learn* that they are helpless, their theory was considered downright absurd by fellow researchers. Nobody at the time took seriously the possibility that dogs could have thoughts that then influenced their behavior. In fact, few psychologists entertained the possibility that *people* had thoughts that influenced their behavior. Instead, the received wisdom was that *all* living animals simply respond mechanically to punishments and rewards.

After a mountain of data had accumulated, ruling out every conceivable alternative explanation, the scientific community was, at long last, convinced.

Having thoroughly plumbed the disastrous consequences of uncontrollable stress in the laboratory, Marty grew more and more interested in what could be done about it. He decided to retrain as a clinical psychologist. Wisely, he chose to do so under the wing of Aaron Beck, a psychiatrist and fellow pioneer in understanding the root causes and practical antidotes for depression.

What followed was a vigorous exploration of the flip side of learned helplessness, which Marty later dubbed *learned optimism*. The crucial insight that seeded Marty's new work was available from the very beginning: While two-thirds of the dogs that had experienced uncontrollable shock later gave up trying to help themselves, about a third remained resilient. Despite their earlier trauma, they kept trying maneuvers that would bring relief from pain.

It was those resilient dogs that led Marty to study the analogous *I won't quit* response to adversity in people. Optimists, Marty soon discovered, are just as likely to encounter bad events as pessimists. Where they diverge is in their explanations: optimists habitually search for temporary and specific causes of their suffering, whereas pessimists assume permanent and pervasive causes are to blame.

Here's an example from the test Marty and his students developed to distinguish optimists from pessimists: *Imagine: You can't get all the work done that others expect of you. Now imagine one major cause for this event. What leaps to mind?* After you read that hypothetical scenario, you write down your response, and then, after you're offered more scenarios, your responses are rated for how temporary (versus permanent) and how specific (versus pervasive) they are.

If you're a pessimist, you might say, *I screw up everything.* Or: *I'm a loser.* These explanations are all permanent; there's not much you can do to change them. They're also pervasive; they're likely to influence lots of life situations, not just your job performance. Permanent and pervasive explanations for adversity turn minor complications into major catastrophes. They make it seem logical to give up. If, on the other hand, you're an optimist, you might say, *I mismanaged my time.* Or: *I didn't work efficiently because of distractions.* These explanations are all temporary and specific; their "fixability" motivates you to start clearing them away as problems.

Using this test, Marty confirmed that, compared to optimists, pessimists are more likely to suffer from depression and anxiety. What's more, optimists fare better in domains not directly related to mental health. For instance, optimistic undergraduates tend to earn higher grades and are less likely to drop out of school. Optimistic young adults stay healthier throughout middle age and, ultimately, live longer than pessimists. Optimists are more satisfied with their marriages. A one-year field study of MetLife insurance agents found that optimists are twice as likely to stay in their jobs, and that they sell about 25 percent more insurance than their pessimistic colleagues. Likewise, studies of salespeople in telecommunications, real estate, office products, car sales, banking, and other industries have shown that optimists outsell pessimists by 20 to 40 percent.

In one study, elite swimmers, many of whom were training for the U.S. Olympic trials, took Marty's optimism test. Next, coaches asked each swimmer to swim in his or her best event and then deliberately told each swimmer they'd swum just a little *slower* than was actually the case. Given the opportunity to repeat their event, optimists did at least as well as in their first attempt, but pessimists performed substantially worse.

How do grit paragons think about setbacks? Overwhelmingly, I've found that they explain events optimistically. Journalist Hester Lacey finds the same striking pattern in her interviews with remarkably creative people. "What has been your greatest disappointment?" she asks each of them. Whether they're artists or entrepreneurs or community activists, their response is nearly identical. "Well, I don't really think in terms of disappointment. I tend to think that everything that happens is something I can learn from. I tend to think, 'Well okay, that didn't go so well, but I guess I will just carry on.' "

———

Around the time Marty Seligman took his two-year hiatus from laboratory research, his new mentor Aaron Beck was questioning his own training in Freudian psychoanalysis. Like most psychiatrists at the time, Beck had been taught that all forms of mental illness were rooted in unconscious childhood conflicts.

Beck disagreed. He had the audacity to suggest that a psychiatrist could actually talk directly to patients about what was bothering them, and that the patients' thoughts—their self-talk—could be the target of therapy. The foundational insight of Beck's new approach was that the *same objective event*—losing a job, getting into an argument with a coworker, forgetting to call a friend—can lead to *very different subjective interpretations*. And it is those interpretations—rather than the objective events themselves—that can give rise to our feelings and our behavior.

Cognitive behavioral therapy—which aims to treat depression and other psychological maladies by helping patients think more objectively and behave in healthier ways—has shown that, whatever our childhood sufferings, we can generally learn to observe our negative self-talk and change our maladaptive behaviors. As with any other skill, we can practice interpreting what happens to us and responding as an optimist would. Cognitive behavioral therapy is now a widely practiced psychotherapeutic treatment for depression, and has proven longer-lasting in its effects than antidepressant medication.

———

A few years after I'd gotten a toehold in grit research, Wendy Kopp, the founder and then CEO of Teach For America, came to visit Marty.

Then still his graduate student, I was eager to join their meeting for two reasons. First, Teach For America was sending hundreds of recent college graduates into disadvantaged school districts across the country. From personal experience, I knew teaching to be a grit-demanding profession, nowhere more so than in the urban and rural classrooms where TFA teachers are assigned. Second, Wendy was herself a paragon of grit. Famously, she'd conceived of TFA during her senior year at Princeton and, unlike so many idealists who eventually give up on their dream, she'd stuck with it, starting from nothing and creating one of the largest and most influential educational nonprofits in the country. "Relentless pursuit" was both a core value of TFA and the phrase often used by friends and coworkers to describe Wendy's leadership style.

At that meeting, the three of us developed a hypothesis: Teachers who have an optimistic way of interpreting adversity have more grit than their more pessimistic counterparts, and grit, in turn, predicts better teaching. For instance, an optimistic teacher might keep looking for ways to help an uncooperative student, whereas a pessimist might assume there was nothing more to be done. To test whether that was true, we decided to measure optimism and grit before teachers set foot in the classroom and, a year later, see how effectively teachers had advanced the academic progress of their students.

That August, four hundred TFA teachers completed the Grit Scale and, in addition, Marty's questionnaire assessing their optimism. To the extent they thought of temporary and specific causes for bad events, and permanent and pervasive causes of good events, we coded their responses as optimistic. To the extent they did the reverse, we coded their responses as pessimistic.

In the same survey, we measured one more thing: happiness. Why? For one thing, there was a small but growing body of scientific evidence that happiness wasn't just the *consequence* of performing well at work, it might also be an important *cause*. Also, we were curious about how happy the grittiest teachers were. Did single-minded passion and perseverance come at a cost? Or could you be gritty and happy at the same time?

One year later, when Teach For America had tabulated effectiveness ratings for each teacher based on the academic gains of their students, we analyzed our data. Just as we'd expected, optimistic teachers were grittier and happier, and grit and happiness in turn explained why optimistic teachers got their students to achieve more during the school year.

After staring at these results for a while, I began reminiscing about my own experience of classroom teaching. I remembered the many afternoons I'd gone home exasperated and exhausted. I remembered battling catastrophic self-talk about my own capabilities—*Oh god, I really am an idiot!*—and those of my young charges—*She got it wrong again? She'll never learn this!* And I remembered the mornings I'd gotten up and decided, after all, that there was one more tactic worth trying: *Maybe if I bring in a Hershey bar and cut it into pieces, they'll get the idea of fractions. Maybe if I have everyone clean out their lockers on Mondays, they'll get in the habit of keeping their lockers clean.*

The data from this study of young teachers, along with Wendy Kopp's intuitions, interviews with grit paragons, and a half century of psychological research all point to the same, commonsense conclusion: When you keep searching for ways to change your situation for the better, you stand a chance of finding them. When you stop searching, assuming they can't be found, you guarantee they won't.

Or as Henry Ford is often quoted as saying, "Whether you think you can, or think you can't—you're right."

———

Around the time Marty Seligman and Steve Maier were linking hopelessness to a lack of perceived control, a young psychology major named Carol Dweck was making her way through college. Carol had always been intrigued that some people persevere while others in identical circumstances give up. Right after graduation, she enrolled in a doctoral program in psychology and pursued this question.

Marty and Steve's work had a profound influence on young Carol. She believed their findings but was unsatisfied. Sure, attributing your misery to causes beyond your control was debilitating, but where did these attributions come from in the first place? Why, she asked, did one person grow up to be an optimist and another a pessimist?

In one of Carol's first studies, she worked with middle schools to identify boys and girls who, by consensus of their teachers, the school principal, and the school psychologist, were especially "helpless" when confronted by failure. Her hunch was that these children believed that a lack of intellectual ability led to mistakes, rather than a lack of effort. In other words, she suspected it wasn't *just* a long string of failures that made these children pessimistic, but rather their core beliefs about success and learning.

To test her idea, Carol divided the children into two groups. Half the children were assigned to a *success only* program. For several weeks, they solved math problems and, at the end of each session, no matter how many they'd completed, they received praise for doing well. The other half of the children in Carol's study were assigned to an *attribution retraining* program. These children also solved math problems, but were occasionally told that they hadn't solved enough problems during that particular session and, crucially, that they "should have tried harder."

Afterward, all the children were given a combination of easy and very difficult problems to do.

Carol reasoned that, if prior failures were the root cause of helplessness, the *success only* program would boost motivation. If, on the other hand, the real problem was how children interpreted their failures, then the *attribution retraining* program would be more effective.

What Carol found is that the children in the *success only* program gave up just as easily after encountering very difficult problems as they had before training. In sharp contrast, children in the *attribution retraining* program tried harder after encountering difficulty. It seems as though they'd learned to interpret failure as a cue to try harder rather than as confirmation that they lacked the ability to succeed.

———

Over the next four decades, Carol probed deeper.

She soon discovered that people of all ages carry around in their minds private theories about how the world works. These points of view are conscious in that if Carol asks you questions about them, you have a ready answer. But like the thoughts you work on when you go to a cognitive behavioral therapist, you may not be aware of them until you're asked.

Here are four statements Carol uses to assess a person's theory of intelligence. Read them now and consider how much you agree or disagree with each:

> Your intelligence is something very basic about you that you can't change very much.

> You can learn new things, but you can't really change how intelligent you are.

> *No matter how much intelligence you have, you can always change it quite a bit.*

> *You can always substantially change how intelligent you are.*

If you found yourself nodding affirmatively to the first two statements but shaking your head in disagreement with the last two, then Carol would say you have more of a fixed mindset. If you had the opposite reaction, then Carol would say you tend toward a growth mindset.

I like to think of a growth mindset this way: Some of us believe, deep down, that people really *can* change. These growth-oriented people assume that it's possible, for example, to get smarter *if* you're given the right opportunities and support and *if* you try hard enough and *if* you believe you can do it. Conversely, some people think you can learn skills, like how to ride a bike or do a sales pitch, but your *capacity* to learn skills—your talent—can't be trained. The problem with holding the latter fixed-mindset view—and many people who consider themselves talented *do*—is that no road is without bumps. Eventually, you're going to hit one. At that point, having a fixed mind-set becomes a tremendous liability. This is when a C–, a rejection letter, a disappointing progress review at work, or any other setback can derail you. With a fixed mindset, you're likely to interpret these setbacks as evidence that, after all, you don't have "the right stuff"—you're not good enough. With a growth mindset, you believe you can learn to do better.

Mindsets have been shown to make a difference in all the same life domains as optimism. For instance, if you have a growth mindset, you're more likely to do well in school, enjoy better emotional and physical health, and have stronger, more positive social relationships with other people.

A few years ago, Carol and I asked more than two thousand high school seniors to complete a growth-mindset questionnaire. We've found that students with a growth mindset are significantly grittier than students with a fixed mindset. What's more, grittier students earn higher report card grades and, after graduation, are more likely to enroll in and persist through college. I've since measured growth mindset and grit in both younger children and older adults, and in every sample, I've found that growth mindset and grit go together.

———

When you ask Carol where our mindsets come from, she'll point to people's personal histories of success and failure and how the people around them, particularly those in a position of authority, have responded to these outcomes.

Consider, for example, what people said to you when, as a child, you did something really well. Were you praised for your talent? Or were you praised for your effort? Either way, chances are you use the same language today when evaluating victories and defeats.

Praising effort and learning over "natural talent" is an explicit target of teacher training in the KIPP schools. KIPP stands for the Knowledge Is Power Program, and it was started in 1994 by Mike Feinberg and Dave Levin, two gritty young Teach For America teachers. Today, KIPP schools serve seventy thousand elementary, middle, and high school students across the country. The vast majority of KIPPsters, as they proudly refer to themselves, come from low-income families. Against the odds, almost all graduate from high school, and more than 80 percent go on to college.

KIPP teachers get a little thesaurus during training. On one side, there are encouragements teachers often use with the best of intentions. On the other, there is language that subtly sends the message that life is about challenging yourself and learning to do what you couldn't do before. See below for examples appropriate for people of any age. Whether you're a parent, manager, coach, or any other type of mentor, I suggest you observe your own language over the next few days, listening for the beliefs your words may be reinforcing in yourself and others.

Undermines Growth Mindset and Grit	Promotes Growth Mindset and Grit
"You're a natural! I love that."	"You're a *learner*! I love that."
"Well, at least you tried!"	"That didn't work. Let's talk about how you approached it and what might work better."
"Great job! You're so talented!"	"Great job! What's one thing that could have been *even* better?"
"This is hard. Don't feel bad if you can't do it."	"This is hard. Don't feel bad if you can't do it *yet*."
"Maybe this just isn't your strength. Don't worry—you have other things to contribute."*	"I have high standards. I'm holding you to them because I know we can reach them together."

Language is one way to cultivate hope. But modeling a growth mindset—demonstrating by our *actions* that we truly believe people can learn to learn—may be even more important.

---

* There's an expression in sports: "Race your strengths and train your weaknesses." I agree with the wisdom of this adage, but I also think it's important that people recognize that skills improve with practice.

Author and activist James Baldwin once put it this way: "Children have never been very good at listening to their elders, but they have never failed to imitate them." This is one of Dave Levin's favorite quotes, and I've watched him begin many KIPP training workshops with it.

A psychologist in my lab, Daeun Park, recently found this to be exactly the case. In a yearlong study of first- and second-grade class-rooms, she found that teachers who gave special privileges to higher-performing students and emphasized how they compared to others inadvertently inculcated a fixed mindset among the young students. Over the year, students of teachers who acted this way grew to prefer games and problems that were easy, "so you can get a lot right." By year's end, they were more likely to agree that "a person is a certain amount smart, and stays pretty much the same."

Similarly, Carol and her collaborators are finding that children develop more of a fixed mindset when their parents react to mistakes as though they're harmful and problematic. This is true even when these parents *say* they have a growth mindset. Our children are watching us, and they're imitating what we do.

The same dynamics apply in a corporate setting. Berkeley professor Jennifer Chatman and her collaborators recently surveyed employees of Fortune 1000 companies about mindset, motivation, and well-being. They found that, in each company, there was a consensus about mindset. In fixed-mindset companies, employees agreed with state-ments like "When it comes to being successful, this company seems to believe that people have a certain amount of talent, and they really can't do much to change it." They felt that only a few star performers were highly valued and that the company wasn't truly invested in other employees' development. These respondents also admitted to keep-ing secrets, cutting corners, and cheating to get ahead. By contrast, in growth-mindset cultures, employees were 47 percent more likely to say their colleagues were trustworthy, 49 percent more likely to say their company fosters innovation, and 65 percent more likely to say their company supports risk taking.

How do *you* treat high achievers? How do you react when others disappoint you?

My guess is that no matter how much you embrace the idea of growth mindset, you often default to a fixed mindset. At least, this is the case for Carol, Marty, and me. All of us know how we'd *like* to react when, say, someone we're supervising brings us work that falls short of expectations. We'd like our knee-jerk reflex to be calm and encouraging. We aspire to have an *Okay, what is there to learn here?* attitude toward mistakes.

But we're human. So, more often than we'd like, we get frustrated. We show our impatience. In judging the person's abilities, we allow a flicker of doubt to distract us momentarily from the more important task of what they could do next to improve.

The reality is that most people have an inner fixed-mindset pessimist in them right alongside their inner growth-mindset optimist. Recognizing this is important because it's easy to make the mistake of changing what we say *without* changing our body language, facial expressions, and behavior.

So what should we do? A good first step is to watch for mismatches between our words and actions. When we slip up—and we *will*—we can simply acknowledge that it's hard to move away from a fixed, pessimistic view of the world. One of Carol's colleagues, Susan Mackie, works with CEOs and encourages them to give names to their inner fixed-mindset characters. Then they can say things like "Oops. I guess I brought Controlling Claire to the meeting today. Let me try that again." Or: "Overwhelmed Olivia is struggling to deal with all the competing demands, can you help me think this through?"

Ultimately, adopting a gritty perspective involves recognizing that people get better at things—they *grow.* Just as we want to cultivate the ability to get up off the floor when life has knocked us down, we want to give those around us the benefit of the doubt when something they've tried isn't a raging success. There's always tomorrow.

———

I recently called Bill McNabb for his perspective. Since 2008, Bill has served as the CEO of Vanguard, the world's largest provider of mutual funds.

"We've actually tracked senior leaders here at Vanguard and asked why some did better in the long run than others. I used to use the word 'complacency' to describe the ones who didn't work out, but the more I reflect on it, the more I realize that's not quite it. It's really a belief that 'I can't learn anymore. I am what I am. This is how I do things.'"

And what about executives who ultimately excelled?

"The people who have continued to be successful here have stayed on a growth trajectory. They just keep surprising you with how much they're growing. We've had people who, if you looked at their résumé coming in, you'd say, 'Wow, how did that person end up so successful?' And we've had other people come in with incredible credentials, and you're wondering, 'Why did they not go further?'"

When Bill discovered the research on growth mindset and grit, it confirmed his intuitions—not just as a corporate leader but as a father, former high school Latin teacher, rowing coach, and athlete. "I really do think people develop theories about themselves and the world, and it determines what they do."

When we got to the question of where, exactly, any of us begin formulating these theories, Bill said, "Believe it or not, I actually started out with more of a fixed mindset." He chalks up that mindset, partly, to his parents enrolling him, while he was still in elementary school, in a research study at a nearby university. He remembers taking a whole battery of intelligence tests and, at the end, being told, "You did really well, and you're going to do really well in school."

For a while, an authoritative diagnosis of talent, in combination

GRIT

with early success, boosted his confidence: "I took great pride in finishing tests faster than anyone else. I didn't always get one hundred percent, but I usually came close, and I took great pleasure in not working that hard to achieve what I did."

Bill attributes his switch to a growth mindset to joining the crew team in college. "I'd never rowed before, but I found I liked being on the water. I liked being outside. I liked the exercise. I sort of fell in love with the sport."

Rowing was the first thing Bill wanted to do well that didn't come easily: "I was not a natural," he told me. "I had a lot of failures early on. But I kept going, and then eventually, I started getting better. Suddenly, it began to make sense: 'Put your head down and go hard. Hard work really, really matters.'" By the end of his freshman season, Bill was in the junior varsity boat. That didn't sound so bad to me, but Bill explained that, statistically, this placement suggested there was no chance of ever making varsity. That summer, he stayed on campus and rowed all summer.

All that practice paid off. Bill was promoted to the "stroke seat" of the junior varsity boat, making him the one who sets the pace for the other seven rowers. During the season, one of the varsity rowers was injured, and Bill had the opportunity to show what he could do. By his account, and also the team captain's, he did terrifically well. Still, when the injured rower recovered, the coach demoted Bill again.

"That coach had a fixed mindset—he just couldn't believe that I'd improved as much as I did."

There were more ups and downs, but Bill's growth mindset kept getting affirmed. "Because I'd come so damn close to quitting and yet hung in there, and because things eventually did work out, I learned a lesson I'd never forget. The lesson was that, when you have setbacks and failures, you can't overreact to them. You need to step back, analyze them, and learn from them. But you also need to stay optimistic."

How did that lesson help Bill later in life? "There have been times in my career where I felt discouraged. I'd watch someone else get promoted before me. I'd want things to go a certain way, and they'd go the opposite. At those points, I'd say to myself, 'Just keep working hard and learning, and it will all work out.' "

————

"What doesn't kill me makes me stronger," Nietzsche once said. Kanye West and Kelly Clarkson echo the same sentiment, and there's a reason we keep repeating it. Many of us can remember a time when, like Bill McNabb, we were confronted with challenge and yet emerged on the other side more confident than when we began.

Consider, for example, the Outward Bound program, which sends adolescents or adults into the wilderness with experienced leaders, usually for a few weeks. From its inception a half century ago, the premise of Outward Bound—so named for the moment a ship leaves harbor for the open seas—has been that challenging outdoor situations develop "tenacity in pursuit" and "undefeatable spirit." In fact, across dozens of studies, the program has been shown to increase independence, confidence, assertiveness, and the belief that what happens in life is largely under your control. What's more, these benefits tend to increase, rather than diminish, in the six months following participation in the program.

All the same, it's undeniable that what doesn't kill us sometimes makes us *weaker*. Consider the dogs who were shocked repeatedly with no control. A third of the dogs were resilient to this adversity, but there was no evidence that any of the dogs in the uncontrollable stress condition benefited from the experience in any way. On the contrary, most were much more vulnerable to suffering in the immediate aftermath.

So, it appears that sometimes what doesn't kill you makes you stronger, and sometimes it does the opposite. The urgent question becomes: When? When does struggle lead to hope, and when does struggle lead to hopelessness?

A few years ago, Steve Maier and his students designed an experiment nearly identical to the one he and Marty Seligman had conducted forty years earlier: One group of rats received electric shocks, but if they turned a small wheel with their front paws, they could turn off the shock until the next trial. A second group received the exact same dose of electric shocks as the first but had no control over their duration.

One crucial difference was that, in the new experiment, the rats were only five weeks old—that's adolescence in the rat life cycle. A second difference was that the effects of this experience were assessed five weeks later, when the rats were fully mature adults. At that point, both groups of rats were subjected to uncontrollable electric shocks and, the next day, observed in a social exploration test.

Here's what Steve learned. Adolescent rats who experienced stress they could *not* control grew up to be adult rats who, after being subjected to uncontrollable shocks a second time, behaved timidly. This was not unusual—they learned to be helpless in the same way that any other rat would. In contrast, adolescent rats who experienced stress they *could* control grew up to be more adventurous and, most astounding, appeared to be inoculated against learned helplessness in adulthood. That's right—when these "resilient rats" grew up, the usual uncontrollable shock procedures no longer made them helpless.

In other words, what didn't kill the young rats, when by their own efforts they could *control* what was happening, made them stronger for life.

————

When I learned about Steve Maier's new experimental work, I just had to talk to him in person. I got on a plane to Colorado.

Steve walked me around his laboratory and showed me the special cages equipped with little wheels that, when turned, cut off the current to the electric shock. Afterward, the graduate student who ran the experiment on adolescent rats that I just described gave a talk on the brain circuits and neurotransmitters involved. Finally, when Steve and I sat down together, I asked him to explain, from this experiment and everything else he'd done in his long and distinguished career, the neurobiology of hope.

Steve thought for a moment. "Here's the deal in a few sentences. You've got lots of places in the brain that respond to aversive experiences. Like the amygdala. In fact, there are a whole bunch of limbic areas that respond to stress."

I nodded.

"Now what happens is that these limbic structures are regulated by higher-order brain areas, like the prefrontal cortex. And so, if you have an appraisal, a thought, a belief—whatever you want to call it—that says, 'Wait a minute, I can do something about this!' or 'This really isn't so bad!' or whatever, then these inhibitory structures in the cortex are activated. They send a message: 'Cool it down there! Don't get so activated. There's something we can do.'"

I got it. But I still didn't understand, fully, why Steve had gone to the trouble of experimenting with adolescent rats.

"The long-term story needs some more explanation," he continued. "We think there is plasticity in that circuitry. If you experience adversity—something pretty potent—that you overcome on your own during your youth, you develop a different way of dealing with adversity later on. It's important that the adversity be pretty potent. Because these brain areas really have to wire together in some fashion, and that doesn't happen with just minor inconveniences."

So you can't *just* talk someone into believing they can master challenges?

"That's right. Just telling somebody they can overcome adversity isn't enough. For the rewiring to happen, you have to activate the control circuitry at the same time as those low-level areas. That happens when you experience mastery at the same time as adversity."

And what about a life history of challenge *without* control?

"I worry a lot about kids in poverty," Steve said. "They're getting a lot of helplessness experiences. They're not getting enough mastery experiences. They're not learning: 'I can do this. I can succeed in that.' My speculation is that those earlier experiences can have really enduring effects. You need to learn that there's a contingency between your actions and what happens to you: 'If I do something, then something will happen.'"

———

The scientific research is very clear that experiencing trauma without control can be debilitating. But I also worry about people who cruise through life, friction-free, for a long, long time before encountering their first real failure. They have so little practice falling and getting up again. They have so many reasons to stick with a fixed mindset.

I see a lot of invisibly vulnerable high-achievers stumble in young adulthood and struggle to get up again. I call them the "fragile perfects." Sometimes I meet fragile perfects in my office after a midterm or a final. Very quickly, it becomes clear that these bright and wonderful people know how to succeed but not how to fail.

Last year, I kept in touch with a freshman at Penn named Kayvon Asemani. Kayvon has the sort of résumé that might make you worry he's a fragile perfect: valedictorian of his high school class, student body president, star athlete . . . the list goes on.

But I assure you that Kayvon is the very embodiment of growth mindset and optimism. We met when he was a senior at the Milton Hershey School, a tuition-free boarding school originally established by chocolatier Milton Hershey for orphan boys and, to this day, a haven for children from severely disadvantaged backgrounds. Kayvon and his siblings ended up at Hershey just before Kayvon entered the fifth grade—one year after his father nearly strangled his mother to death, leaving her in a permanent coma.

At Hershey, Kayvon thrived. He discovered a passion for music, playing the trombone in two school bands. And he discovered leadership, giving speeches to state politicians, creating a student-run school news website, chairing committees that raised tens of thousands of dollars for charity, and in his senior year, serving as student body president.

In January, Kayvon emailed to let me know how his first semester had gone. "I finished the first semester with a 3.5," he wrote. "Three A's and one C. I'm not completely satisfied with it. I know what I did right to get the A's and I know what I did wrong to get the C."

As for his poorest grade? "That C in Economics caught up to me because I was in a hole from my conflicted thoughts about this place and whether I fit in. . . . I can definitely do better than a 3.5, and a 4.0 is not out of the question. My first semester mentality was that I have a lot to learn from these kids. My new mentality is that I have a lot to teach them."

The spring semester wasn't exactly smooth sailing, either. Kayvon earned a bunch of A's but didn't do nearly as well as he'd hoped in his two quantitative courses. We talked, briefly, about the option of transferring out of Wharton, Penn's highly competitive business school, and I pointed out that there was no shame in switching into a different major. Kayvon was having none of it.

Here's an excerpt from his email to me in June: "Numbers and executing quantitative concepts have always been difficult for me. But I embrace the challenge, and I'm going to apply all the grit I have to improving myself and making myself better, even if it means graduating with a GPA less than what I would have earned if I just majored in something that didn't require me to manipulate numbers."

I have no doubt that Kayvon will keep getting up, time and again, always learning and growing.

———

Collectively, the evidence I've presented tells the following story: A fixed mindset about ability leads to pessimistic explanations of adversity, and that, in turn, leads to both giving up on challenges and avoiding them in the first place. In contrast, a growth mindset leads to optimistic ways of explaining adversity, and that, in turn, leads to perseverance and seeking out new challenges that will ultimately make you even stronger.

growth mindset → **optimistic self-talk** → **perseverance over adversity**

My recommendation for teaching yourself hope is to take each step in the sequence above and ask, *What can I do to boost this one?*

My first suggestion in that regard is to *update your beliefs about intelligence and talent.*

When Carol and her collaborators try to convince people that intelligence, or any other talent, can improve with effort, she starts by explaining the brain. For instance, she recounts a study published in the top scientific journal *Nature* that tracked adolescent brain development. Many of the adolescents in this study increased their IQ scores from age fourteen, when the study started, to age eighteen, when it concluded. This fact—that IQ scores are not entirely fixed over a person's life span—usually comes as a surprise. What's more, Carol continues, these same adolescents showed sizable changes in brain structure: "Those who got better at math skills strengthened the areas of the brain related to math, and the same was true for English skills."

Carol also explains that the brain is remarkably adaptive. Like a muscle that gets stronger with use, the brain changes itself when you struggle to master a new challenge. In fact, there's never a time in life when the brain is completely "fixed." Instead, all our lives, our neurons retain the potential to grow new connections with one another and to strengthen the ones we already have. What's more, throughout adulthood, we maintain the ability to grow myelin, a sort of insulating sheath that protects neurons and speeds signals traveling between them.

My next suggestion is to *practice optimistic self-talk*.

The link between cognitive behavioral therapy and learned helplessness led to the development of "resilience training." In essence, this interactive curriculum is a preventative dose of cognitive behavioral therapy. In one study, children who completed this training showed lower levels of pessimism and developed fewer symptoms of depression over the next two years. In a similar study, pessimistic college students demonstrated less anxiety over the subsequent two years and less depression over three years.

If, reading this chapter, you recognize yourself as an extreme pessimist, my advice is to find a cognitive behavioral therapist. I know how unsatisfying this recommendation might sound. Many years ago, as a teenager, I wrote to Dear Abby about a problem I was having. "Go see a therapist," she wrote back. I recall tearing up her letter, angry she didn't propose a neater, faster, more straightforward solution. Nevertheless, suggesting that reading twenty pages about the science of hope is enough to remove an ingrained pessimistic bias would be naive. There's much more to say about cognitive behavioral therapy and resilience training than I can summarize here.

The point is that you can, in fact, modify your self-talk, and you can learn to not let it interfere with you moving toward your goals. With practice and guidance, you can change the way you think, feel, and, most important, act when the going gets rough.

As a transition to the final section of this book, "Growing Grit from the Outside In," let me offer one final suggestion for teaching yourself hope: *Ask for a helping hand*.

A few years ago, I met a retired mathematician named Rhonda Hughes. Nobody in Rhonda's family had gone to college, but as a girl, she liked math a whole lot more than stenography. Rhonda eventually earned a PhD in mathematics and, after seventy-nine of her eighty applications for a faculty position were rejected, she took a job at the single university that made her an offer.

One reason Rhonda got in touch was to tell me that she had an issue with an item on the Grit Scale. "I don't like that item that says, 'Setbacks don't discourage me.' That makes no sense. I mean, who doesn't get discouraged by setbacks? I certainly do. I think it should say, 'Setbacks don't discourage me *for long. I get back on my feet.'*"

Of course, Rhonda was right, and in so many words, I changed the item accordingly.

But the most important thing about Rhonda's story is that she almost never got back up all by herself. Instead, she figured out that asking for help was a good way to hold on to hope.

Here's just one of the stories she told me: "I had this mentor who knew, even before I did, that I was going to be a mathematician. It all started when I'd done very poorly on one of his tests, and I went to his office and cried. All of a sudden, he jumped up out of his chair and, without a word, ran out of the room. When, finally, he came back he said, 'Young lady, you should go to graduate school in mathematics. But you're taking all of the wrong courses.' And he had all of the courses I *should* have been taking mapped out, and the personal promises of other faculty that they'd help."

About twenty years ago, Rhonda cofounded the EDGE Program with Sylvia Bozeman, a fellow mathematician. EDGE stands for Enhancing Diversity in Graduate Education, and its mission is to support women and minority students pursuing doctoral training in mathematics. "People assume you have to have some special talent to do mathematics," Sylvia has said. "They think you're either born with it, or you're not. But Rhonda and I keep saying, 'You actually *develop* the ability to do mathematics. *Don't give up!*'"

"There have been so many times in my career when I wanted to pack it in, when I wanted to give up and do something easier," Rhonda told me. "But there was always someone who, in one way or another, told me to keep going. I think everyone needs somebody like that. Don't you?"

Part III

GROWING GRIT FROM THE OUTSIDE IN

➡ *Chapter 10*

PARENTING FOR GRIT

What can I do to encourage grit in the people I care for?

I'm asked this question at least once a day.

Sometimes it's a coach who asks; sometimes it's an entrepreneur or a CEO. Last week, it was a fourth-grade teacher, and the week before, a math professor at a community college. I've had army generals and navy admirals toss me this question, too, but most often it's a mother or father who worries that their child isn't close to realizing their potential.

All the people quizzing me are thinking as parents would, of course—even if they're *not* parents. The word *parenting* derives from Latin and means "to bring forth." You're acting in a parentlike way if you're asking for guidance on how to best bring forth interest, practice, purpose, and hope in the people you care for.

———

When I turn the tables and ask people for their own intuitions on how to "parent for grit," I get different answers.

Some believe grit is forged in the crucible of adversity. Others are quick to paraphrase Nietzsche: "What doesn't kill you makes you stronger."* Such invocations conjure an image of scowling mothers and fathers dispensing endless criticism on the sidelines of games that had better be victories, or chaining their children to the piano bench or violin stand, or grounding them for the sin of an A–.

This perspective assumes that offering loving support and demanding high standards are two ends of a continuum, with the authoritarian parents of the gritty far to the right of center.

Had I been around to seek opinions a century ago, such would have been the perspective of John Watson, then chair of psychology at Johns Hopkins University.

In his best-selling 1928 parenting guide, *Psychological Care of Infant and Child*, Watson holds forth on how to raise a child "who loses himself in work and play, who quickly learns to overcome the small difficulties in his environment . . . and who finally enters manhood so bulwarked with stable work and emotional habits that no adversity can quite overwhelm him."

Here's Watson's advice: "Never hug and kiss them. Never let them sit in your lap. If you must, kiss them once on the forehead when they say good night. Shake hands with them in the morning. Give them a pat on the head if they have made an extraordinarily good job of a difficult task." Watson further recommends letting children cope with problems on their own "almost from the moment of birth," rotating different caregivers to prevent unhealthy attachment to any one adult, and otherwise avoiding the coddling affection that prevents a child from "conquering the world."

Occasionally, of course, people take the opposite stance.

They're convinced that perseverance and especially passion bloom when children are lavished with unconditional affection and sup-

---

* When I hear that, I sometimes interrupt with a précis of Steve Maier's research showing that, in fact, finding a way *out* of the suffering is what does the strengthening.

port. These champions of kinder and gentler parenting advocate big hugs and long leashes and point out that children are by their nature challenge-seeking creatures whose innate desire for competence needs only our unconditional love and affection to reveal itself. Once unfettered by the demands of imperious parents, children will follow their own intrinsic interests, and disciplined practice and resilience in the face of setbacks will follow.

On the continuum between supportive and demanding parenting, proponents of this permissive "child-centered" approach fall to the left of center.

———

So which is it? Is grit forged in the crucible of unrelentingly high standards or is it nurtured in the warm embrace of loving support?

As a scientist, I'm tempted to answer that we need more research on the topic. There's a lot of research on parenting, and some research on grit, but no research yet on parenting *and* grit.

But as a mother of two teenagers, I don't have time for all the data to come in. Like the parents asking *me* this question, I have to make decisions today. My girls are growing up, and each day of their lives, my husband and I are parenting them, for better or for worse. What's more, as a professor and a lab director, I interact with dozens of young people—and I'd like to encourage their grit, too.

So, as a step toward resolving the debate, I've probed the evidence for each side. An advocate of old-fashioned, strict parenting suggested I talk to grit paragon Steve Young, the record-breaking quarterback whose Mormon upbringing included a daily paper route, Bible classes before school, and absolutely no cussing or drinking. Meanwhile, an advocate with a more liberal bent pointed me toward Francesca Martinez, the outspoken British stand-up comic whose writer father and environmentalist mother allowed her to drop out of school when she was sixteen and didn't bat an eye when she titled her memoir *What the **** Is Normal?!*

Let's begin with Steve Young.

The legendary quarterback of the San Francisco 49ers was twice named Most Valuable Player in the National Football League. And he was selected Most Valuable Player of Super Bowl XXIX, during which he completed a record-breaking six touchdown passes. At retirement, he was the highest-rated quarterback in NFL history.

"My parents were my foundation," Steve has said. "Good parenting is something I wish everyone could have."

Here's a story to illustrate his point.

Though Steve had been the star of his high school football team and was heavily recruited by colleges across the country, he entered Brigham Young University as their eighth-string quarterback. Since seven other quarterbacks stood between Steve and playing time, his coach relegated him to the "hamburger squad"—a unit composed of the least valuable players whose primary role was to run plays so the BYU defensive line could practice.

"Man, I wanted to go home," Steve recalled. "I went to school my whole first semester with my bags packed. . . . I remember calling [my dad] and just saying, 'Coaches don't know my name. I'm just a big tackling dummy for the defense. Dad, it's horrible. And this is just not what I expected . . . and I think I'd like to come home.' "

Steve's father, whom Steve describes as "the ultimate tough guy," told him: "You can quit. . . . But you can't come home because I'm not going to live with a quitter. You've known that since you were a kid. You're not coming back here." Steve stayed.

All season, Steve was first to practice and last to leave. After the team's last game, he stepped up his private workouts: "There was a huge net hanging at the far end of the field house. I squatted behind an imaginary center; took the snap; did the three-step drop, and threw into the net. From the beginning of January to the end of February, I threw over 10,000 spirals. My arm hurt. But I wanted to be a quarterback."

By sophomore year, Steve moved up from number-eight quarterback to number two. By his junior year, he was BYU's starting quarterback. In his senior year, Steve received the Davey O'Brien award for the most outstanding quarterback in the country.

There were several other times in his athletic career when his confidence faltered. Each time, he wanted desperately to quit. Each time, he appealed to his father—who wouldn't let him.

One early challenge came while playing baseball in middle school. "I was thirteen," Steve recalled. "I didn't get a hit the whole year, and it just got more and more embarrassing. . . . Game after game, I couldn't get a hit." When the season ended, Steve informed his dad that he'd had it. "My dad looked me straight in the eye and said, 'You cannot quit. You have the ability, so you need to go back and work this out.'" So Steve and his dad went back to the field. "I remember it being really cold and miserable and rainy and sleet and snow, and he'd be pitching the ball and I'd be hitting them." By his senior year in high school, as captain of the varsity baseball team, Steve was batting .384.

The lesson that persistence eventually delivers rewards was one on which Steve relied in the four years he sat on the bench with the San Francisco 49ers. Rather than request a trade, Steve apprenticed himself to Joe Montana, the starting quarterback who captained the team to four Super Bowl victories. "If I was ever going to find out just how good I could get, I needed to stay in San Francisco and learn, even if it was brutally hard to do. . . . I many times thought about quitting. . . . I heard boos during my sleepless nights, but I feared calling my dad. I knew what he'd say: 'Endure to the end, Steve.'"

At this point in my narrative of Steve Young's improbable ascent, you might conclude that parents of gritty children are authoritarian. You might leap to the conclusion that they're centered on their own standards and fairly insensitive to their children's particular needs.

Before you issue a final verdict, though, sit down with Steve's parents, Sherry and LeGrande Young. And before you do, take note that LeGrande prefers the childhood nickname that aptly captures his approach to life: "Grit." "He's all about hard work and being tough and not whining," Steve's brother Mike once said of his father. "The name really fits him."

As a corporate attorney, Grit Young seldom missed a day of work. About twenty-five years ago, Grit was working out at his local YMCA when a fellow gym-goer challenged him to an ongoing sit-up competition. After a year, each man could do about a thousand sit-ups each, at which point the challenger bowed out. By then, Grit was competing against himself. He kept on, for years, until he could do ten thousand sit-ups in a row.

When I called to talk to Steve's parents about their famous son and the way they'd raised him, I expected sternness and formality. The first thing Sherry said was "We're delighted to talk to you! Our Steve is a great kid!" Grit then joked that, given my chosen field of study, he was surprised it had taken me so long to get to them.

My shoulders softened a bit, and I sat back as each told me how they'd learned to work hard early in life. "We were one generation off the farm," Sherry explained. "There were expectations." Sherry was picking cherries by age ten. Grit did the same, and to earn money for baseball mitts and clothes, he mowed lawns, delivered newspapers on his bike to houses miles apart, and picked up whatever farm work he could.

When it came time to raise their children, both Sherry and Grit very deliberately set out to provide the same challenges. "My goal was to teach them discipline," Grit said, "and to go at things hard like I learned to do. You have to learn those things. They don't just happen. It was important to me to teach the kids to finish what you begin."

In no uncertain terms, Steve and his siblings were made to understand that, whatever they signed up for, they *had* to see it through to the end. "We told them, you've got to go to all the practices. You can't say, 'Oh, I'm tired of this.' Once you commit, you discipline yourself to do it. There's going to be times you don't want to go, but you've got to go."

Sounds strict, right? It was. But if you listen closely, you'll discover that the Youngs were also tremendously supportive.

Steve tells the story of getting tackled playing Pop Warner football as a nine-year-old and looking up to see his mom, still carrying her purse, striding right past him to grab a boy on the opposing team by the shoulder pads to tell him that he would *not* be illegally neck tackling Steve again. As Steve and his siblings got older, their home became a favorite hangout. "Our basement was always filled with kids," Sherry says.

As a corporate attorney, Grit traveled often. "Most guys I knew would stay for the weekend, wherever we were, because you wouldn't be finished with your business on Friday, and you had to start again on Monday. Not me. I always, *always* did everything I could to get home for the weekend." Occasionally, weekend trips home were also demonstrations of the character that had earned Grit his nickname: "Once I was in Montana negotiating with an aluminum plant. Friday night, I take a taxi down to the airport, and it's all fogged in. All the flights were canceled."

I considered what I might do in the same situation, and then blushed a bit as I listened to the rest of the story. Grit rented a car, drove to Spokane, took a flight to Seattle, then a second flight to San Francisco, and finally a third flight—a red-eye that arrived at JFK the next morning at dawn. He then got in another rental car and drove back to Greenwich, Connecticut. "I'm not patting myself on the back," Grit said. "It's just that I thought it was important to be with the kids, to support them, whether it was athletic activities or anything else."

Sherry and Grit were also attuned to their children's emotional needs. Steve, for example, was especially anxious. "We noticed there were things he wouldn't do," Grit said. "When he was in second grade, he refused to go to school. When he was twelve, he wouldn't go to Boy Scout camp. He never slept over at another kid's house. He just wouldn't do it."

It was hard for me to square the image of Steve Young, fearless all-star quarterback, with the timid boy Sherry and Grit were describing. Likewise, neither Sherry nor Grit had any idea what to make of their oldest son's fearfulness. One time, Grit says, he went to pick up Steve from school to take him to his uncle and aunt's house for the day, and Steve simply couldn't stop sobbing. He was petrified to be away from his own home. Grit was flabbergasted. I waited to hear how he and Sherry reacted. Did they tell their son to man up? Did they remove some of his privileges?

No and no. Grit's description of the talk he had with his son when Steve refused to go to school makes it clear Grit did more questioning and listening than lecturing and criticizing: "I said, 'Well, is somebody picking on you?' He says, 'No.' Do you like your teacher? 'I love my teacher.' Well, why don't you go to school? 'I don't know. I just don't want to go to school.'"

Sherry ended up sitting in Steve's second-grade classroom for weeks until, at long last, Steve felt comfortable going to school by himself.

"It was separation anxiety," Sherry told me. "At the time, we didn't know what to call it. But we could tell he was all tight inside, and we knew that he needed to work through all that."

Later, when I asked Steve to elaborate on his first troubled semester at BYU, I pointed out that, if someone heard only that anecdote and nothing else, they might conclude that his father, Grit, was a tyrant. What kind of parent could refuse a son his plea to return home?

"Okay," Steve said. "All right. Everything is contextual, right?"

I listened.

"The context was that my dad *knew* me. He knew all I wanted to do was sprint home, and he knew that if he let me do that, it would be letting me give into my fears.

"It was a loving act," Steve concluded. "It was tough, but it was loving."

But it's a fine line between tough love and bullying, isn't it? What's the difference?

"I knew the decision was mine," Steve said. "And I knew my dad didn't want me to be him. Number one, a parent needs to set a stage that proves to the child, 'I'm not trying to just have you do what I say, control you, make you be like me, make you do what I did, ask you to make up for what I didn't do.' My dad showed me early that it wasn't about him and what he needed. It truly was 'I'm giving you all I got.'

"There was an underlying selflessness to the tough love," Steve continued. "I think that's vital. If any of the tough love is about the parent just trying to control you, well, kids smell it out. In every way possible, I knew my parents were saying, 'We're looking to see *your* success. We've left ourselves behind.' "

If getting to know the Youngs helps you understand that "tough love" isn't necessarily a contradiction in terms, hold that thought—and meet Francesca Martinez and her parents, Tina and Alex.

Named by the *Observer* as one of the funniest comics in Britain, Francesca performs to sold-out audiences around the world. In a typical routine, she breaks the no-cussing rule of the Young family, and after the show, she's sure to violate the drinking prohibition. Like her parents, Francesca is a lifelong vegetarian, not religious, and politically, somewhere to the left of progressive.

Francesca was diagnosed with cerebral palsy at age two. She prefers the term "wobbly." Told that their brain-damaged daughter would "never lead a normal life," Tina and Alex quickly decided that no doctor could foretell who their daughter might become. Achieving comedic stardom takes grit no matter who you are, but perhaps more so when it's a challenge merely to enunciate your consonants or walk to the stage. So, like other aspiring comics, Francesca has endured four-hour drives (each way) to perform for ten minutes for no pay and made countless cold calls to impassive and busy television producers. But unlike most of her peers, she needs to do breathing and voice exercises before each show.

"I don't take credit for my hard work and passion," she told me. "I think these qualities came from my family, which was very loving and very stable. Their overwhelming support and positivity are why there is no limit to my ambition."

Not surprisingly, counselors at Francesca's school were doubtful of entertainment as a career path for a girl who struggled to walk and talk at a normal cadence. They were even more wary of her dropping out of high school to do so. "Oh, Francesca," they'd say with a sigh, "think about something more sensible. Like computers." The thought of an office job was about as horrible a fate as Francesca could imagine. She asked her parents what she should do.

"Go and follow your dreams," Alex told his daughter, "and if they don't work out, then you can reassess."

"My mum was just as encouraging," Francesca said. Then, with a smile: "Basically, they were happy for me to leave formal education at sixteen to act on television. They let me spend my weekends clubbing with friends, surrounded by leery men and cocktails with sexually explicit names."

I asked Alex about his "follow your dream" advice. Before explaining, he reminded me that Francesca's brother Raoul was also allowed to drop out of high school—to apprentice himself to a renowned portrait painter. "We never put pressure on either of them to become doctors or lawyers or anything like that. I truly believe that when you do something you really want to do, it becomes a vocation. Francesca and her brother are incredibly hard workers, but they feel passionately about their subjects, so to them it's not at all oppressive."

Tina agreed entirely: "I've always had an instinctive sense that life and nature and evolution have planted in children their own capabilities—their own destiny. Like a plant, if they're fed and watered in the right way, they will grow up beautiful and strong. It's just a question of creating the right environment—a soil that is nurturing, that is listening and responsive to their needs. Children carry within them the seeds of their own future. Their own interests will emerge if we trust them."

Francesca connects the unconditional support that her "absurdly cool" parents lavished on her to the hope she maintained even when hope seemed lost: "So much of sticking with things is believing you can do it. That belief comes from self-worth. And that comes from how others have made us feel in our lives."

So far, Alex and Tina seem the epitome of permissive parenting. I asked them whether they see themselves as such.

"Actually," Alex said, "I think I'm allergic to spoiled children. Children must be loved and accepted, but then, without complications, they need to be taught: 'No, you cannot hit your sister on the head with that stick. Yes, you must share. No, you don't get to have everything you want when you want it.' It's no-nonsense parenting."

As an example, Alex pushed Francesca to do the physical therapy exercises prescribed by her doctors. She hated them. For years, she and her father battled. Francesca couldn't understand why she couldn't simply work around her limitations, and Alex believed his responsibility was to stand firm. As she says in her book: "Though happy in many ways, the next few years were punctuated with intense rows replete with door-banging and tears and the throwing of objects."

Whether these skirmishes could have been handled more skillfully is an open question—Alex believes he could have done a better job explaining to his young daughter *why* he was so insistent. That may be so, but what really strikes me about this aspect of Francesca's child-hood is the notion that an affectionate, follow-your-dreams parent can nevertheless feel compelled to lay down the law on matters of discipline. Suddenly, the one-dimensional view of Alex and Tina as hippy-dippy parents seems incomplete.

It was telling, for example, to hear Alex, who is a writer, talk about the work ethic he modeled for his children: "To finish things, you have to put the work in. When I was younger, I'd meet many people who were writing stuff. They'd say to me, 'Oh yeah, I am a writer as well but I've never finished anything.' Well, in that case, you are not a writer. You are just somebody who sits down and writes things on a bit of paper. If you've got something to say, go ahead and say it and finish it."

Tina agrees that as much as children need freedom, they also need limits. She's a tutor as well as an environmental activist, and she's watched a lot of parents engage in what she calls begging-and-pleading negotiations with their children. "We taught our children to live by clear principles and moral guidelines," she said. "We explained our reasoning, but they always knew where the boundaries were.

"And there was no television," she added. "I felt it was a hypnotic medium, and I didn't want it to replace interactions with people. So we simply didn't have a television. If the children wanted to watch something special, they would walk over to their grandparents'."

———

What can we learn from the stories of Steve Young and Francesca Martinez? And what can we glean from how other grit paragons describe their parents?

In fact, I've noticed a pattern. For those of us who want to parent for grit, the pattern is a helpful blueprint, a guide for making the many decisions we must grapple with while raising our children.

Before I say more, let me repeat the caveat that, as a scientist, I'd like to collect many more data points before coming to firm conclusions. In a decade, I should know a lot more about parenting for grit than I do now. But because there's no pause button for parenting the people we care about, I'll go ahead and tell you my hunches. In large part, I'm encouraged to do so because the pattern I've observed matches up with dozens of carefully executed research studies on parenting (but not grit). The pattern also makes sense, given what's been learned about human motivation since John Watson dispensed his *Don't Coddle 'em* advice. And, finally, the pattern I see matches up with the interviews of world-class athletes, artists, and scholars completed by psychologist Benjamin Bloom and his team thirty years ago. Though parenting was not the explicit focus of the Bloom study—parents were originally included as "observers to verify" biographical details—the importance of parenting ended up as one of its major conclusions.

Here is what I see.

First and foremost, there's no either/or trade-off between supportive parenting and demanding parenting. It's a common misunderstanding to think of "tough love" as a carefully struck balance between affection and respect on the one hand, and firmly enforced expectations on the other. In actuality, there's no reason you can't do both. Very clearly, this is exactly what the parents of Steve Young and Francesca Martinez did. The Youngs were tough, but they were also loving. The Martinezes were loving, but they were also tough. Both families were "child-centered" in the sense that they clearly put their children's interests first, but neither family felt that children were always the better judge of what to do, how hard to work, and when to give up on things.

Below is a figure representing how many psychologists now categorize parenting styles. Instead of one continuum, there are two. In the upper right-hand quadrant are parents who are both demanding and supportive. The technical term is "authoritative parenting," which, unfortunately is easily confused with "authoritarian parenting." To avoid such confusion, I'll refer to authoritative parenting as *wise par-*

enting, because parents in this quadrant are accurate judges of the psychological needs of their children. They appreciate that children need love, limits, and latitude to reach their full potential. Their authority is based on knowledge and wisdom, rather than power.

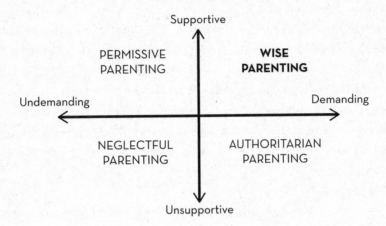

In the other quadrants are three other common parenting styles, including the undemanding, unsupportive approach to raising children exemplified by neglectful parents. Neglectful parenting creates an especially toxic emotional climate, but I won't say much more about it here because it's not even a plausible contender for how parents of the gritty raise their children.

Authoritarian parents are demanding and unsupportive, exactly the approach John Watson advocated for strengthening character in children. Permissive parents, by contrast, are supportive and undemanding.

When psychologist Larry Steinberg delivered his 2001 presidential address to the Society for Research on Adolescence, he proposed a moratorium on further research on parenting styles because, as he saw it, there was so much evidence for the benefits of supportive and demanding parenting that scientists could profitably move on to thornier research questions. Indeed, over the past forty years, study after carefully designed study has found that the children of psychologically wise parents fare better than children raised in any other kind of household.

In one of Larry's studies, for example, about ten thousand American teenagers completed questionnaires about their parents' behavior. Regardless of gender, ethnicity, social class, or parents' marital status, teens with warm, respectful, and demanding parents earned higher grades in school, were more self-reliant, suffered from less anxiety and depression, and were less likely to engage in delinquent behavior. The same pattern replicates in nearly every nation that's been studied and at every stage of child development. Longitudinal research indicates that the benefits are measurable across a decade or more.

———

One of the major discoveries of parenting research is that what matters more than the messages parents aim to deliver are the messages their children receive.

What may *appear* to be textbook authoritarian parenting—a no-television policy, for example, or a prohibition against swearing—may or may not be coercive. Alternatively, what may *seem* permissive—say, letting a child drop out of high school—may simply reflect differences in the rules parents value as important. In other words, don't pass judgment on that parent lecturing their child in the supermarket cereal aisle. In most cases, you don't have enough context to understand how the child interprets the exchange, and, at the end of the day, it's the child's experience that really matters.

Are you a psychologically wise parent? Use the parenting assessment on the next page, developed by psychologist and parenting expert Nancy Darling, as a checklist to find out. How many of these statements would your child affirm without hesitation?

You'll notice that some of the items are italicized. These are "reverse-coded" items, meaning that if your child agrees with them, you may be less psychologically wise than you think.

Supportive: Warm

I can count on my parents to help me out if I have a problem.

My parents spend time just talking to me.

My parents and I do things that are fun together.

My parents don't really like me to tell them my troubles.

My parents hardly ever praise me for doing well.

Supportive: Respectful

My parents believe I have a right to my own point of view.

My parents tell me that their ideas are correct and that I shouldn't question them.

My parents respect my privacy.

My parents give me a lot of freedom.

My parents make most of the decisions about what I can do.

Demanding

My parents really expect me to follow family rules.

My parents really let me get away with things.

My parents point out ways I could do better.

When I do something wrong, my parents don't punish me.

My parents expect me to do my best even when it's hard.

———

Growing up with support, respect, and high standards confers a lot of benefits, one of which is especially relevant to grit—in other words, wise parenting encourages children to *emulate* their parents.

To a certain extent, of course, young children *imitate* their mothers and fathers. When we have nothing else to go by, what other choice do we have, really, than to mimic the accents, habits, and attitudes of the people around us? We talk like they talk. We eat what they eat. We adopt their likes and dislikes.

A young child's instinct to copy adults is very strong. In a classic psychology experiment conducted more than fifty years ago at Stanford University, for example, preschoolers watched adults play with a variety of toys and then were given the opportunity to play with the toys themselves. Half of the boys and girls watched an adult quietly play with Tinkertoys while ignoring a child-size, inflatable doll in the same room. The other half of the children watched the adult begin assembling the Tinkertoys and, after a minute, turn to viciously attack the doll. The adult pummeled the doll with his fists and then a mallet, tossed the doll up in the air and, finally, while screaming and yelling, aggressively kicked the doll about the room.

When given an opportunity to play with the same toys, children who'd seen adults play quietly followed suit. In contrast, children who'd watched adults beat up the doll were likewise aggressive, in many cases so closely imitating violent adults they'd seen earlier that researchers described their behavior as virtual "carbon copies."

And yet, there's a world of difference between *imitation* and *emulation*.

As we grow older, we develop the capacity to reflect on our actions and pass judgment on what we admire and disdain in others. When our parents are loving, respectful, and demanding, we not only follow their example, we revere it. We not only comply with their requests, we understand why they're making them. We become especially eager to pursue the same interests—for instance, it's no coincidence that Steve Young's father was himself a standout football player at BYU, or that Francesca Martinez, like her father, developed an early love of writing.

Benjamin Bloom and his team noted the same pattern in their studies of world-class performers. Almost without exception, the supportive and demanding parents in Bloom's study were "models of the work ethic in that they were regarded as hard workers, they did their best in whatever they tried, they believed that work should come before play, and that one should work toward distant goals." Further, "most of the parents found it natural to encourage their children to participate in their favored activities." Indeed, one of Bloom's summary conclusions was that "parents' own interests somehow get communicated to the child. . . . We found over and over again that the parents of the pianists would send their child to the tennis lessons but they would take their child to the piano lessons. And we found just the opposite for the tennis homes."

It's indeed remarkable how many paragons of grit have told me, with pride and awe, that their parents are their most admired and influential role models. And it's just as telling that so many paragons have, in one way or another, developed very similar interests to those of their parents. Clearly, these exemplars of grit grew up not just imitating their parents but also emulating them.

This logic leads to the speculative conclusion that not *all* children with psychologically wise parents will grow up to be gritty, because not all psychologically wise parents *model* grittiness. Though they may be both supportive and demanding, upper-right-quadrant moms and dads may or may not show passion and perseverance for long-term goals.

If you want to bring forth grit in your child, first ask how much passion and perseverance you have for your own life goals. Then ask yourself how likely it is that your approach to parenting encourages your child to emulate you. If the answer to the first question is "a great deal," and your answer to the second is "very likely," you're already parenting for grit.

—————

It's not just mothers and fathers who lay the foundation for grit.

There's a larger ecosystem of adults that extends beyond the nuclear family. All of us are "parents" to young people other than our own children in the sense that, collectively, we are responsible for "bringing forth" the next generation. In this role of supportive but demanding mentors to other people's children, we can have a huge impact.

Technology entrepreneur Tobi Lütke is a grit paragon who had such a mentor in his life. Tobi dropped out of his German high school when he was sixteen without any memorably positive learning experiences. As an apprentice at an engineering company in his hometown, he met Jürgen, a programmer who worked in a small room in the basement. Tobi affectionately described Jürgen as "a long-haired, fifty-something, grizzled rocker who would have been right at home in any Hells Angels gang." Under his tutelage, Tobi discovered that the learning disabilities he'd been diagnosed with as a failing student did nothing to hamper his progress as a computer programmer.

"Jürgen was a master teacher," Tobi said. "He created an environment in which it was not only possible but easy to move through ten years of career development every year."

Each morning, Tobi would arrive at work to find a printout of the code he'd written the day before, covered in red marker with comments, suggestions, and corrections. Jürgen was unsparing in pointing out specific ways Tobi's work could be better. "This taught me not to tangle my ego up in the code I write," Tobi said. "There are always ways to improve it and getting this feedback is a gift."

One day, Jürgen asked Tobi to lead a software assignment for General Motors. The company gave Tobi extra money to buy his first suit for the presentation and installation. Tobi expected Jürgen to do all the talking, but the day before the installation, Jürgen casually turned to Tobi and told him he had somewhere else to be. Tobi would be visiting General Motors alone. Full of trepidation, Tobi went. The installation was a success.

"This pattern kept on repeating itself," Tobi said. "Jürgen somehow knew the extent of my comfort zone and manufactured situations which were slightly outside it. I overcame them through trial and error, through doing. . . . I succeeded."

Tobi went on to found Shopify, a software company that powers tens of thousands of online stores and recently exceeded $100 million in revenue.

———

In fact, emerging research on teaching suggests uncanny parallels to parenting. It seems that psychologically wise teachers can make a huge difference in the lives of their students.

Ron Ferguson is a Harvard economist who has collected more data comparing effective and ineffective teachers than anyone I know. In one recent study, Ron partnered with the Gates Foundation to study students and teachers in 1,892 different classrooms. He found that teachers who are demanding—whose students say of them, "My teacher accepts nothing less than our best effort," and "Students in this class behave the way my teacher wants them to"—produce measurable year-to-year gains in the academic skills of their students. Teachers who are supportive and respectful—whose students say, "My teacher seems to know if something is bothering me," and "My teacher wants us to share our thoughts"—enhance students' happiness, voluntary effort in class, and college aspirations.

It's possible, Ron finds, to be a psychologically wise teacher, just as it's possible to be permissive, authoritarian, or negligent. And it's the wise teachers who seem to promote competence in addition to well-being, engagement, and high hopes for the future.

Recently, psychologists David Yeager and Geoff Cohen ran an experiment to see what effect the message of high expectations in conjunction with unflagging support had on students. They asked seventh-grade teachers to provide written feedback on student essays, including suggestions for improvement and any words of encouragement they would normally give. Per usual, teachers filled the margins of the students' essays with comments.

Next, teachers passed all of the marked-up essays to researchers, who randomly sorted them into two piles. On half of the essays, researchers affixed a Post-it note that read: *I'm giving you these comments so that you'll have feedback on your paper.* This was the placebo control condition.

On the other half of the essays, researchers affixed a Post-it note that read: *I'm giving you these comments because I have very high expectations and I know that you can reach them.* This was the wise feedback condition.

So that teachers would not see which student received which note, and so that students would not notice that some of their classmates had received a different note than they had, researchers placed each essay in a folder for teachers to hand back to the students during class.

Students were then given the option to revise their essays the following week.

When the essays were collected, David discovered that about 40 percent of the students who'd received the placebo control Post-it note decided to turn in a revised essay, compared to about *twice* that number—80 percent of the students—who'd received the Post-it note communicating wise feedback.

In a replication study with a different sample, students who received the wise feedback Post-it—"I'm giving you these comments because I have very high expectations and I know that you can reach them"—made twice as many edits to their essays as students in the placebo control condition.

Most certainly, Post-it notes are no substitute for the daily gestures, comments, and actions that communicate warmth, respect, and high expectations. But these experiments do illuminate the powerful motivating effect that a simple message can have.

———

Not every grit paragon has had the benefit of a wise father and mother, but every one I've interviewed could point to *someone* in their life who, at the right time and in the right way, encouraged them to aim high and provided badly needed confidence and support.

Consider Cody Coleman.

A couple of years ago, Cody sent me an email. He'd seen my TED talk on grit and wanted to know if we could talk sometime. He thought perhaps his personal story might be helpful. He was majoring in electrical engineering and computer science at MIT and was on the cusp of graduating with a near-perfect GPA. From his perspective, talent and opportunity had very little to do with his accomplishments. Instead, success had been all about passion and perseverance sustained over years and years.

"Sure, I said, "let's talk." Here's what I learned.

Cody was born thirty miles east of Trenton, New Jersey, at the Monmouth County Correctional Institution. His mother was declared insane by the FBI and, when Cody came along, was imprisoned for threatening to kill a senator's child. Cody has never met his father. Cody's grandmother took legal custody of Cody and his brothers, and probably saved his life by doing so. But she was not a prototypically wise parent. She may have *wanted* to be loving and strict, but both her body and mind were in decline. As Cody describes it, he was soon doing more parenting—and cooking and cleaning—than she was.

"We were poor," Cody explained. "When my school did food drives, the food went to my family, because we were the poorest in the neighborhood. And the neighborhood itself wasn't all that great. My school district scored below average in every category imaginable.

"To make matters worse," Cody continued, "I wasn't really an athletic or smart person. I started out in remedial English classes. My math scores were average, at best."

And then what happened?

"One day, my oldest brother—he was eighteen years older than me—he comes home. It was the summer after my freshman year in high school. He drove up from Virginia to pick me up to spend two weeks with him, and on the drive back to his place, he turns and asks me, 'Where do you want to go to college?'"

Cody told him, "I don't know. . . . I want to go to a good school. Maybe somewhere like Princeton." And then immediately, he took it back: "There's no way a school like Princeton would accept me."

"Why wouldn't Princeton take you?" Cody's brother asked him. "You're doing all right in school. If you work harder, if you keep pushing yourself, you can get to that level. You have nothing to lose by trying."

"That's when a switch flipped in my head," Cody said. "I went from 'Why bother?' to 'Why not?' I knew I might not get into a really good college, but I figured, if I try, I have a chance. If I never try, then I have no chance at all."

The next year, Cody threw himself into his schoolwork. By junior year he was earning straight As. As a senior, Cody set about finding the best college in the country for computer science and engineering. He changed his dream school from Princeton to MIT. During this transformative period, he met Chantel Smith, an exceptionally wise math teacher who all but adopted him.

It was Chantel who paid for Cody's driving lessons. It was Chantel who collected a "college dorm fund" to pay for the supplies he'd need once he moved. It was Chantel who mailed sweaters, hats, gloves, and warm socks to him for the cold Boston winters, who worried about him every day, who welcomed him home each holiday break, who stood by Cody at his grandmother's funeral. It was in Chantel's home that Cody first experienced waking on Christmas morning to presents with his name on them, where he decorated Easter eggs for the first time, and where, at the age of twenty-four, he had his first family birthday party.

MIT wasn't entirely smooth sailing, but the new challenges came with an "ecosystem of support," as Cody put it. Deans, professors, older students in his fraternity, roommates, and friends—compared to what he'd experienced growing up, MIT was a haven of attention.

After graduating with top honors, Cody stayed on to get his master's in electrical engineering and computer science, earning a perfect GPA while doing so and, at the same time, fielding offers from doctoral programs and Silicon Valley recruiters.

In deciding between an immediately lucrative career and graduate school, Cody did some hard thinking about how he'd gotten to where he was. Next fall, he'll begin a PhD program in computer science at Stanford. Here's the first sentence from his application essay: "My mission is to utilize my passion for computer science and machine learning to benefit society at large, while serving as an example of success that will shape the future of our society."

So, Cody Coleman did not have a psychologically wise mother, father, or grandparent. I wish he had. What he *did* have was a brother who said the right thing at the right time, an extraordinarily wise and wonderful high school math teacher, and an ecosystem of other teachers, mentors, and fellow students who collectively showed him what's possible and helped him to get there.

Chantel refuses to take credit for Cody's success. "The truth is that Cody has touched my life more than I've touched his. He's taught me that nothing is impossible and no goal is beyond reach. He's one of the kindest human beings I have ever met, and I couldn't be prouder when he calls me 'Mom.' "

A local radio station recently interviewed Cody. Toward the end of the conversation, Cody was asked what he had to say to listeners struggling to overcome similar life circumstances. "Stay positive," Cody said. "Go past those negative beliefs in what's possible and impossible and just give it a try."

Cody had these final words: "You don't need to be a parent to make a difference in someone's life. If you just care about them and get to know what's going on, you can make an impact. Try to understand what's going on in their life and help them through that. That's something I experienced firsthand. It made the difference."

Chapter 11

THE PLAYING FIELDS OF GRIT

One day, when she was about four years old, my daughter Lucy sat at the kitchen table, struggling to open a little box of raisins. She was hungry. She wanted those raisins. But the top of that box stubbornly resisted her efforts. After a minute or so, she put down the unopened box with a sigh and wandered off. I was watching from another room, and I nearly gasped. *Oh god, my daughter has been defeated by a box of raisins! What are the odds she'll grow up to have any grit?*

I rushed over and encouraged Lucy to try again. I did my best to be both supportive and demanding. Nevertheless, she refused.

Not long after, I found a ballet studio around the corner and signed her up.

Like a lot of parents, I had a strong intuition that grit is enhanced by doing activities like ballet . . . or piano . . . or football . . . or really any structured extracurricular activity. These activities possess two important features that are hard to replicate in any other setting. First, there's an adult in charge—ideally, a supportive and demanding one—who is *not* the parent. Second, these pursuits are *designed* to cultivate interest, practice, purpose, and hope. The ballet studio, the recital hall, the dojo, the basketball court, the gridiron—these are the playing fields of grit.

––––

The evidence on extracurricular activities is incomplete. I cannot point to a single study in which kids have been randomly assigned to play a sport or musical instrument, compete on the debate team, hold an after-school job, or work on the school newspaper. If you think about it for a moment, you'll realize why. No parent wants to volunteer their kids to do things (or not) by the flip of a coin, and for ethical reasons, no scientist can really force kids to stay in (or out) of activities.

Nevertheless, as a parent and as a social scientist, I would recommend that, as soon as your child is old enough, you find something they might enjoy doing *outside of class* and sign them up. In fact, if I could wave a magic wand, I'd have all the children in the world engage in at least one extracurricular activity of their choice, and as for those in high school, I'd require that they stick with at least one activity for more than a year.

Do I think every moment of a child's day should be scripted? Not at all. But I do think kids thrive when they spend at least some part of their week doing hard things that interest them.

––––

Like I said, the evidence for such a bold recommendation is incomplete. But the research that *has* been done is, in my view, highly suggestive. Put it all together, and you have a compelling case for kids learning grit at the elbow of a wise ballet instructor, football coach, or violin teacher.

For starters, a few researchers have equipped kids with beepers so that, throughout the day, they can be prompted to report on what they're doing and how they feel at that very moment. When kids are in class, they report feeling challenged—but especially unmotivated. Hanging out with friends, in contrast, is not very challenging but super fun. And what about extracurricular activities? When kids are playing sports or music or rehearsing for the school play, they're *both* challenged and having fun. There's no other experience in the lives of young people that reliably provides this combination of challenge and intrinsic motivation.

The bottom line of this research is this: School's hard, but for many kids it's not intrinsically interesting. Texting your friends is interesting, but it's not hard. But ballet? Ballet can be both.

———

In-the-moment experience is one thing, but what about long-term benefits? Do extracurriculars pay off in any measurable way?

There are countless research studies showing that kids who are more involved in extracurriculars fare better on just about every conceivable metric—they earn better grades, have higher self-esteem, are less likely to get in trouble and so forth. A handful of these studies are longitudinal, meaning that researchers waited to see what happened to kids later in life. These longer-term studies come to the same conclusion: more participation in activities predicts better outcomes.

The same research clearly indicates that *overdosing* on extracurriculars is pretty rare. These days, the average American teenager reports spending more than three hours a day watching television and playing video games. Additional time is drained away checking social media feeds, texting friends links to cat videos, and tracking the Kardashians as they figure out which outfit to wear—which makes it hard to argue that time can't be spared for the chess club or the school play, or just about any other structured, skill-focused, adult-guided activity.

But what about grit? What about accomplishing something that takes years, as opposed to months, of work? If grit is about sticking with a goal for the long-term, and if extracurricular activities are a way of practicing grit, it stands to reason that they're especially beneficial when we do them *for more than a year.*

In fact, lessons learned while working to improve from one season to the next come up repeatedly in my interviews with paragons of grit.

Here's an example: After a lackluster passing season his junior year of high school football, future NFL Hall of Famer Steve Young went down to the high school woodshop and fashioned a wooden football with tape for laces. In one end, he screwed in an eye hook and used that to latch the football to a weight machine in the high school gym. Then, gripping the ball, he'd move it back and forth in a passing motion, the added resistance developing his forearms and shoulders. His passing yardage doubled the next year.

Even more convincing evidence for the benefits of long-term extracurricular activities comes from a study conducted by psychologist Margo Gardner. Margo and her collaborators at Columbia University followed eleven thousand American teenagers until they were twenty-six years old to see what effect, if any, participating in high school extracurriculars for two years, as opposed to just one, might have on success in adulthood.

Here's what Margo found: kids who spend more than a year in extracurriculars are significantly more likely to graduate from college and, as young adults, to volunteer in their communities. The hours per week kids devote to extracurriculars also predict having a job (as opposed to being unemployed as a young adult) and earning more money, but *only* for kids who participate in activities for two years rather than one.

———

One of the first scientists to study the importance of following through with extracurricular activities—as opposed to just dabbling—was Warren Willingham.

In 1978, Willingham was the director of the Personal Qualities

Project. Even today, this study remains the most ambitious attempt ever to identify the determinants of success in young adulthood.

The project was funded by the Educational Testing Service. ETS, as it's more commonly called, occupies a sprawling campus in Princeton, New Jersey, and employs more than a thousand statisticians, psychologists, and other scientists—all devoted to the development of tests that predict achievement in school and the workplace. If you've taken the SAT, you've taken an ETS test. Ditto for the GRE, TOEFL, Praxis, and any one of three dozen advanced placement exams. Basically, ETS is to standardized testing what Kleenex is to tissues: Sure, there are other organizations that make standardized tests, but most of us are hard-pressed to think of their names.

So, what motivated ETS to look beyond standardized tests?

Better than anyone, Willingham and other scientists at ETS knew that, together, high school grades and test scores did only a half-decent job of predicting success later in life. It's very often the case that two kids with identical grades and test scores will end up faring very differently later in life. The simple question Willingham set out to answer was *What other personal qualities matter?*

To find out, Willingham's team followed several thousand students for five years, beginning in their senior year of high school.

At the start of the study, college application materials, questionnaires, writing samples, interviews, and school records were collected for each student. This information was used to produce numerical ratings for *more than one hundred* different personal characteristics. These included family background variables, like parent occupation and socioeconomic status, as well as self-declared career interests, motivation for a college degree, educational goals, and many more.

Then, as the students progressed through college, objective measures of success were collected across three broad categories: First, did the student distinguish him or herself academically? Next, as a young adult, did this individual demonstrate leadership? And, finally, to what extent could these young men and women point to a significant accomplishment in science and technology, the arts, sports, writing and speaking, entrepreneurism, or community service?

In a sense, the Personal Qualities Project was a horse race. Each of the hundred-plus measures at the start of the study could have ended up as the strongest predictor of later success. It's clear from reading the first report, completed several years before the final data were collected, that Willingham was entirely dispassionate on the issue. He methodically described each variable, its rationale for being included, how it was measured, and so on.

But when all the data were finally in, Willingham was unequivocal and emphatic about what he'd learned. One horse did win, and by a long stretch: *follow-through*.

This is how Willingham and his team put a number on it: "The follow-through rating involved evidence of purposeful, continuous commitment to certain types of activities (in high school) versus sporadic efforts in diverse areas."

Students who earned a top follow-through rating participated in two different high school extracurricular activities for several years each and, in both of those activities, advanced significantly in some way (e.g., becoming editor of the newspaper, winning MVP for the volleyball team, winning a prize for artwork). As an example, Willingham described a student who was "on his school newspaper staff for three years and became managing editor, and was on the track team for three years and ended up winning an important meet."

In contrast, students who hadn't participated in a single multiyear activity earned the lowest possible follow-through rating. Some students in this category didn't participate in any activities at all in high school. But many, many others were simply itinerant, joining a club or team one year but then, the following year, moving on to something entirely different.

The predictive power of follow-through was striking: After controlling for high school grades and SAT scores, follow-through in high school extracurriculars predicted graduating from college with academic honors better than any variable. Likewise, follow-through was the single best predictor of holding an appointed or elected leadership position in young adulthood. And, finally, better than any of the more than one hundred personal characteristics Willingham had measured, follow-through predicted notable accomplishments for a young adult in all domains, from the arts and writing to entrepreneurism and community service.

Notably, the *particular* pursuits to which students had devoted themselves in high school didn't matter—whether it was tennis, student government, or debate team. The key was that students had signed up for *something*, signed up *again* the following year, and during that time had made some kind of *progress*.

———

I learned about the Personal Qualities Project a few years after I started studying grit. When I got my hands on the original study report, I read it cover to cover, put it down for a moment, and then started again on page one.

That night, I couldn't sleep. Instead, I lay awake thinking: *Holy smokes! What Willingham calls "follow-through" sounds a lot like grit!*

Immediately—desperately—I wanted to see if I could replicate his findings.

One motive was practical.

Like any self-report questionnaire, the Grit Scale is ridiculously fakeable. In research studies, participants have no real incentive to lie, but it's hard to imagine using the Grit Scale in a high-stakes setting where, in fact, there's something to gain by pretending that "I finish whatever I begin." Quantifying grit as Willingham had done was a measurement strategy that could not easily be gamed. Not, at least, without outright lying. In Willingham's own words: "Looking for clear signs of productive follow-through is a useful way to mine the student's track record."

But the more important goal was to see whether follow-through would predict the same showing-up-instead-of-dropping-out outcomes that are the hallmark of grit.

For the support of a new longitudinal study, I turned to the largest philanthropic funder in education: the Bill and Melinda Gates Foundation.

I soon learned that the foundation is especially interested in why college students drop out in such large numbers. At present, the dropout rate for two- and four-year colleges in the United States is among the highest in the world. Escalating tuitions and the byzantine labyrinth of financial aid in this country are two contributing factors. Woefully inadequate academic preparation is another. Still, students with similar financial circumstances and identical SAT scores drop out at very different rates. Predicting who will persist through college and earn their degree and who won't is among the most stubborn problems in all of social science. Nobody has a very satisfying answer.

In a meeting with Bill and Melinda Gates, I had an opportunity to explain my perspective in person. Learning to follow through on something hard in high school, I said, seemed the best-possible preparation for doing the same thing later in life.

In that conversation, I learned that Bill himself has long appreciated the importance of competencies other than talent. Back in the days when he had a more direct role in hiring software programmers at Microsoft, for instance, he said he'd give applicants a programming task he knew would require hours and hours of tedious troubleshooting. This wasn't an IQ test, or a test of programming skills. Rather, it was a test of a person's ability to muscle through, press on, get to the finish line. Bill only hired programmers who finished what they began.

With generous support from the Gates Foundation, I recruited 1,200 seniors and, just as Willingham had done, asked them to name their extracurricular activities (if they *had* any), when they'd participated in them, and how they'd distinguished themselves doing them, if at all. Around the lab, while we were doing this study, we began calling this measure what it looks like: the Grit Grid.

Directions: Please list activities in which you spent a significant amount of time outside of class. They can be any kind of pursuit, including sports, extracurricular activities, volunteer activities, research/academic activities, paid work, or hobbies. If you do not have a second or third activity, please leave those rows blank:

Activity	Grade levels of participation 9-10-11-12	Achievements, awards, leadership positions, if any
	☐—☐—☐—☐	
	☐—☐—☐—☐	
	☐—☐—☐—☐	

Following Willingham's lead, my research team calculated Grit Grid scores by quantifying multiyear commitment and advancement in up to two activities.

Specifically, each activity students did for two years or more earned a grit point; activities students did for only one year earned no points and weren't scored further. Activities that students pursued for *multiple* years and in which they could point to some kind of advancement (for example, member of the student government one year and treasurer the next) each earned a second point. Finally, when advancement could reasonably be deemed "high" versus just "moderate" (president of the student body, MVP of the basketball team, employee of the month), we awarded a third grit point.

In sum, students could score anywhere from zero on the Grit Grid (if they'd participated in no multiyear commitments at all) to six points (if they pursued two different multiyear commitments and, in both, demonstrated high achievement).

As expected, we found that students with higher Grit Grid scores rated themselves higher in grit, and so did their teachers.

Then we waited.

After graduating from high school, students in our sample ended up at dozens of colleges throughout the country. After two years, only 34 percent of the 1,200 students in our study were enrolled in a two- or four-year college. Just as we expected, the odds of staying in school depended heavily on Grit Grid scores: 69 percent of students who scored 6 out of 6 on the Grit Grid were still in college. In contrast, just 16 percent of students who scored 0 out 6 were still on track to get their college degrees.

In a separate study, we applied the same Grit Grid scoring system to the college extracurriculars of novice teachers. The results were strikingly similar. Teachers who, in college, had demonstrated productive follow-through in a few extracurricular commitments were more likely to stay in teaching and, furthermore, were more effective in producing academic gains in their students. In contrast, persistence and effectiveness in teaching had absolutely no measurable relationship with teachers' SAT scores, their college GPAs, or interviewer ratings of their leadership potential.

———

Considered together, the evidence I've presented so far could be interpreted in two different ways. I've been arguing that extracurricular activities are a way for young people to practice, and therefore develop passion and perseverance for long-term goals. But it's also possible that following through with extracurriculars is something only gritty people do. These explanations aren't mutually exclusive: it's entirely possible that *both* factors—cultivation and selection—are at play.

My best guess is that following through on our commitments while we grow up both *requires* grit and, at the same time, *builds* it.

One reason I think so is that, in general, the situations to which people gravitate tend to enhance the very characteristics that brought us there in the first place. This theory of personality development has been dubbed the *corresponsive principle* by Brent Roberts, the foremost authority on what leads to enduring changes in how people think, feel, and act in different situations.

When Brent was a psychology graduate student at Berkeley, the prevailing view was that, after childhood, personalities are more or less "set like plaster." Brent and other personality researchers have since collected enough longitudinal data—following, literally, *thousands* of people across years and decades—to show that personalities do, in fact, change after childhood.

Brent and other personality researchers have found that a key process in personality development involves situations and personality traits reciprocally "calling" each other. The corresponsive principle suggests that the very traits that steer us toward certain life situations are the very same traits that those situations encourage, reinforce, and amplify. In this relationship there is the possibility of virtuous and vicious cycles.

For instance, in one study, Brent and his collaborators followed a thousand adolescents in New Zealand as they entered adulthood and found jobs. Over the years, hostile adolescents ended up in lower-prestige jobs and reported difficulties paying their bills. These conditions, in turn, led to *increases* in levels of hostility, which further eroded their employment prospects. By contrast, more agreeable adolescents entered a virtuous cycle of psychological development. These "nice kids" secured higher-status jobs offering greater financial security—outcomes that *enhanced* their tendency toward sociability.

So far, there hasn't been a corresponsive principle study of grit.

Let me speculate, though. Left to her own devices, a little girl who, after failing to open a box of raisins and saying to herself, "This is too hard! I quit!" might enter a vicious cycle that reinforces giving up. She might learn to give up one thing after another, each time missing the opportunity to enter the virtuous cycle of struggle, followed by progress, followed by confidence to try something even harder.

But what about a little girl whose mother takes her to ballet, even though it's hard? Even though the little girl doesn't really *feel* like putting on her leotard at that moment, because she's a little tired. Even though, at the last practice, her ballet teacher scolded her for holding her arms the wrong way, which clearly stung a bit. What if that little girl was nudged to try and try again and, at one practice, experienced the satisfaction of a breakthrough? Might that victory encourage the little girl to practice *other* difficult things? Might she learn to welcome challenge?

———

The year after Warren Willingham published the Personal Qualities Project, Bill Fitzsimmons became the dean of admissions at Harvard.

Two years later, when I applied to Harvard, it was Bill who reviewed my application. I know because, at some point as an undergraduate, I found myself involved in a community service project with Bill. "Oh, Miss School Spirit!" he exclaimed when we were introduced. And then he ticked off, with remarkable accuracy, the various activities I'd pursued in high school.

I recently called Bill to ask what he thought about extracurricular follow-through. Not surprisingly, he was intimately familiar with Willingham's research.

"I have it here somewhere," he said, seemingly scanning his bookshelf. "It's never far from reach."

Okay, so did he agree with Willingham's conclusions? Did Harvard admissions really care about anything other than SAT scores and high school grades?

I wanted to know, because Willingham's opinion, at the time he published his findings, was that college admissions offices weren't weighing follow-through in extracurriculars as heavily as his research suggested they ought to be.

Each year, Bill Fitzsimmons explained, several hundred students are admitted to Harvard on the merits of truly outstanding academic credentials. Their early scholarly accomplishments suggest they will at some point become world-class academics.

But Harvard admits at least as many students who, in Bill's words, "have made a commitment to pursue something they love, believe in, and value—and [have done] so with singular energy, discipline, and plain old hard work."

Nobody in the admissions office wants or needs these students to pursue the same activities when they get to campus. "Let's take athletics as an example," Bill said. "Let's say the person gets hurt, or decides not to play, or doesn't make the team. What we have tended to find is that all that energy, drive, and commitment—all that grit—that was developed through athletics can almost always be transferred to something else."

Bill assured me that, in fact, Harvard was paying the utmost attention to follow-through. After describing our more recent research confirming Willingham's findings, he told me they are using a very similar rating scale: "We ask our admissions staff to do exactly what it appears you're doing with your Grit Grid."

This helped explain why he'd maintained such a clear memory, more than a year after he'd read my application, of how I'd spent my time outside of classes in high school. It was in my *activities*, as much as anything else in my record, that he found evidence that I'd prepared myself for the rigors—and opportunities—of college.

"My sense, from being in admissions for over forty years," Bill concluded, "is that most people are born with tremendous potential. The real question is whether they're encouraged to employ their good old-fashioned hard work and their grit, if you will, to its maximum. In the end, those are the people who seem to be the most successful."

I pointed out that extracurricular follow-through might be a mere signal of grit, rather than something that would develop it. Bill agreed, but reaffirmed his judgment that activities aren't *just* a signal. His intuition was that following through on hard things teaches a young person powerful, transferable lessons. "You're learning from others, you're finding out more and more through experience what your priorities are, you're developing character.

"In some cases," Bill continued, "students get into activities because somebody else, maybe the parent, maybe the counselor, suggests it. But what often happens is that these experiences are actually *transformative*, and the students actually learn something very important, and then they jump in and contribute to these activities in ways that they and their parents and their counselor never would've imagined."

———

What surprised me most about my conversation with Bill was how much he worried about the kids who'd been denied the opportunity to practice grit in extracurricular activities.

"More and more high schools have diminished or eliminated arts and music and other activities," Bill told me, and then explained that, of course, it was primarily schools serving poor kids who were making these cuts. "It's the least level playing field one could possibly imagine."

Research by Harvard political scientist Robert Putnam and his collaborators reveals that affluent American high school students have been participating in extracurricular activities at consistently high rates for the past few decades. In contrast, participation among poor students has been dropping precipitously.

The widening gap in extracurricular participation between rich and poor has a few contributing factors, Putnam explains. Pay-to-play sports activities like traveling soccer teams are one obstacle to equal participation. Even when participation is "free," not all parents can afford the uniforms. Not all parents are able or willing to drive their kids to and from practices and games. For music, the cost of private lessons and instruments can be prohibitive.

Just as Putnam would have predicted, there is a worrisome correlation between family income and Grit Grid scores. On average, Grit Grid scores for the high school seniors in our sample who qualified for federally subsidized meals were a full point lower than those for students who were more privileged.

———

Like Robert Putnam, Geoffrey Canada is a Harvard-trained social scientist.

Geoff is about as gritty as they come. His passion is enabling kids growing up in poverty to realize their potential. Recently, Geoff has become something of a celebrity. But for decades he toiled in relative obscurity as the director of a radically intensive education program in New York City called the Harlem Children's Zone. The first kids to make it all the way through are now in college, and the program's unusually comprehensive approach, coupled with unusually successful results, has attracted national attention.

A few years ago, Geoff came to Penn to deliver our commencement speech. I managed to shoehorn a private meeting into his busy schedule. Given our limited time, I got straight to the point.

"I know you're trained as a social scientist," I began. "And I know there are things we have tons of evidence for and aren't doing in education, and there are things we have no evidence for and keep doing anyway. But I want to know, from all you've seen and done, what you *really* think is the way to dig kids out of poverty."

Geoff sat forward and put his hands together like he was about to pray. "I'll tell you straight. I'm a father of four. I've watched many, many kids who were not my own grow up. I may not have the random-assignment, double-blind studies to prove it, but I can tell you what poor kids need. They need all the things you and I give to our own children. What poor kids need is a lot. But you can sum it up by saying that what they need is a decent childhood."

About a year later, Geoff gave a TED talk, and I was lucky enough to be in the audience. Much of what Harlem Children's Zone did, Canada explained, was based on rock-solid scientific evidence— preschool education, for instance, and summer enrichment activities. But there's one thing his program provided without sufficient scientific evidence to justify the expense: extracurricular activities.

"You know why?" he asked. "Because I actually like kids."

The audience laughed, and he said it again: *"I actually like kids."*

"You've never read a study from MIT that says giving your kid dance instruction is going to help them do algebra better," he admitted. "But you will give that kid dance instruction, and you will be thrilled that that kid wants to do dance instruction, and it will make your day."

———

Geoffrey Canada is right. All the research I talked about in this chapter is nonexperimental. I don't know if there'll ever be a day when scientists figure out the logistics—and ethics—of randomly assigning kids to years of ballet class and then waiting to see if the benefit transfers to mastering algebra.

But, in fact, scientists *have* done short-term experiments testing whether doing hard things teaches a person to do other hard things.

Psychologist Robert Eisenberger at the University of Houston is the leading authority on this topic. He's run dozens of studies in which rats are randomly assigned to do something hard—like press a lever twenty times to get a single pellet of rat chow—or something easy, like press that lever two times to get the same reward. Afterward, Bob gives *all* the rats a different difficult task. In experiment after experiment, he's found the same results: Compared to rats in the "easy condition," rats who were previously required to work hard for rewards subsequently demonstrate more vigor and endurance on the second task.

My favorite of Bob's experiments is among his most clever. He noticed that laboratory rats are generally fed in one of two ways. Some researchers use wire-mesh hoppers filled with chow, requiring rats to gnaw at the food pellets through small openings in the mesh. Other researchers just scatter pellets on the floor of the cage. Bob figured that working for your supper, so to speak, might teach rats to work harder on an effortful training task. In fact, that's exactly what he found. He began his experiment by training young rats to run down a narrow plank for a reward. Then, he divided the rats into two groups. One group lived in cages with hopper feeders, and the other in cages where food pellets were scattered about the floor. After a month of working to obtain food from the hopper, rats performed better on the runway task than rats who instead merely wandered over to their food when they were hungry.

Because his wife was a teacher, Bob had the opportunity to try short-term versions of the same experiments with children. For instance, in one study, he gave pennies to second and third graders for counting objects, memorizing pictures, and matching shapes. For some children, Bob rapidly increased the difficulty of these tasks as the children improved. Other children were repeatedly given easy versions of the same tasks.

All the children got pennies and praise.

Afterward, the children in both conditions were asked to do a tedious job that was entirely different from the previous tasks: copying a list of words onto a sheet of paper. Bob's findings were exactly the same as what he'd found with rats: children who'd trained on difficult (rather than easy) tasks worked harder on the copying task.

Bob's conclusion? With practice, industriousness can be learned.

In homage to the earlier work of Seligman and Maier on learned helplessness, where the inability to escape punishment led animals to give up on a second challenging task, Bob dubbed this phenomenon *learned industriousness*. His major conclusion was simply that the association between working hard and reward can be learned. Bob will go further and say that *without* directly experiencing the connection between effort and reward, animals, whether they're rats or people, default to laziness. Calorie-burning effort is, after all, something evolution has shaped us to avoid whenever possible.

———

My daughter Lucy was still a baby when I first read Bob's work on learned industriousness, and her sister, Amanda, was a toddler. With both girls, I soon discovered I was ill-suited to play the role Bob had in his experiments. It was difficult for me to create the necessary contingency for learning—in other words, an environment in which the acknowledged rule was *If you work hard, you'll be rewarded. If you don't, you won't.*

Indeed, I struggled to provide the sort of feedback I knew my children needed. I found myself enthusiastically praising them no matter what they did. And this is one of the reasons extracurricular activities offer superior playing fields for grit—coaches and teachers are tasked with bringing forth grit in children who are not their own.

At the ballet class where I dropped off the girls each week, there was a terrific teacher waiting to receive them. This teacher's passion for ballet was infectious. She was every bit as supportive as I was, and, frankly, a heck of a lot more demanding. When a student ambled in late to class, they got a stern lecture about the importance of respecting other people's time. If a student forgot to wear their leotard that day, or left their ballet shoes at home, they sat and watched the other children for the entire class and weren't allowed to participate. When a move was executed incorrectly, there were endless repetitions and adjustments until, at last, this teacher's high standards were satisfied. Sometimes, these lessons were accompanied by short lectures on the history of ballet, and how each dancer is responsible for carrying on that tradition.

Harsh? I don't think so. High standards? Absolutely.

And so it was in ballet class, more than at home, that Lucy and Amanda got to rehearse developing an interest, diligently practice things they couldn't yet do, appreciate the beyond-the-self purpose of their efforts, and, when bad days eventually became good ones, acquire the hope to try, try again.

———

In our family, we live by the Hard Thing Rule. It has three parts. The first is that everyone—including Mom and Dad—has to do a hard thing. A hard thing is something that requires daily deliberate practice. I've told my kids that psychological research is my hard thing, but I also practice yoga. Dad tries to get better and better at being a real estate developer; he does the same with running. My oldest daughter, Amanda, has chosen playing the piano as her hard thing. She did ballet for years, but later quit. So did Lucy.

This brings me to the second part of the Hard Thing Rule: You can quit. But you can't quit until the season is over, the tuition payment is up, or some other "natural" stopping point has arrived. You must, at least for the interval to which you've committed yourself, finish whatever you begin. In other words, you can't quit on a day when your teacher yells at you, or you lose a race, or you have to miss a sleepover because of a recital the next morning. You can't quit on a bad day.

And, finally, the Hard Thing Rule states that *you* get to pick your hard thing. Nobody picks it for you because, after all, it would make no sense to do a hard thing you're not even vaguely interested in. Even the decision to try ballet came after a discussion of various other classes my daughters could have chosen instead.

Lucy, in fact, cycled through a half-dozen hard things. She started each with enthusiasm but eventually discovered that she *didn't* want to keep going with ballet, gymnastics, track, handicrafts, or piano. In the end, she landed on viola. She's been at it for three years, during which time her interest has waxed rather than waned. Last year, she joined the school and all-city orchestras, and when I asked her recently if she wanted to switch her hard thing to something else, she looked at me like I was crazy.

Next year, Amanda will be in high school. Her sister will follow the year after. At that point, the Hard Thing Rule will change. A fourth requirement will be added: each girl must commit to at least one activity, either something new or the piano and viola they've already started, for at least *two years*.

Tyrannical? I don't believe it is. And if Lucy's and Amanda's recent comments on the topic aren't disguised apple-polishing, neither do my daughters. They'd like to grow grittier as they get older, and, like any skill, they know grit takes practice. They know they're fortunate to have the opportunity to do so.

For parents who would like to encourage grit without obliterating their children's capacity to choose their own path, I recommend the Hard Thing Rule.

Chapter 12

A CULTURE OF GRIT

The first football game I ever watched from beginning to end was Super Bowl XLVIII. The game took place on February 2, 2014, and pitted the Seattle Seahawks against the Denver Broncos. The Seahawks won, 43–8.

The day after their victory, Seahawks head coach Pete Carroll was interviewed by a former member of the San Francisco 49ers.

"I know when I was with the (Forty-) Niners," the interviewer began, "you were there. . . . It meant something to be a Niner, not a football player. When you and John Schneider are looking for a player, tell me: What is that philosophy, what does it mean to be a Seahawk?"

Pete chuckled softly. "I'm not going to give it all to you, but . . ."

"Come on, man. Give it to me, Pete."

"I will tell you that we're looking for great competitors. That's really where it starts. And that's the guys that really have *grit*. The mindset that they're always going to succeed, that they've got something to prove. They're resilient, they're not going to let setbacks hold them back. They're not going to be deterred, you know, by challenges and hurdles and things. . . . It's that attitude—we really refer to it as *grit*."

I can't say I was surprised, either by Pete's comments or by his team's triumphant performance the day before.

Why not? Because nine months earlier, I'd received a call from Pete. Apparently, he'd just watched my TED talk on grit. What prompted his call were two urgent emotions.

First, he was curious—eager to learn more about grit than I'd been able to convey in the six minutes TED had allotted me.

Second, he was annoyed. Not by most of what I had to say. It was just the part at the end that irked him. Science, I'd confessed in that talk, had at that point disappointingly little to say about building grit. Pete later told me that he just about jumped out of his chair, practically yelling at my on-screen image that building grit is *exactly* what the Seahawks culture is all about.

We ended up talking for roughly an hour: me on one end of the line, sitting at my desk in Philadelphia, and Pete and his staff on the other, huddled around a speakerphone in Seattle. I told him what I was learning in my research, and Pete reciprocated by telling me about what he was trying to accomplish with the Seahawks.

"Come and watch us. All we do is help people be great competitors. We teach them how to persevere. We unleash their passion. That's *all* we do."

———

Whether we realize it or not, the culture in which we live, and with which we identify, powerfully shapes just about every aspect of our being.

By culture, I don't mean the geographic or political boundaries that divide one people from another as much as the invisible psychological boundaries separating *us* from *them*. At its core, a culture is defined by the shared norms and values of a group of people. In other words, a distinct culture exists anytime a group of people are in consensus about how we do things around here and why. As for how the rest of the world operates, the sharper the contrast, the stronger the bonds among those in what psychologists call the "in-group."

So it is that the Seattle Seahawks and the KIPP charter schools—as much as any nation—are bona fide cultures. If you're a Seahawk, you're not just a football player. If you're a KIPPster, you're not just a student. Seahawks and KIPPsters do things in a certain way, and they do so for certain reasons. Likewise, West Point has a distinct culture—one that is more than two centuries old, and yet, as we'll soon discover, continues to evolve.

For many of us, the companies we work for are an important cultural force in our lives. For instance, growing up, my dad liked to refer to himself as a DuPonter. All the pencils in our house were company-issued, embossed with phrases like *Safety First*, and my dad would light up every time a DuPont commercial came on television, sometimes even chiming in with the voice-over: "Better things for better living." I think my dad only met the CEO of DuPont a handful of times, but he'd tell stories of his good judgment the way you might speak of a family war hero.

How do you know you're part of a culture that, in a very real sense, has become part of you? When you adopt a culture, you make a *categorical* allegiance to that in-group. You're not "sort of" a Seahawk, or "sort of" a West Pointer. You either are or you aren't. You're *in* the group, or *out* of it. You can use a noun, not just an adjective or a verb, to describe your commitment. So much depends, as it turns out, on which in-group you commit to.

The bottom line on culture and grit is: *If you want to be grittier, find a gritty culture and join it. If you're a leader, and you want the people in your organization to be grittier, create a gritty culture.*

———

I recently called Dan Chambliss, the sociologist we met in chapter 3 who spent the first six years of his professional life studying swimmers.

My question for Dan was whether, in the three decades since his landmark study of expertise, he'd changed his mind about any of its provocative conclusions.

Did he, for example, still believe talent was largely a red herring when it came to understanding the origins of world-class excellence? Did he stand by the observation that going from your local club team to being competitive at the state and national levels and, finally, to world-class, Olympic-level expertise necessitated qualitative improvements in skill, not just "more hours" in the pool? And was mystifying excellence, at the end of the day, really the confluence of countless, perfectly executed yet mundane, doable acts?

Yes, yes, and yes.

"But I left out the most important thing," Dan said. "The real way to become a great swimmer is to join a great team."

That logic might strike you as strange. You might assume that *first* a person becomes a great swimmer and *then* he or she joins a great team. And it's true, of course, that great teams don't take just anyone. There are tryouts. There are a limited number of spots. There are standards. And the more elite the team, the fiercer the desire of those already on the team to keep those standards high.

What Dan was getting at is the reciprocal effect of a team's particular culture on the person who joins it. In his many years in and out of the pool, he'd seen the arrow of causality between a great team and a great individual performer go both ways. In effect, he'd witnessed the corresponsive principle of personality development: he'd seen that the very characteristics that are selected for certain situations are, in turn, enhanced by them.

"Look, when I started studying Olympians, I thought, 'What kind of oddball gets up every day at four in the morning to go to swimming practice?' I thought, 'These must be extraordinary people to do that sort of thing.' But the thing is, when you go to a place where basically *everybody* you know is getting up at four in the morning to go to practice, that's just what you do. It's no big deal. It becomes a habit."

Over and over, Dan had observed new swimmers join a team that did things a notch or two better than what they'd been used to. Very quickly, the newcomer conformed to the team's norms and standards.

"Speaking for myself," Dan added, "I don't have that much self-discipline. But if I'm surrounded by people who are writing articles and giving lectures and working hard, I tend to fall in line. If I'm in a crowd of people doing things a certain way, I follow along."

The drive to fit in—to conform to the group—is powerful indeed. Some of the most important psychology experiments in history have demonstrated how quickly, and usually without conscious awareness, the individual falls in line with a group that is acting or thinking a different way.

"So it seems to me," Dan concluded, "that there's a hard way to get grit and an easy way. The hard way is to do it by yourself. The easy way is to use conformity—the basic human drive to fit in—because if you're around a lot of people who are gritty, you're going to act grittier."

———

Short-term conformity effects are not what excite me about the power of culture to influence grit. Not exactly.

What excites me most is the idea that, in the long run, culture has the power to shape our identity. Over time and under the right circumstances, the norms and values of the group to which we belong become our own. We internalize them. We carry them with us. *The way we do things around here and why* eventually becomes *The way I do things and why*.

Identity influences every aspect of our character, but it has special relevance to grit. Often, the critical gritty-or-not decisions we make— to get up one more time; to stick it out through this miserable, exhausting summer; to run five miles with our teammates when on our own we might only run three—are a matter of identity more than anything else. Often, our passion and perseverance do not spring from a cold, calculating analysis of the costs and benefits of alternatives. Rather, the source of our strength is the person we know ourselves to be.

James March, an expert on decision making at Stanford University, explains the difference this way: Sometimes, we revert to cost-benefit analyses to make choices. Of course, March doesn't mean that, in deciding what to order for lunch or when to go to bed, we take out a pad of paper and a calculator. What he means is that, sometimes when making choices, we take into consideration how we might benefit, and what we'll have to pay, and how likely it is that these benefits and costs will be what we think they'll be. We can do all of this in our heads, and indeed, when I'm deciding what to order for lunch or when to go to bed, I often think through the pros and the cons before making a decision. It's very logical.

But other times, March says, we don't think through the conse-quences of our actions at all. We don't ask ourselves: *What are the ben-efits? What are the costs? What are the risks?* Instead, we ask ourselves: *Who am I? What is this situation? What does someone like me do in a situation like this?*

Here's an example:

Tom Deierlein introduced himself to me this way: "I am a West Pointer, Airborne Ranger, and two-time CEO. I founded and run a nonprofit. I am not special or extraordinary in any way. Except one: grit."

On active duty in Baghdad during the summer of 2006, Tom was shot by a sniper. The bullet shattered his pelvis and sacrum. There was no way to know how the bones would knit back together and what sort of functionality Tom might have when they did. Doctors told him he might never walk again.

"You don't know me," Tom replied simply. And then, to himself, he made a promise to run the Army Ten-Miler, a race he'd been training to run before he was shot.

When, seven months later, he was finally well enough to get out of bed and begin physical therapy, Tom worked fiercely, unrelentingly, doing all the assigned exercises and then more. Sometimes, he'd grunt in pain or shout out encouragements to himself. "The other patients were a little startled at first," Tom says, "but they got used to it, and then—all in good fun—they'd mock me with fake grunts of their own."

After a particularly tough workout, Tom got "zingers," sharp bolts of pain that shot down his legs. "They'd only last a second or two," Tom says, "but they'd come back at random times throughout the day, literally making me jump from the shock." Without fail, each day, Tom set a goal, and for a few months, the pain and perspiration were paying off. Finally, he could just barely walk with a walker, then with just a cane, then on his own. He walked faster and farther, then was able to run on the treadmill for a few seconds while holding onto the railings, and then for a full minute, and on and on until, after four months of improving, he hit a plateau.

"My physical therapist said, 'You're done. Good job.' And I said, 'I'm still coming.' And she said, 'You did what you needed to do. You're good.' And I said, 'No, no, I'm still coming.'"

And then Tom kept going for a full eight months beyond the point where there were any noticeable improvements. Technically, his physical therapist wasn't allowed to treat him anymore, but Tom came back on his own to use the equipment anyway.

Was there any benefit to those extra months? Maybe. Maybe not. Tom can't say for sure that the extra exercises did any good. He *does* know that he was able to start training for the Army Ten-Miler the next summer. Before getting shot, he'd aimed to run seven-minute miles, completing the race in seventy minutes or less. After getting shot, he revised his goal: he hoped to run twelve-minute miles and to finish in two hours. His finish time? One hour and fifty-six minutes.

Tom can't say that running the Army Ten-Miler—and, after that, two triathlons—were decisions rooted in costs and benefits, either. "I simply wasn't going to fail because I didn't care or didn't try. That's not who I am."

Indeed, the calculated costs and benefits of passion and perseverance don't always add up, at least in the short run. It's often more "sensible" to give up and move on. It can be years or more before grit's dividends pay off.

And that's exactly why culture and identity are so critical to understanding how gritty people live their lives. The logic of anticipated costs and benefits doesn't explain their choices very well. The logic of identity does.

———

The population of Finland is just over five million. There are fewer Finns in the world than New Yorkers. This tiny, cold Nordic country—so far north that, in the depth of winter, they get barely six hours of daylight—has been invaded numerous times by larger, more powerful neighbors. Whether those meteorological and historical challenges contribute to how Finns see themselves is a good question. Regardless, it is undeniable that the Finns see themselves as among the world's grittiest people.

The closest word to *grit* in Finnish is *sisu* (pronounced *see-sue*). The translation isn't perfect. Grit specifies having a passion to accomplish a particular top-level goal *and* the perseverance to follow through. *Sisu*, on the other hand, is really just about perseverance. In particular, *sisu* refers to a source of inner strength—a sort of psychological capital—that Finns believe they're born with by dint of their Finnish heritage. Quite literally, *sisu* refers to the insides of a person, their guts.

In 1939, Finland was the underdog in the Winter War, battling a Soviet army that boasted three times as many soldiers, thirty times as many aircraft, and a hundred times as many tanks. Finnish troops held their ground for several months—dramatically longer than the Soviets or anyone else might have expected. In 1940, *Time* magazine ran a feature on *sisu*:

> The Finns have something they call *sisu*. It is a compound of bravado and bravery, of ferocity and tenacity, of the ability to keep fighting after most people would have quit, and to fight with the will to win. The Finns translate *sisu* as "the Finnish spirit" but it is a much more gutful word than that.

In the same year, the *New York Times* ran a feature called "Sisu: A Word That Explains Finland." A Finn explained his countrymen to the journalist this way: "A typical Finn is an obstinate sort of fellow who believes in getting the better of bad fortune by proving that he can stand worse."

When I lecture on grit to my undergraduate classes, I like to include a brief digression on *sisu*. I ask my students the rhetorical question: Can we forge a culture—as Seahawks coach Pete Carroll clearly thinks we can—that celebrates and supports such qualities as *sisu* and grit?

A few years ago, by complete coincidence, a young Finnish woman named Emilia Lahti was in the audience when I mentioned *sisu*. After the lecture, she rushed to greet me and confirmed that my outsider view of *sisu* was correct. We agreed there was a pressing need for a systematic investigation of *sisu*, how Finns think about it, how it's propagated.

Emilia became my graduate student the next year, completing her master's thesis on exactly those questions. She asked a thousand Finns how they thought about *sisu* and discovered that most have a growth mindset about its development. When asked, "Do you think *sisu* can be learned or developed through conscious effort?" 83 percent said, "Yes." One respondent then offered: "For example, participation in Finnish scouting association jaunts, where thirteen-year-olds may be in charge of ten-year-olds alone in the woods, seems to have some correlation with *sisu*."

As a scientist, I don't take seriously the notion that Finns, or members of any other nationality, have actual reserves of energy hidden in their intestines, awaiting release at the critical moment. Still, there are two powerful lessons we can take from *sisu*.

First, thinking of yourself as someone who is able to overcome tremendous adversity often leads to behavior that confirms that self-conception. If you're a Finn with that "*sisu* spirit," you get up again no matter what. Likewise, if you're a Seattle Seahawk, you're a competitor. You have what it takes to succeed. You don't let setbacks hold you back. Grit is who you are.

Second, even if the idea of an actual inner energy source is preposterous, the metaphor couldn't be more apt. It sometimes feels like we have nothing left to give, and yet, in those dark and desperate moments, we find that if we just keep putting one foot in front of the other, there *is* a way to accomplish what all reason seems to argue against.

———

The idea of *sisu* has been integral to Finnish culture for centuries. But cultures can be created in much shorter time frames. In my quest to understand what gives rise to grit, I've encountered a few organizations with especially gritty leaders at the helm who, in my view, have successfully forged a culture of grit.

Consider, for example, Jamie Dimon, the CEO of JPMorgan Chase. Jamie isn't the only one of the bank's 250,000-plus employees who says, "I wear this jersey and I bleed this blood." Other employees much lower in the ranks say things like "What I do every day for our clients actually matters. No one here is insignificant. And every detail, every employee, matters. . . . I am proud to be part of this great company."

Jamie has been the CEO of JPMorgan Chase, the largest bank in the United States, for more than a decade. In the 2008 financial crisis, Jamie steered his bank to safety, and while other banks collapsed entirely, JPMorgan Chase somehow turned a $5 billion profit.

Coincidentally, the motto of Jamie's prep school alma mater, the Browning School, is "grytte," an Old English version of *grit* defined in an 1897 yearbook as "firmness, courage, determination . . . which alone win the crown of genuine success in all undertakings." In Jamie's senior year at Browning, his calculus teacher had a heart attack, and the substitute teacher didn't know calculus. Half the boys quit; the other half, including Jamie, decided to stick with it and spent the entire year in a separate classroom, alone, teaching themselves.

"You have to learn to get over bumps in the road and mistakes and setbacks," he told me when I called to talk about the culture he's built at JPMorgan Chase. "Failures are going to happen, and how you deal with them may be the most important thing in whether you succeed. You need fierce resolve. You need to take responsibility. You call it grit. I call it fortitude."

Fortitude is to Jamie Dimon what *sisu* is to Finland. Jamie recalls that getting fired from Citibank at age forty-two, and then taking a full year to ponder what lessons to take from the episode, made him a better leader. And he believes in fortitude enough to make it a core value for the entire JPMorgan Chase bank. "The ultimate thing is that we need to grow over time."

Is it really possible, I asked, for a leader to influence the culture of such an enormous corporation? True, the culture of JPMorgan Chase has, with some affection, been described as "the cult of Jamie." But there are literally thousands and thousands of JPMorgan Chase employees Jamie has never met in person.

"Absolutely," Jamie says. "It takes relentless—absolutely relentless—communication. It's what you say and how you say it."

It may also be how *often* you say it. By all accounts, Jamie is a tireless evangelist, crossing the country to appear at what he calls town hall meetings with his employees. At one meeting he was asked, "What do you look for in your leadership team?" His answer? "Capability, character, and how they treat people." Later, he told me that he asks himself two questions about senior management. First: "Would I let them run the business without me?" Second: "Would I let my kids work for them?"

Jamie has a favorite Teddy Roosevelt quote he likes to repeat:

> It is not the critic who counts; not the man who points out how the strong man stumbles, or where the doer of deeds could have done them better. The credit belongs to the man who is actually in the arena, whose face is marred by dust and sweat and blood; who strives valiantly; who errs, who comes short again and again, because there is no effort without error and shortcoming; but who does actually strive to do the deeds; who knows great enthusiasms, the great devotions; who spends himself in a worthy cause; who at the best knows in the end the triumph of high achievement, and who at the worst, if he fails, at least fails while daring greatly, so that his place shall never be with those cold and timid souls who neither know victory nor defeat.

And here is how Jamie translates the poetry of Roosevelt into the prose of a JPMorgan Chase manual, titled *How We Do Business*: "Have a fierce resolve in everything you do." "Demonstrate determination, resiliency, and tenacity." "Do not let temporary setbacks become permanent excuses." And, finally, "Use mistakes and problems as opportunities to get better—not reasons to quit."

––––––

Anson Dorrance has the challenge of instilling grit in considerably fewer people. Thirty-one women, to be exact, which is the full roster of the women's soccer team at the University of North Carolina at Chapel Hill. Anson is the winningest coach in women's soccer history.

His record includes twenty-two national championships in thirty-one years of competition. In 1991, he coached the U.S. Women's National Team to its first world title.

During his younger, playing days, Anson was the captain of the UNC men's soccer team. He wasn't especially talented, but his full-throttle, aggressive playing in every minute of practice and competition earned the admiration of his teammates, who nicknamed him Hack and Hustle. His father once declared, "Anson, you're the most confident person without any talent I've ever met." To which Anson quickly replied, "Dad, I'm taking that as a compliment." Many years later, as a coach, Anson observed that "talent is common; what you invest to develop that talent is the critical final measure of greatness."

Many of Anson's admirers attribute his unprecedented success to recruitment. "That's simply incorrect," he told me. "We're out-recruited by five or six schools on a regular basis. Our extraordinary success is about what we do once the players get here. It's our culture."

Culture building, Anson said, is a matter of continuous experimentation. "Basically, we'll try anything, and if it works, we'll keep doing it."

For instance, after learning about my research on grit, Anson asked each of his players to fill out the Grit Scale and made sure each received their score. "To be honest, I was absolutely shocked. With only one or two exceptions, the grit ranking on your test is the way *I* would have evaluated their grit." Anson now makes sure the entire team scores themselves on grit each spring so that they have "a deeper appreciation for the critical qualities of successful people." Each player gets to see her score because, as Anson put it, "in some cases the scale captures them, and in some cases it *exposes* them." Returning players take the scale again—and again—each year so they can compare their grit now to what it used to be.

Another experiment that stuck is the Beep Test, which begins every Tar Heel season. All the players line up, shoulder to shoulder, and at the sound of an electronic beep, jog to a line twenty meters away, arriving in time for the sound of another beep, which signals them to turn around and jog back to where they started. Back and forth they run, picking up the pace as the interval between the beeps gets shorter and shorter. Within minutes, the players are in a flat-out sprint—at which point, the beeps come faster still. One by one, players drop out, invariably falling to all fours in utter exhaustion when they do. How far they get, like everything else the players do in training and competition, is carefully recorded and, without delay, posted in the locker room for everyone to see.

The Beep Test was originally designed by Canadian exercise physiologists as a test of maximal aerobic capacity, but gauging fitness is only one reason Anson likes it. Like the researchers at the Harvard Fatigue Laboratory who, in 1940, designed a treadmill test to assess perseverance through physical pain, Anson sees the Beep Test as a twofold test of character. "I give a little speech beforehand about what this is going to prove to me," he told me. "If you do well, either you have self-discipline because you've trained all summer, or you have the mental toughness to handle the pain that most people can't. Ideally, of course, you have both." Just before the first beep, Anson announces, "Ladies, this is a test of your mentality. *Go!*"

How else does Anson build a culture of grit? Like Jamie Dimon, he puts a lot of stock in communication. It's certainly not the only thing that he does, but as a philosophy and English major he has a special appreciation for the power of words: "For me, language is everything."

Over the years, Anson has developed a list of twelve carefully worded core values that define what it means to be a UNC Tar Heel, as opposed to just any run-of-the-mill soccer player. "If you want to create a great culture," he told me, "you have to have a collection of core values that everyone lives." Half the team's core values are about teamwork. Half are about grit. Together, they define a culture Anson and his players refer to as "the competitive cauldron."

But a lot of organizations have core values, I pointed out, that are flagrantly ignored on a daily basis. Anson agreed. "Of course, there's nothing motivational about the statement that within your culture you work hard. I mean, it's so *banal*."

His solution to rescuing core values from banality was in some ways entirely unpredictable and in other ways exactly what you might expect from someone with Anson's humanities background.

Inspiration struck while Anson was reading an article about Joseph Brodsky, the Russian exile and Nobel laureate poet. Brodsky, Anson learned, required his graduate students at Columbia University to memorize scores of Russian poems each semester. Naturally, most students considered this demand unreasonable and antiquated, and they marched into his office to tell him so. Brodsky said they could do what they liked, but if they didn't memorize the required verses, they wouldn't get their PhDs. "So they walked out of his office," Anson recalled, "with their tails tucked firmly between their legs, and they got to work." What happened next was, as Anson put it, "simply transformational." Quite suddenly, upon committing a verse to memory, Brodsky's students "felt and lived and breathed Russia." What was dead on the page had come to life.

Rather than read this anecdote and quickly forget it, Anson immediately appreciated its relevance to the top-level goal he was trying to accomplish. Like just about everything else he reads, sees, or does, he asked himself, *How can this help me develop the culture I want?*

Each year that you play soccer for Anson Dorrance, you must memorize three different literary quotes, each handpicked to communicate a different core value. "You will be tested in front of the team in preseason," his memo to the team reads, "and then tested again in every player conference. Not only do you have to memorize them, but you have to understand them. So reflect on them as well. . . ."

By senior year, Anson's athletes know all twelve by heart, beginning with the first core value—*We don't whine*—and its corresponding quote, courtesy of playwright George Bernard Shaw: "The true joy in life is to be a force of fortune instead of a feverish, selfish little clod of ailments and grievances complaining that the world will not devote itself to making you happy."

———

Verbatim memorization is a proud, centuries-old tradition at West Point. You can find the very, very long list of songs, poems, codes, creeds, and miscellany that all first-year cadets—"plebes" in West Point parlance—are required to memorize in a document West Point calls the Bugle Notes.

But West Point's current superintendent, Lieutenant General Robert Caslen, is the first to point out that words, even those committed to memory, don't sustain a culture when they diverge from actions.

Take, for example, Schofield's Definition of Discipline. These words, first spoken in an 1879 address to the cadets by then superintendent John Schofield, are the sort you'd expect a West Pointer to know by heart. The passage that cadets must memorize begins: "The discipline which makes the soldiers of a free country reliable in battle is *not* to be gained by harsh or tyrannical treatment. On the contrary, such treatment is far more likely to destroy than to make an army."

Schofield goes on to say—and the cadets must memorize this, too—that the very same commands can be issued in a way that inspires allegiance or seeds resentment. And the difference comes down to one essential thing: respect. Respect of subordinates for their commander? No, Schofield says. The origin of great leadership begins with the respect of the commander for his subordinates.

The irony of reciting Schofield's uplifting words, even as you're being yelled and screamed at by upperclassmen, was not lost on Caslen when he committed them to memory as an eighteen-year-old plebe in 1971. In that era, hazing was not only tolerated but encouraged. "It was the survivalists who succeeded," Caslen recalled. "It wasn't so much the physical challenges as the mental toughness required to cope with all the yelling and screaming."

Indeed, forty years ago, 170 of the cadets who started Beast Barracks quit before it was over. That's 12 percent, double the proportion who dropped out of Beast by the time I came to West Point to study grit a decade ago. Last year, attrition was down to less than 2 percent.

One explanation for this downward trend is hazing, or, rather, the lack thereof. The practice of inflicting physical and psychological stress on first-year cadets was long considered a necessary part of toughening up future officers. A second benefit, so the logic went, was to cull the weak, effectively eliminating weakness in the corps by pushing out those who couldn't handle it. Over the decades, the list of approved hazing rituals was progressively curtailed, and in 1990, hazing was officially banned altogether.

So, eliminating hazing might explain declining Beast attrition in the late twentieth century, but what explains the last decade's precipitous drop? Is West Point admissions doing a better job of selecting for grit? From the year-to-year data on grit I've seen, absolutely not. The average grit scores of incoming cadets haven't changed since West Point began collecting them.

According to General Caslen, what's happened at the academy is a deliberate change in culture. "When only the survivalists succeed, that's an *attrition model*," he explained. "There's another kind of leadership. I call it a *developmental model*. The standards are exactly the same—high—but in one case, you use fear to get your subordinates to achieve those standards. And in the other case, you lead from the front."

On the battlefield, leading from the front means, quite literally, getting out in front with your soldiers, doing the same hard work, and facing the same mortal risks. At West Point, it means treating cadets with unconditional respect and, when they fall short of meeting the academy's extraordinarily high standards, figuring out the support they need to develop.

"For example," Caslen explained, "on the physical fitness test, if there are cadets that struggle with the two-mile run and I'm their leader, what I'm going to do is sit down with them and put together a training program. I'm going to make sure the plan is sensible. Some afternoons, I'm going to say, 'Okay, let's go run,' or 'Let's go workout,' or 'Let's go do intervals.' I will lead from the front to get the cadet to the standard. Very often, the cadet who was unable to do it on their own all of a sudden is now motivated, and once they start to improve, their motivation increases, and when they meet those objectives they gain even more confidence. At some point, they figure out how to do things on their own."

Caslen's example brought to mind a story West Pointer Tom Deierlein told me of the even-tougher-than-Beast training he endured to become an Airborne Ranger. At one point in the training, he was hanging off a rock face—a climb he'd already failed once—with every muscle in his body shaking in rebellion. "I can't!" Tom shouted to the Ranger instructor on the plateau above. "I expected him to shout back, 'That's right. Quit! You're a loser!' This guy, for whatever reason, instead says, 'Yes you can! Get up here!' And I did. I climbed up, and I swore to myself I'd never say 'I can't' again."

As for critics of West Point's new developmental culture, Caslen points out that the academic, physical, and military standards for graduating from West Point have, if anything, grown more stringent over time. He's convinced that the academy is producing finer, stronger, and more capable leaders than ever before. "If you want to measure West Point by how much yelling and screaming goes on around here, then I'm just going to let you complain. Young men and women today just don't respond to yelling and screaming."

Other than objective standards of performance, what else *hasn't* changed at West Point in the last ten years? Norms of politeness and decorum remain so strong that, during my visit, I found myself checking my watch to make sure I was a few minutes early for each appointment and, without thinking, addressed every man and woman I met by "sir" and "ma'am." Also, the gray full-dress uniforms worn by cadets on formal occasions remain the same, making today's cadets part of the "long gray line" of West Pointers stretching back two centuries before them. Finally, cadet slang is still spoken fluently by West Pointers and includes such improbably defined terms as *firsties* for "fourth-year cadets," *spoony* for "neat in physical appearance," and *huah* for everything from "I understand you" to "gung ho" to "agreed" to "great job."

Caslen isn't so naive as to think that four years of developmental culture at West Point will reliably turn 2s and 3s on the Grit Scale into 5s. But then again, the varsity athletes, class presidents, and valedictorians who make it through West Point's two-year admissions process aren't exactly the bottom of the barrel in grit. Importantly, he's seen people change. He's watched cadets develop. He has a growth mindset. "You never really know who is going to become a Schwarzkopf or a MacArthur."

———

Two years after Pete Carroll called to talk about grit, I got on a plane to Seattle. I wanted to see firsthand what Pete meant when he said the Seahawks were building the grittiest culture in the NFL.

By then I'd read his autobiography, *Win Forever*, in which he talks about discovering the power of passion and perseverance in his own life:

> Personally, I have learned that if you create a *vision* for yourself and stick with it, you can make amazing things happen in your life. My experience is that once you have done the work to create the clear vision, it is the *discipline* and *effort* to maintain that vision that can make it all come true. The two go hand in hand.

The moment you've created that vision, you're on your way, but it's the diligence with which you stick to that vision that allows you to get there.

Getting that across to players is a constant occupation.

I'd also watched Pete talk about grit and culture in his many interviews. In one, Pete is onstage in an auditorium at the University of Southern California, returning as an honored guest to the school where he'd coached the USC Trojans to a record six wins in seven championship games over nine years. "What's new? What are you learning?" Pete's interviewer asked. Pete recounted discovering my research on grit and its resonance with his own decades-in-the-making approach to coaching. "In our program," Pete said, his coaching staff reinforces a culture of grit through innumerable "competitive opportunities and moments and illustrations. . . . Really what we're doing is we're just trying to make them more gritty. We're trying to teach them how to persevere. We're trying to illustrate to them how they can demonstrate more passion."

Then he gave an example. In practice, Seahawks play to win—offensive and defensive players compete against each other with the full-throated aggression and destroy-the-enemy intensity of a real game. The ritual of weekly competition-level practice, dubbed Competition Wednesdays, can be traced back to Anson Dorrance, whose book on coaching Pete devoured when he was crafting his own approach. "If you thought of it as who was winning and who was losing, you'd miss the whole point. . . . It's really the guy across from us that makes us who we are." Our opponent, Pete explained, creates challenges that help us become our best selves.

Outsiders to Seahawks culture easily miss that point. "Guys don't understand it right away," Pete said. "They don't get it, but in time we work our way through it." For Pete, this means sharing—in the most transparent way—everything that goes on in his own head, his objectives, the reasoning behind his approach. "If I didn't talk about it, they wouldn't know that. They'd be thinking, 'Am I going to win or am I going to lose?' But when we talk about it enough, they come to an appreciation of *why* they compete."

Pete admitted that some players may have more to teach than they have to learn. Seahawk free safety Earl Thomas, for example, came to him as "the most competitive, gritty guy you could ever imagine. . . . He pushes and practices with marvelous intensity. He focuses, studies, does everything." But the magic of culture is that one person's grit can provide a model for others. On a daily basis, Earl "demonstrates in so many different ways what he's all about." If each person's grit enhances grit in others, then, over time, you might expect what social scientist Jim Flynn calls a "social multiplier" effect. In a sense, it's the motivational analogue of the infinity cube of self-reflecting mirrors Jeff Bezos built as a boy—one person's grit enhances the grit of the others, which in turn inspires more grit in that person, and so on, without end.

What does Earl Thomas have to say about being a Seahawk? "My teammates have been pushing me since day one. They're helping me to get better, and vice versa. You have to have a genuine appreciation for teammates who are willing to put in hard work, buy into the system, and never be satisfied with anything but continuing to evolve. It's incredible to see the heights we're reaching from that humble attitude."

———

By the time I got around to visiting the Seahawks' training facility, my curiosity had doubled. Making it to the championship game in successive years is notoriously hard, but the Seahawks had defied the odds and made it to the Super Bowl again that year. In sharp contrast to the prior year's win, which Seattle fans celebrated with a blue and green ticker-tape parade that was the largest public gathering in Seattle's history, this year's loss resulted in howling, weeping, and the gnashing of teeth—over what sports commentators deemed "the worst call in NFL history."

Here's a recap: With twenty-six seconds on the clock, the Seahawks have possession of the ball and are one yard away from a game-winning touchdown. Everyone expects Pete to call a running play. It's not just that the end zone is so close. It's also because the Seahawks have Marshawn Lynch, whose nickname is Beast Mode and who's widely agreed to be the single best running back in the entire NFL.

Instead, Seahawks quarterback Russell Wilson throws a pass, the ball is intercepted, and the New England Patriots take home the trophy.

Since Super Bowl XLIX was only the third football game I'd watched without interruption in my entire life—the second being the NFC championship game the Seahawks had won the week before—I can't offer an expert opinion on whether, indeed, passing instead of running was the epitome of coaching misjudgment. What interested me more when I arrived in Seattle was Pete's reaction and that of the whole team.

Pete's idol, basketball coach John Wooden, was fond of saying, "Success is never final; failure is never fatal. It's courage that counts." What I wanted to know is how a culture of grit continues not just in the afterglow of success, but in the aftermath of failure. What I wanted to know is how Pete and the Seahawks found the courage to continue.

———

As I look back on it now, my visit has an "in the moment" feel:

My appointment begins with a meeting in Pete's office—yes, it's the corner office, but no, it's not huge or fancy, and the door is apparently *always* open, literally, allowing loud rock music to spill out into the hallway. "Angela," Pete leans in to ask, "how can this day be helpful to you?"

I explain my motive. Today I'm an anthropologist, here to take notes on Seahawks culture. If I had a pith helmet, I'd be wearing it.

And that, of course, gets Pete all excited. He tells me that it's not just one thing. It's a million things. It's a million details. It's substance and it's style.

After a day with the Seahawks, I have to agree. It's countless small things, each doable—but each so easy to botch, forget, or ignore. And though the details are countless, there are some themes.

The most obvious is language. One of Pete's coaches once said, "I speak fluent Carroll." And to speak Carroll is to speak fluent Seahawk: *Always compete. You're either competing or you're not. Compete in everything you do. You're a Seahawk 24-7. Finish strong. Positive self-talk. Team first.*

During my day with the team, I can't tell you how many times someone—a player, a coach, a scout—enthusiastically offers up one of these morsels, but I can tell you I don't once hear variations. One of Pete's favorite sayings is "No synonyms." Why not? "If you want to communicate effectively, you need to be clear with the words you use."

Everybody I meet peppers their sentences with these Carrollisms. And while nobody has quite the neutron-powered, teenage energy of the sixty-three-year-old head coach, the rest of the Seahawks family, as they like to call themselves, are just as earnest in helping me decode what these dictums actually mean.

"Compete," I'm told, is not what I think it is. It's not about triumphing over others, a notion I've always been uneasy about. Compete means excellence. "Compete comes from the Latin," explains Mike Gervais, the competitive-surfer-turned-sports-psychologist who is one of Pete's partners in culture building. "Quite literally, it means *strive together*. It doesn't have anything in its origins about another person losing."

Mike tells me that two key factors promote excellence in individuals and in teams: "deep and rich support and relentless challenge to improve." When he says that, a lightbulb goes on in my head. Supportive and demanding parenting is psychologically wise and encourages children to emulate their parents. It stands to reason that supportive and demanding leadership would do the same.

I begin to get it. For this professional football team, it's not solely about defeating other teams, it's about pushing beyond what you can do today so that tomorrow you're just a little bit better. It's about excellence. So, for the Seahawks, *Always compete* means *Be all you can be, whatever that is for you. Reach for your best.*

After one of the meetings, an assistant coach catches up to me in the hallway and says, "I don't know if anyone's mentioned *finishing* to you."

Finishing?

"One thing we really believe in here is the idea of finishing strong." Then he gives me examples: Seahawks finish a game strong, playing their hearts out to the last second on the clock. Seahawks finish the season strong. Seahawks finish every drill strong. And I ask, "But why just finish strong? Doesn't it make sense to start strong, too?"

"Yes," the coach says, "but starting strong is easy. And for the Seahawks, 'finishing' doesn't literally mean 'finishing.'"

Of course not. Finishing strong means consistently focusing and doing your absolute best at every moment, from start to finish.

Soon enough, I realize it's not only Pete doing the preaching. At one point, during a meeting attended by more than twenty assistant coaches, the entire room spontaneously breaks out into a chant, in perfect cadence: *No whining. No complaining. No excuses.* It's like being in a choir of all baritones. Before this, they sang out: *Always protect the team.* Afterward: *Be early.*

Be early? I tell them that, after reading Pete's book, I made "Be early" a resolution. So far, I had yet to be early for almost anything. This elicited some chuckles. Apparently, I'm not the only who struggles with that one. But just as important, this confession gets one of the guys talking about why it's important to be early: "It's about respect. It's about the details. It's about excellence." Okay, okay, I'm getting it.

Around midday, I give a lecture on grit to the team. This is after giving similar presentations to the coaches and the scouts, and before talking to the entire front-office staff.

After most of the team has moved on to lunch, one of the Seahawks asks me what he should do about his little brother. His brother's very smart, he says, but at some point, his grades started slipping. As an incentive, he bought a brand-new Xbox video-game console and placed it, still in its packaging, in his brother's bedroom. The deal was that, when the report card comes home with A's, he gets to unwrap the game. At first, this scheme seemed to be working, but then his brother hit a slump. "Should I just give him the Xbox?" he asks me.

Before I can answer, another player says, "Well, man, maybe he's just not *capable* of A's."

I shake my head. "From what I've been told, your brother is plenty smart enough to bring home A's. He was doing it before."

The player agrees. "He's a smart kid. Trust me, he's a smart kid."

I'm still thinking when Pete jumps up and says, with genuine excitement: "First of all, there is absolutely no way you give that game to your brother. You got him motivated. Okay, that's a start. That's a beginning. Now what? He needs some *coaching*! He needs someone to explain what he needs to do, specifically, to get back to good grades! He needs a plan! He needs your help in figuring out those next steps."

This reminds me of something Pete said at the start of my visit: "Every time I make a decision or say something to a player, I think, 'How would I treat my own kid?' You know what I do best? I'm a great dad. And in a way, that's the way I coach."

At the end of the day, I'm in the lobby, waiting for my taxi. Pete is there with me, making sure I get off okay. I realize I haven't asked him directly how he and the Seahawks found the courage to continue after he'd made "the worst call ever." Pete later told *Sports Illustrated* that it wasn't the worst decision, it was the "worst possible outcome." He explained that like every other negative experience, and every positive one, "it becomes part of you. I'm not going to ignore it. I'm going to face it. And when it bubbles up, I'm going to think about it and get on with it. And use it. *Use it!*"

Just before I leave, I turn and look up. And there, twenty feet above us, in foot-high chrome letters, is the word CHARACTER. In my hand, I'm holding a bag of blue and green Seahawk swag, including a fistful of blue rubber bracelets stamped in green with LOB: Love Our Brothers.

Chapter 13

CONCLUSION

This book has been about the power of grit to help you achieve your potential. I wrote it because what we accomplish in the marathon of life depends tremendously on our grit—our passion and perseverance for long-term goals. An obsession with talent distracts us from that simple truth.

This book has been my way of taking you out for a coffee and telling you what I know.

I'm almost done.

Let me close with a few final thoughts. The first is that you *can* grow your grit.

I see two ways to do so. On your own, you can grow your grit "from the inside out": You can cultivate your interests. You can develop a habit of daily challenge-exceeding-skill practice. You can connect your work to a purpose beyond yourself. And you can learn to hope when all seems lost.

You can also grow your grit "from the outside in." Parents, coaches, teachers, bosses, mentors, friends—developing your personal grit depends critically on other people.

———

My second closing thought is about happiness. Success—whether measured by who wins the National Spelling Bee, makes it through West Point, or leads the division in annual sales—is not the only thing you care about. Surely, you also want to be happy. And while happiness and success are related, they're not identical.

You might wonder, If I get grittier and become more successful, will my happiness plummet?

Some years ago, I sought to answer this question by surveying two thousand American adults. The graph below shows how grit relates to life satisfaction, measured on a scale that ranged from 7 to 35 and included items such as, "If I could live my life over, I would change almost nothing." In the same study, I measured positive emotions such as excitement and negative emotions such as shame. I found that the grittier a person is, the more likely they'll enjoy a healthy emotional life. Even at the top of the Grit Scale, grit went hand in hand with well-being, no matter how I measured it.

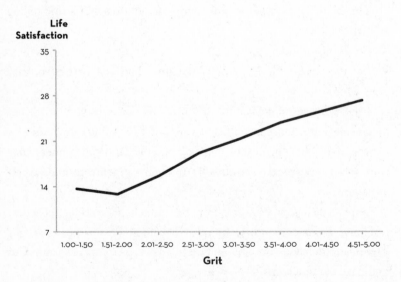

When my students and I published this result, we ended our report this way: "Are the spouses and children of the grittiest people also happier? What about their coworkers and employees? Additional inquiry is needed to explore the possible downsides of grit."

I don't yet have answers to those questions, but I think they're good ones to ask. When I talk to grit paragons, and they tell me how thrilled they are to work as passionately as they do for a purpose greater than themselves, I can't tell whether their families feel the same way.

I don't know, for example, whether all those years devoted to a top-level goal of singular importance comes at a cost I haven't yet measured.

What I *have* done is ask my daughters, Amanda and Lucy, what it's like to grow up with a gritty mom. They've watched me attempt things I've never done before—like write a book—and they've seen me cry when it got really rough. They've seen how torturous it can be to hack away at innumerable doable, but hard-to-do, skills. They've asked, at dinner: "Do we *always* have to talk about deliberate practice? Why does *everything* have to come back to your research?"

Amanda and Lucy wish I'd relax a little and, you know, talk more about Taylor Swift.

But they don't wish their mother was anything other than a paragon of grit.

In fact, Amanda and Lucy aspire to achieve the same. They've glimpsed the satisfaction that comes from doing something important—for yourself and others—and doing it well, and doing it even though it's so very hard. They want more of that. They recognize that complacency has its charms, but none worth trading for the fulfillment of realizing their potential.

———

Here's another question I haven't quite answered in my research: Can you have *too* much grit?

Aristotle argued that too much (or too little) of a good thing is bad. He speculated, for example, that too little courage is cowardice but too much courage is folly. By the same logic, you can be too kind, too generous, too honest, and too self-controlled. It's an argument that psychologists Adam Grant and Barry Schwartz have revisited. They speculate that there's an inverted-U function that describes the benefits of any trait, with the optimal amount being somewhere between the extremes.

So far, with grit I haven't found the sort of inverse U that Aristotle predicted or that Barry and Adam have found for other traits, like extroversion. Regardless, I recognize that there are trade-offs to any choice, and I can appreciate how that might apply to grit. It isn't hard to think of situations in which giving up is the best course of action. You may recall times you stuck with an idea, sport, job, or romantic partner longer than you should have.

In my own experience, giving up on piano when it became clear I had neither interest in it nor obvious talent was a great decision. I could have given up even earlier, actually, and saved my teacher from having to listen to me sight-read all the pieces I hadn't practiced the week before. Giving up on becoming fluent in French was also a good idea, even though I did enjoy it and picked it up more quickly than I did piano. Less time spent on piano and French freed up time for pursuits I found more gratifying.

So, finishing whatever you begin *without exception* is a good way to miss opportunities to start different, possibly better, things. Ideally, even if you're discontinuing one activity and choosing different lower-order goals, you're still holding fast to your ultimate concern.

One reason I don't worry much about an epidemic of grit is that such a prospect seems so removed from our current reality. How many days have you come home from work and said to your partner, "Gosh, everyone at the office is just too gritty! They stick with their most valued goals too long! They try too hard! I wish they were less passionate!"

Recently, I asked three hundred American adults to take the Grit Scale and, after receiving their scores, to tell me how they felt. Many said they were happy with their scores, and some wanted to be grittier. Nevertheless, in the entire sample, there wasn't a single person who, upon reflection, aspired to be *less* gritty.

I'm certain most of us would be better off with more grit, not less. There may be exceptions—grit outliers who don't need to be any grittier—but those exceptions are rare.

———

I've been asked, on more than one occasion, why I feel grit is the only thing that matters. In fact, I don't.

I can tell you, for example, that grit is *not* the only thing I want my children to develop as they round the corner from childhood to maturity. Do I want them to be great at whatever they do? Absolutely. But greatness and goodness are different, and if forced to choose, I'd put goodness first.

As a psychologist, I can confirm that grit is far from the only—or even the most important—aspect of a person's character. In fact, in studies of how people size up others, morality trumps all other aspects of character in importance. Sure, we take notice if our neighbors seem lazy, but we're especially offended if they seem to lack qualities like honesty, integrity, and trustworthiness.

So, grit isn't everything. There are many other things a person needs in order to grow and flourish. Character is plural.

One way to think about grit is to understand how it relates to other aspects of character. In assessing grit along with other virtues, I find three reliable clusters. I refer to them as the intrapersonal, interpersonal, and intellectual dimensions of character. You could also call them strengths of will, heart, and mind.

Intrapersonal character includes grit. This cluster of virtues also includes self-control, particularly as it relates to resisting temptations like texting and video games. What this means is that gritty people tend to be self-controlled and vice versa. Collectively, virtues that make possible the accomplishment of personally valued goals have also been called "performance character" or "self-management skills." Social commentator and journalist David Brooks calls these "resume virtues" because they're the sorts of things that get us hired and keep us employed.

Interpersonal character includes gratitude, social intelligence, and self-control over emotions like anger. These virtues help you get along with—and provide assistance to—other people. Sometimes, these virtues are referred to as "moral character." David Brooks prefers the term "eulogy virtues" because, in the end, they may be more important to how people remember us than anything else. When we speak admiringly of someone being a "deeply good" person, I think it's this cluster of virtues we're thinking about.

And, finally, intellectual character includes virtues like curiosity and zest. These encourage active and open engagement with the world of ideas.

My longitudinal studies show these three virtue clusters predict different outcomes. For academic achievement, including stellar report card grades, the cluster containing grit is the most predictive. But for positive social functioning, including how many friends you have, interpersonal character is more important. And for a positive, independent posture toward learning, intellectual virtue trumps the others.

In the end, the plurality of character operates against any one virtue being uniquely important.

––––––

I'm often asked whether encouraging grit does children a disservice by setting expectations unreasonably high. "Careful, Dr. Duckworth, or children will all grow up thinking they can be Usain Bolt, Wolfgang Mozart, or Albert Einstein."

If we can't be Einstein, is it worth studying physics? If we can't be Usain Bolt, should we go for a run this morning? Is there any point in trying to run a little faster or longer than we did yesterday? In my view, these are absurd questions. If my daughter says to me, "Mom, I shouldn't practice my piano today because I'll never be Mozart," I'll say in reply, "You're not practicing piano to be Mozart."

We all face limits—not just in talent, but in opportunity. But more often than we think, our limits are self-imposed. We try, fail, and conclude we've bumped our heads against the ceiling of possibility. Or maybe after taking just a few steps we change direction. In either case, we never venture as far as we might have.

To be gritty is to keep putting one foot in front of the other. To be gritty is to hold fast to an interesting and purposeful goal. To be gritty is to invest, day after week after year, in challenging practice. To be gritty is to fall down seven times, and rise eight.

I was interviewed recently by a journalist. As he was packing up his notes, he said, "So, it's obvious you could have talked all day. You really love this subject."

"Oh, gosh. Is there *anything* as interesting as the psychology of achievement? Could there be *anything* more important?"

He chuckled. "You know," he said, "I absolutely love what I do, too. It's amazing to me how many people I know who're well into their forties and haven't really committed to anything. They don't know what they're missing."

———

One final thought.

Earlier this year, the latest MacArthur genius awards were announced. One of the winners was Ta-Nehisi Coates, the journalist whose second book, *Between the World and Me*, has been an extraordinary best seller.

Eight years ago, Coates was unemployed, recently laid off by *Time* magazine, and scrambling to get freelance work. It was a hard time. He guesses he gained thirty pounds from the strain. "I knew what kind of writer I wanted to be. I was not becoming that kind of writer. I was banging my head against a wall and nothing was coming out."

His wife, he says, was "unerringly supportive." Still, they had a young son. There were practical realities. "I was considering driving a cab."

He finally got back on his feet, and after pushing through the "extraordinary stress" of his book, he began to hit his stride. "The writing was very, very different. The sentences had much more power."

In his three-minute video posted on the MacArthur website, the first thing Coates says is: "Failure is probably the most important factor in all of my work. Writing *is* failure. Over and over and over again." Then he explains, that as a boy, he was insatiably curious. Growing up in Baltimore, he was particularly obsessed with the idea of physical safety, and the lack thereof, and has remained so since. Journalism, he says, lets him keep asking the questions that interest him.

Toward the end of the video, Coates offers the best description of what it's like to write that I've ever heard. To give you a sense of his intonation, and the cadence, I've laid out the words as *I* heard them—as a poem:

The challenge of writing
Is to see your horribleness on page.
To see your terribleness
And then to go to bed.

And wake up the next day,
And take that horribleness and that terribleness,
And refine it,

And make it not so terrible and not so horrible.
And then to go to bed again.

And come the next day,
And refine it a little bit more,
And make it not so bad.
And then to go to bed the next day.

And do it again,
And make it maybe average.
And then one more time,
If you're lucky,
Maybe you get to good.

And if you've done that,
That's a success.

You might think Coates is especially modest. He *is*. But he's also especially gritty. And I've yet to meet a MacArthur Fellow, Nobel laureate, or Olympic champion who says that what they achieved came in any other way.

"You're no genius," my dad used to say when I was just a little girl. I realize now he was talking to himself as much as he was talking to me.

If you define genius as being able to accomplish great things in life without effort, then he was right: I'm no genius, and neither is he.

But if, instead, you define genius as working toward excellence, ceaselessly, with every element of your being—then, in fact, my dad *is* a genius, and so am I, and so is Coates, and, if you're willing, so are you.

SEVEN QUESTIONS I GET ASKED ABOUT GRIT

What followed the debut of *Grit* was a blizzard of talks, interviews, and signings. In parallel, there was a flurry of book reviews and, from various public intellectuals, a number of think pieces—some admiring and others critical. Though many commentators waved the flag of grit, others wanted to burn it. The only point of unanimity was that "grit" was the new buzzword in the business world and in education.

More meaningful to me than these public plaudits or critiques were the hundreds of personal stories and questions I received from readers. A few topics have come up again and again. Here they are, along with my answers:

What about work-life balance? Doesn't grit come at a cost?

Like any investment, gritty devotion to a single top-level goal comes at a cost. In particular, the time you devote to thinking about and working toward your goal is time you're *not* doing other things you also care about. For instance, the time I spend in the lab, reading or writing at home, and traveling for meetings, adds up to about seventy hours in an average week. Many of the high achievers I've studied put in close to that number. Others work even more.

In those hours, I'm not focused on my husband, our teenage daughters, my best friend, or my extended family. In those hours, I'm not relaxing, catching up on world events, exercising, or sleeping. If I didn't work such long hours, dinner last night at the Duckworth home might have been more sophisticated than reheated frozen meatballs and spaghetti sauce from a jar. If I dialed back a little, I'd probably know more people at my college reunion and our family would probably receive more greeting cards at holiday time.

So yes, grit involves a tradeoff. The root of the word passion is *pati*, Latin for "to suffer." And it's not only you, personally, who pays the cost. It's also your family and friends.

Must you work seventy hours per week to be gritty? No. But when you really love what you do, you might find that you *want* to. You might feel, as I do, that nearly everything you see, hear, read, or experience is in some way relevant to your work. You might find that you don't want to take a vacation from your calling.

How to allocate your time, energy, and attention is a decision only you can make. And no matter your choices, some degree of conflict between your personal and professional goals is inevitable.

Of the 168 hours you have in a week, you may end up devoting seven, seventy, or seventy-seven to work. Whatever you choose, I have one suggestion: Like the paragons of grit I study, consider curating your many, many low-level professional goals such that they align with a single top-level professional goal. A good start would be to write down your "ultimate concern" on a piece of paper. Give yourself a max of ten words. But the shorter, the better. If you've read this book, you have a few examples. Mine is seven words long: "Use psychological science to help children thrive." For Pete Carroll there are just two: "Always compete." And Will Smith lives by these three: "Create and relate."

Why do this? Because the process will help you achieve clarity.

You'll have a clearer sense of who you are, what you care about, and how to align your effort with your identity.

Just recently, I learned of a study of young adults who kept daily diaries for forty days. Each day, they were asked to complete a short adaptation of the Grit Scale and, in addition, to reflect on what the researchers called clarity of self-concept, measured with items like "Today I had a clear picture of what I am." When analyzed longitudinally, the data showed that increases in clarity of self-knowledge predicted increases in grit and vice versa. "Having a clear sense of oneself," the researchers concluded, "galvanizes subsequent perseverance for one's goal engagements."

Clarity won't give you more hours in the week, but it will help you get more out of your hours. As Will Smith once told me, "Harmony is aerodynamic."

Can you lose your grit? I was passionate about something before but, for some reason, I feel like I no longer have it in me.

When I get an email asking, in so many words, "What do I do when passion has given way to burnout?" I think of my cousin Tom.

Tom hasn't lost his grit but has seen many others who have. A physician and researcher, Tom is among the keenest observers of human nature I know. He tells me—and statistics back him up—that there is a virtual epidemic of burnout in the health-care sector. Compared to medical practitioners of the past, and compared to those in many other professions, today's doctors and nurses report alarming levels of burnout.

Of course, in any profession you can name—from the most glamorous to the most mundane—there is burnout. If this question particularly interests you, it may be because you've lost your mojo and are wondering what the heck happened.

Here's what I think. No matter what you've fallen in love with doing, it's possible to fall *out* of love, too. Burnout is not an illusion or a myth. It's a psychological reality.

Scientists who study burnout agree that its cardinal feature is the feeling of exhaustion. In surveys of burnout in the workplace, what usually accompanies exhaustion is depersonalization—the sense that you're unconnected to the people you're serving or working with—and also helplessness—the sense that no matter what you do or how hard you try, you're not making progress.

As we learned in chapter 9, feelings are downstream from thoughts. So, the feeling of exhaustion, in my view, is what happens when you think, "I'm trying my best to be useful, but no matter what I do, I'm not really making a difference."

Though burnout is a psychological problem, the solution isn't always between the ears. In other words, it's very often the *objective* situation itself that urgently needs changing. Maybe your boss is a bully or a bigot, the absolute antithesis of the supportive-yet-demanding leaders I described in chapter 12. Maybe you're working for a company whose core mission conflicts with your most deeply cherished values. In these cases, my advice is to change the situation: look for another boss, another company, or another position.

But what if your whole industry, like health care or journalism, is undergoing seismic changes? What if these changes are eroding your capacity to feel joy and satisfaction the way you used to?

In new research with my collaborator Lauren Eskreis-Winkler, we're finding that giving advice to others about staying gritty helps renew our *own* grit. Why? To be honest, we're not entirely sure. One possibility is that when encouraging another person in need, we direct attention to what can be changed about a situation. As some coaches like to say, when advising others, we focus less on the many things we can't fix on our own and instead concentrate on "controlling the controllables."

Another benefit, perhaps, is that sometimes what we need most is a reminder of lessons learned but easily forgotten.

My favorite explanation is that providing counsel may satisfy a deep human motivation to be useful. In other words, if the feeling of being "burned out" comes from the thought "I'm not helping no matter how hard I try," then perhaps giving advice to someone in a similarly difficult situation shows us that, in fact, what we do makes a difference.

Is there a relationship between grit and socioeconomic opportunity? Is it easier to grow up gritty in poverty or in affluence?

Kayvon Asemani and Cody Coleman—paragons of grit whom you met in earlier chapters—have taught me that developing passion and perseverance is possible for anyone and everyone.

Even so, trauma is not the royal road to grit. On the contrary, it's well-documented that poverty, discrimination, and uncertainty can have a crushing effect on physical health, psychological well-being, and character development.

A recently published study of athletes directly tested the idea that "talent needs trauma" to bloom. Researchers interviewed professional athletes classified as Super Champions, Champions, or Almosts. A Super Champion, as judged by this study, plays at the very highest level—an average of seventy-three appearances for a national team in the sport's most elite league. Champions play at the same level but, on average, have made only four appearances. Almosts are players who, in their youth, achieved similar accomplishments as the other athletes but eventually top out in their sport's second-highest league.

Following a standardized script to explore, in depth, each athlete's life history, "No evidence was found for the necessity of major trauma as a feature of development. . . . If anything, there seems to be a higher incidence of such trauma in lower rather than higher achievers."

At the other end of the spectrum are children of extreme privilege. Parents in the wealthiest families often worry they might be "overparenting." The same study of athletes suggests this concern is indeed legitimate. Super Champions surveyed by the researchers tend to have parents who are supportive in the least intrusive way. Said one: "They were supportive, but they didn't drive me, they didn't push me at all . . ." In contrast, Champions have parents who are more hands-on, and Almosts describe their parents as more dedicated to their athletic achievements than the athletes themselves: "Once there [on my own at university] I seemed to lose my way. No one telling me what to do . . . I just lost interest."

If you've made a habit of driving back to your child's school to retrieve a forgotten history textbook or scolding your child's coach for not putting them into the game, ask yourself whether you're parenting wisely or parenting permissively.

Permissive parents are exceedingly supportive but, unfortunately, not demanding enough to develop their children's competence. And while this feels good for both parents and children in the short run, the long-run cost is children who are less likely to develop into independent, confident, and successful adults.

Here's how Anson Dorrance, the coach we met in chapter 12, puts it:

> Sometimes, we aren't willing to make that emotional investment in our kids at home or in the kids we are teaching because to do so we have to be somewhat demanding and critical. It causes stressful moments of conflict, and that's a taxing price. Even in my own home, I can see what happens when my wife and I come home from a long day at work and are very tired. Donovan, our four-and-a-half-year-old son, has just been eating in front of the television, and he decides to leave his dish there and go play in his bedroom. Well, the correct behavior is . . . to go find Donovan and say, "Donovan, your dish is sitting there in the living room, and that's not where you leave it. When you are finished eating, you bring it to the kitchen and put it in the dishwasher." Then there

is a moment of confrontation with Donovan that is emotionally taxing—in a very small way. He will roll his eyes, object, and say he'll do it later. Well, now you're getting a little angry because he's trying to blow you off, and it's not a very pleasant experience. It's not an issue about getting the dish in the dishwasher, but we're not in the mood for this type of dispute. And if we are the sort of parent, educator, or coach who doesn't have the strength to constantly have these battles, we pick up the dish and put it in the dishwasher. OK, now the dish is in the dishwasher, but Donovan has a lower standard of expectation.

Whatever their parents' education or income, all children really need the same thing: *appropriately demanding challenges* in combination with *consistently warm and respectful support.* I worry that some kids— especially those growing up in poverty—get too much challenge and not enough support. On the other hand, I worry that many kids—especially those with permissive parents—get a lot of "I love you, sweetie" without enough "I know you can do better. Let's see what you can do tomorrow."

The realities of class and opportunity in society surely have an influence on the development of grit. The question is, what will we do as a society to ensure that all children grow up with daily opportunities to try, fail, learn, and grow?

What about grit and romantic relationships?

I must have broken up with a dozen boyfriends before I met and married my husband. I'm sure glad I did because, in the end, I'm crazy about Jason and have a hard time imagining life with anyone else.

So, if you want to know if I think sticking it out to the bitter end with your current romantic partner is always the right thing to do, my answer is, "Of course not!" In fact, cutting your losses may be exactly the way you should think about a relationship where you don't share the same values, interests, or life goals.

At the same time, it's true that romantic relationships are their own kind of work. There are days you can't stand this love-of-your-life. As a couple, there are weaknesses that each of you, and both of you together, must work on. In romance, as in school and at work, it seems that the best outcomes require a willingness to persevere and the capacity to sustain passion for years and years.

This, in fact, was the view of Paul Glick, a scientist who studied census data in the 1950s. Glick noticed that high school and college dropouts had significantly higher divorce rates than the general population—a phenomenon later dubbed "the Glick Effect." Many years later, psychologists studying personality and divorce found that men and women who score higher on conscientiousness also have marriages that last longer.

I've only done one study of grit and the longevity of romantic relationships. What I found in a sample of over six thousand adults who had at some point been married is that less-gritty men are more likely to be divorced or separated. Interestingly, among women, I found that grit didn't affect marital status at all. In other words, I only have evidence for "half" of the Glick effect.

Why might grit link to marital status for men but not for women? I'm not sure. Women in that sample were no grittier than men, so the explanation can't be a general male deficit in grit. Maybe men find it more challenging to stick with committed relationships? That's certainly possible, but there are other explanations, too. It's been suggested, for example, that women are more likely to leave less gritty, less successful husbands. If you have a theory to explain this data, let me know!

Meanwhile, my intuition is that a commitment to long-term goals is as important to relationships as it is to professional success. As writer

Pamela Druckerman once observed: "*Soul mate* isn't a preexisting condition. It's an earned title. They're made over time."

It seems that cell phones and social media provide immediate gratification in a way I didn't experience growing up. As a result, do we live in an especially "ungritty" era?

It's a plain fact that kids growing up today face a lot more competition for their attention than at any other time in history.

Sure, distractions have tempted humanity since the beginning. This is exactly why every major religious tradition has a version of "Lead us not into temptation." But our parents, grandparents, and distant ancestors didn't have to contend 24-7 with effortlessly available text messages, cat videos, tweets from Selena Gomez, and Candy Crush. There weren't whole marketing divisions in Silicon Valley and on Madison Avenue working day and night to produce, in ever more potent forms, immediate gratification.

An esteemed mathematician once told me that when he was a young boy he'd spend hours just staring at the wood beams in his bedroom, thinking. There wasn't much else to do, he said, in his rural town in Germany. So, he learned to think about something and continue thinking about it for hours and days, and it is this continuity of focus that he thinks has enabled him to make a contribution in mathematics. His own two girls, he added worriedly, were growing up without a moment's boredom. At the slightest twinge of ennui, they were able to find relief in one form of button pressing or another.

As I mentioned in chapter 5, we ought not forget that the next generation differs from us not only in age and experience but also in culture. I don't have a time machine, so I can't know for sure whether my teenage girls would grow up with more passion and perseverance if they'd been born in the 1950s, when nobody had cell phones super-glued to their palms.

If I did have a time machine, I'd go back a few decades and run the same experiment that Tim Wilson and his colleagues recently ran on millennials. Intrigued by how people seem attached to modern technology, Tim gave young adults a simple task: sit in a quiet room with nothing to do for several minutes. Participants generally found the experience difficult—to the point that they found mundane tasks to be far more enjoyable than doing nothing. In fact, one in four young women and two out of three young men voluntarily administered electric shocks to themselves instead of sitting alone with their thoughts.

Here's what we do in the Duckworth home. For our girls—and in my research, for most teenagers—cell phones are the single most potent distraction from homework, putting away laundry, viola practice, reading, and even dinner-table conversation. So, we have rules: Cell phones stay in the nook in the kitchen until everything that needs to get done gets done. No cell phones at meals. No cell phones when sitting in a restaurant with relatives or family friends, even if you're bored out of your skull.

Do we enforce these rules with 100 percent consistency? I wish. But we're trying and, more importantly, we've discussed as a family *why* these rules are necessary. We all agree, and we sometimes say aloud, that these distractions are like heroin: addictive. We all recognize effortless entertainment is the enemy of long-term passion and perseverance.

If anything, the bells and whistles of the future will be louder than those of the present. Amid the cacophony, some individuals will nevertheless learn to pursue depth over breadth. How? Rules imposed by others (*no texting while practicing your viola*) eventually become cherished personal principles (*I don't let distractions get in the way of my work*). And for those who become true paragons of grit, there will eventually be the singular satisfaction of loving what you do and continually working to get better at it.

I want my kid to develop grit. When should I expect him or her to have the single-minded focus of mature world-class achievers?

My husband Jason and I are raising our girls according to the Hard Thing Rule: Do something that requires deliberate practice, don't quit in the middle of the season or the semester, and pick the hard thing yourself. We thought this third requirement—pick the hard thing yourself— would enable our girls to explore intrinsic interests that, eventually, might develop and deepen into lifelong passions.

As I mentioned in chapter 10, Lucy cycled through a half-dozen pursuits before deciding to stick with viola. This pattern—what performance psychologists call *sampling*—paradoxically affords young people the experience and self-knowledge to commit to a single pursuit later on. Contrary to popular wisdom, both professional and Olympic athletes don't specialize early. Instead, they spend much of their youth sampling from a variety of sports before eventually committing to just one.

Around the time that *Grit was* published, I realized that my daughter Lucy was doggedly pursuing viola when, in fact, her heart was in baking. "Maybe chocolate cupcakes with vanilla buttercream," she'd muse aloud at breakfast. "Or maybe biscotti. Maybe chocolate biscotti with pistachios and chocolate chips."

"What?"

"Oh, I'm planning what to bake on Friday after school."

After her turn on the family iPad, the browser tabs were DIY cupcake videos on YouTube. For Christmas, she asked for cookbooks and a new set of baking pans. She read cookbooks the way other kids read Harry Potter. Our pantry was burgeoning with four kinds of flour and every imaginable shade of food coloring.

What about viola? Deliberate practice and great teachers have paid off. Lucy has been getting better and better. And every season, when we ask if she wants to quit or keep going, she chooses to keep going.

But if an interest is that which spontaneously draws our attention, then it's clear that Lucy is much more interested in baking than music. Or, I should say, it's *now* clear to Lucy. At first, when I pointed out what I thought was obvious, she said, "I have no idea what you're talking about." Budding interests, you'll recall from chapter 6, are sometimes more apparent to observers than the interested parties themselves.

"Mom, you can't deliberately practice baking," Lucy protested when I suggested she switch her hard thing.

"Really?" I asked? "What about Rose Beranbaum?"

If ever there was a paragon of grit, it's Rose Beranbaum: three-time winner of the James Beard award and author of a dozen cookbooks and countless newspaper and magazine articles. Described by the *New York Times* as "the most meticulous cook who ever lived," she supposedly dreams new recipes in her sleep.

Apparently, I've convinced Lucy that a hard thing can be fun, too. This summer, she's taking a two-week cooking class and volunteering to help a local pastry chef.

For *your* child there may be a long succession of fun-but-not-yet-hard things, each an opportunity to explore and, eventually, be something to pursue with seriousness.

I'd like to propose that parents who want to cultivate grit in their children abide by the Hard Thing Rule and, in addition, the Fun Thing Rule. Ask your kids to do something that will teach them, through experience, deliberate practice and resilience. But also make sure they're doing things that they find interesting and enjoyable, even if it doesn't seem that they could ever lead to anything more serious.

Why? Because the ultimate goal is to grow up to develop a calling—a fun thing that is *also* a hard thing.

Is grit the only psychological factor that determines success?

Not at all. A lot of factors determine success. Emotional intelligence. Physical talent. Intelligence. Conscientiousness. Self-control. Imagination. The list goes on.

For everyday functioning, my research suggests that grit isn't as important as self-control in the face of distractions and temptations. For making friends, emotional intelligence is probably more useful. And as I mentioned in chapter 13, there is a long list of character strengths more consequential than grit in a moral sense. Greatness is wonderful but goodness ever so much more so.

And, of course, there is luck. And opportunity. Grit isn't everything.

So, why a whole book—and a whole research career—centered on grit?

Because grit holds special significance for the achievement of excellence. This is true whether the endeavor in question is physical, mental, entrepreneurial, civic, or artistic. When you look at the best of the best across domains, the combination of passion and perseverance sustained over the long term is a common denominator.

It's often said that the last mile is the longest. Grit keeps you on the path.

ACKNOWLEDGMENTS

When I pick up a book for the first time, I immediately flip to the Acknowledgments. Like many readers, I'm eager to peek behind the curtain; I want to meet the cast and crew responsible for the show. Writing my own book has only deepened my appreciation for the team effort that any work represents. If you like this book, please know that credit for its creation is shared among the wonderful human beings recognized here. It's time for these many supporters to step out into the footlights for a moment and take a well-deserved bow. If I've left anyone in the wings, I apologize; any omissions are inadvertent.

First and foremost, I want to thank my collaborators. I wrote this book in the first-person singular, using "I" when, in fact, pretty much everything I've done as a researcher or writer was accomplished by a plurality. The "we" who deserve credit—in particular coauthors on published research—are named individually in the Notes. On their behalf, I extend a heartfelt thanks to our research teams who, collectively, made this research possible.

As for the book itself, I have three individuals to thank in particular: First and foremost, I am eternally grateful to my editor, Rick Horgan, who improved my writing and thinking more than I thought was possible. If I'm lucky, he'll let me work with him again (and again). Max Nesterak was my day-to-day editor, research assistant, and conscience.

Put simply, were it not for Max, this book would not be in your hands today. And, finally, my fairy godfather and agent, Richard Pine, is the person who originally, and finally, made this book a reality. Eight years ago, Richard wrote me an email asking, "Has anyone ever told you that you ought to write a book?" I demurred. Gritty and gallant, he kept asking, but never pushing, until I was ready. Thank you, Richard, for everything.

The following scholars were kind enough to review drafts of this book, discuss their relevant work, or both—of course, any errors that remain are mine: Elena Bodrova, Mihály Csíkszentmihályi, Dan Chambliss, Jean Côté, Sidney D'Mello, Bill Damon, Nancy Darling, Carol Dweck, Bob Eisenberger, Anders Ericsson, Lauren Eskreis-Winkler, Ronald Ferguson, James Flynn, Brian Galla, Margo Gardner, Adam Grant, James Gross, Tim Hatton, Jerry Kagan, Scott Barry Kaufman, Dennis Kelly, Emilia Lahti, Reed Larson, Luc Leger, Deborah Leong, Susan Mackie, Steve Maier, Mike Matthews, Darrin McMahon, Barbara Mellers, Cal Newport, Gabrielle Oettingen, Daeun Park, Pat Quinn, Ann Renninger, Brent Roberts, Todd Rogers, James Rounds, Barry Schwartz, Marty Seligman, Paul Silvia, Larry Steinberg, Rong Su, Phil Tetlock, Chia-Jung Tsay, Eli Tsukayama, Elliot Tucker-Drob, George Vaillant, Rachel White, Dan Willingham, Warren Willingham, Amy Wrzesniewski, and David Yeager.

I was shocked, and so deeply moved, that the following individuals were willing to share their stories for this book; even when I wasn't able to include details in the book itself, their perspectives deepened my understanding of grit and its development: Hemalatha Annamalai, Kayvon Asemani, Michael Baime, Jo Barsh, Mark Bennett, Jackie Bezos, Juliet Blake, Geoffrey Canada, Pete Carroll, Robert Caslen, Ulrik Christensen, Kerry Close, Roxanne Coady, Kat Cole, Cody Coleman, Daryl Davis, Joe de Sena, Tom Deierlein, Jamie Dimon, Anson Dorrance, Aurora Fonte, Franco Fonte, Bill Fitzsimmons, Rowdy Gaines, Antonio Galloni, Bruce Gemmell, Jeffrey Gettleman,

Jane Golden, Temple Grandin, Mike Hopkins, Rhonda Hughes, Michael Joyner, Noa Kageyama, Paige Kimble, Sasha Kosanic, Hester Lacey, Emilia Lahti, Terry Laughlin, Joe Leader, Michael Lomax, David Luong, Tobi Lütke, Warren MacKenzie, Willy MacMullen, Bob Mankoff, Alex Martinez, Francesca Martinez, Tina Martinez, Duff McDonald, Bill McNabb, Bernie Noe, Valerie Rainford, Mads Rasmussen, Anthony Seldon, Will Shortz, Chantel Smith, Are Traasdahl, Marc Vetri, Chris Wink, Grit Young, Sherry Young, Steve Young, Sam Zell, and Kai Zhang.

Many friends and family members helped improve earlier drafts. For their invaluable comments, I thank Steve Arnold, Ben Malcolmson, Erica Dewan, Feroz Dewan, Joe Duckworth, Jordan Ellenberg, Ira Handler, Donald Kamentz, Annette Lee, Susan Lee, Dave Levin, Felicia Lewis, Alyssa Matteucci, David Meketon, Evan Nesterak, Rick Nichols, Rebecca Nyquist, Tanya Schlam, Robert Seyfarth, Naomi Shavin, Paul Solman, Danny Southwick, Sharon Parker, Dominic Randolph, Richard Shell, Paolo Terni, Paul Tough, Amy Wax, and Rich Wilson.

The figures in this book are courtesy of Stephen Few. A world expert on data visualization, Stephen is also the soul of generosity and patience.

I am immensely grateful for the unflagging support of so many outstanding individuals at Simon & Schuster. The only hard thing about writing this book was the writing; everything else, these remarkable folks made easy. In particular, I'd like to thank Nan Graham, whose optimism, energy, and genuine affection for her authors have no parallel. Katie Monaghan and Brian Belfiglio masterfully orchestrated a world-class publicity campaign, ensuring that this book would end up in your hands. For masterful handling of this book's production, I thank Carla Benton and her team. David Lamb, you're a total pro; your commitment to excellence at every stage of the editorial process made all the difference. And, finally, for this book's beautiful cover, I am grateful to Jaya Miceli.

ACKNOWLEDGMENTS

Huge thanks to the world-class team at InkWell Management, including Eliza Rothstein, Lyndsey Blessing, and Alexis Hurley. You handle so much so well, and with utter grace and professionalism.

Like the grit paragons profiled in this book, I've benefited from especially supportive and demanding teachers. Matthew Carr taught me to write and to love words. Kay Merseth reminded me, at so many critical junctures, that each of us is the author of our own life story. Marty Seligman taught me that the right question is at least as important as the right answer. The late Chris Peterson showed me that a true teacher is one who puts students first. Sigal Barsade showed me, in innumerable ways, what it means to be a professor and how to be a good one. Walter Mischel showed me that at its apogee, science is an art. And Jim Heckman taught me that genuine curiosity is the best companion to true grit.

I am deeply grateful to the institutions and individuals who have supported my research, including the National Institute on Aging, the Bill & Melinda Gates Foundation, the Pinkerton Foundation, the Robert Wood Johnson Foundation, the KIPP Foundation, the John Templeton Foundation, the Spencer Foundation, the Lone Pine Foundation, the Walton Family Foundation, the Richard King Mellon Family Foundation, the University of Pennsylvania Research Foundation, Acco Brands, the Michigan Retirement Research Center, the University of Pennsylvania, Melvyn and Carolyn Miller, Ariel Kor, and Amy Abrams.

The board and staff of the Character Lab deserve special thanks because they are the past, present, and most definitely the future of all I do.

And, finally, thank you to my family. Amanda and Lucy, your patience, good humor, and stories made this book possible. Mom and Dad, you gave up everything for your children, and we love you for that. Jason, you make me a better person every day—this book is for you.

RECOMMENDED READING

Brooks, David. *The Road to Character*. New York: Random House, 2015.

Brown, Peter C., Henry L. Roediger III, and Mark A. McDaniel. *Make It Stick: The Science of Successful Learning*. Cambridge, MA: Belknap Press, 2014.

Damon, William. *The Path to Purpose: How Young People Find Their Calling in Life*. New York: Free Press, 2009.

Deci, Edward L. with Richard Flaste. *Why We Do What We Do: Understanding Self-Motivation*. New York: Penguin Group, 1995.

Duhigg, Charles. *The Power of Habit: Why We Do What We Do in Life and Business*. New York: Random House, 2012.

Dweck, Carol. *Mindset: The New Psychology of Success*. New York: Random House, 2006.

Emmons, Robert A. *Thanks!: How the New Science of Gratitude Can Make You Happier*. New York: Houghton Mifflin Harcourt, 2007.

Ericsson, Anders and Robert Pool. *Peak: Secrets from the New Science of Expertise*. New York: Houghton Mifflin Harcourt, 2016.

Heckman, James J., John Eric Humphries, and Tim Kautz (eds.). *The Myth of Achievement Tests: The GED and the Role of Character in American Life*. Chicago: University of Chicago Press, 2014.

Kaufman, Scott Barry and Carolyn Gregoire. *Wired to Create: Unraveling the Mysteries of the Creative Mind*. New York: Perigee, 2015.

Lewis, Sarah. *The Rise: Creativity, the Gift of Failure, and the Search for Mastery.* New York: Simon and Schuster, 2014.

Matthews, Michael D. *Head Strong: How Psychology is Revolutionizing War.* New York: Oxford University Press, 2013.

McMahon, Darrin M. *Divine Fury: A History of Genius.* New York: Basic Books, 2013.

Mischel, Walter. *The Marshmallow Test: Mastering Self-Control.* New York: Little, Brown, 2014.

Oettingen, Gabriele. *Rethinking Positive Thinking: Inside the New Science of Motivation.* New York: Penguin Group, 2014.

Pink, Daniel H. *Drive: The Surprising Truth About What Motivates Us.* New York: Riverhead Books, 2009.

Renninger, K. Ann and Suzanne E. Hidi. *The Power of Interest for Motivation and Engagement.* New York: Routledge, 2015.

Seligman, Martin E. P. *Learned Optimism: How To Change Your Mind and Your Life.* New York: Alfred A. Knopf, 1991.

Steinberg, Laurence. *Age of Opportunity: Lessons from the New Science of Adolescence.* New York: Houghton Mifflin Harcourt, 2014.

Tetlock, Philip E. and Dan Gardner. *Superforecasting: The Art and Science of Prediction.* New York: Crown, 2015.

Tough, Paul. *How Children Succeed: Grit, Curiosity, and the Hidden Power of Character.* New York: Houghton Mifflin Harcourt, 2012.

Willingham, Daniel T. *Why Don't Students Like School: A Cognitive Scientist Answers Questions About How the Mind Works and What It Means for the Classroom.* San Francisco: Jossey-Bass, 2009.

NOTES

CHAPTER 1: SHOWING UP

3 **more than 14,000 applicants:** For more information on West Point, including its admissions process, see www.usma.edu.

3 **drop out before graduation:** Data provided by the United States Military Academy.

4 **"new cadet to Soldier":** "Information for New Cadets and Parents," United States Military Academy–West Point, 2015, www.usma.edu/parents/SiteAssets /Info-4-New-Cadets_Class-of-19.pdf.

5 **"West Point toughens you":** Ibid.

5 **and who would leave:** For more on Jerry's views about predicting West Point outcomes, see Jerome Kagan, *An Argument for Mind* (New Haven, CT: Yale University Press, 2006), 49–54.

6 **West Point admissions:** For more information on the Whole Candidate Score and its history, see Lawrence M. Hanser and Mustafa Oguz, *United States Service Academy Admissions: Selecting for Success at the Military Academy /West Point and as an Officer* (Santa Monica, CA: RAND Corporation, 2015).

6 **those with the lowest:** Angela L. Duckworth, Christopher Peterson, Michael D. Matthews, and Dennis R. Kelly, "Grit: Perseverance and Passion for Long-term Goals," *Journal of Personality and Social Psychology* 92 (2007): 1087–1101.

6 **"I was tired, lonely, frustrated":** Michael D. Matthews, *Head Strong: How Psychology Is Revolutionizing War* (New York: Oxford University Press, 2014), 16.

7 **"never give up" attitude:** Mike Matthews, professor of engineering psychology at the U.S. Military Academy at West Point, in conversation with the author, May 25, 2015.

10 **physical fitness marks:** Hanser and Oguz, *Selecting for Success.*

10 **seventy-one cadets had dropped out:** Duckworth et al., "Grit."

11 **55 percent of the salespeople:** Lauren Eskreis-Winkler, Elizabeth P. Shulman, Scott A. Beal, and Angela L. Duckworth, "The Grit Effect: Predicting Retention in the Military, the Workplace, School and Marriage," *Frontiers in Psychology* 5 (2014): 1–12.

11 **graduate degree were grittier:** Duckworth, et al., "Grit."

11 **as high as 80 percent:** For more information on college dropout rates in the United States, see "Institutional Retention and Graduation Rates for Undergraduate Students," National Center for Education Statistics, last updated May 2015, http://nces.ed.gov/programs/coe/indicator_cva.asp.

12 **"where we decide":** Dick Couch, *Chosen Soldier: The Making of a Special Forces Warrior* (New York: Three Rivers Press, 2007), 108.

12 **42 percent of the candidates:** Eskreis-Winkler et al., "The Grit Effect."

12 **Success in the military, business, and education:** Ibid. Importantly, the bivariate associations between grit and outcomes were in all cases significant as well.

13 **to all 273 spellers:** Duckworth et al., "Grit."

14 **SAT scores and grit:** Ibid. See also Kennon M. Sheldon, Paul E. Jose, Todd B. Kashdan, and Aaron Jarden, "Personality, Effective Goal-Striving, and Enhanced Well-Being: Comparing 10 Candidate Personality Strengths," *Personality and Social Psychology Bulletin* 1 (2015), 1–11. In this one-year longitudinal study, grit emerged as a more reliable predictor of goal attainment than any other measured personality strength. Likewise, my colleagues Phil Tetlock and Barbara Mellers have found in their longitudinal research that people who forecast future events with astonishing accuracy are considerably grittier than others: "The strongest predictor of rising into the ranks of superforecasters is perpetual beta, the degree to which one is committed to belief updating and self-improvement. It is roughly three times as powerful a predictor as its closest rival, intelligence." See Philip E. Tetlock and Dan Gardner, *Superforecasting: The Art and Science of Prediction* (New York: Crown, 2015), page 192.

CHAPTER 2: DISTRACTED BY TALENT

15 **in the classroom:** The school I taught at was created by Teach For America alumnus Daniel Oscar, and in my view, the best teacher in the school was a guy named Neil Dorosin. Both Daniel and Neil are still in the vanguard of education reform.

19 **"I was a little behind":** David Luong, in an interview with the author, May 8, 2015.

20 **learning came easy:** Karl Pearson, *The Life, Letters and Labours of Francis Galton*, vol. 1 (Cambridge, UK: Cambridge University Press, 1930), 66.

21 **"capacity for hard labor":** Francis Galton, *Hereditary Genius* (London: Macmillan, 1869), 38. It's important to note here that Galton's fascination

with heredity was misguided. While his conclusions about the importance of zeal and hard work and ability have been supported by modern research, his erroneous conclusions about heredity and race have not.

21 *"eminently* **important difference"**: Charles Darwin, Letter to Francis Galton, December 23, 1869. Frederick Burkhardt et al., ed., *The Correspondence of Charles Darwin*, vol. 17, 1869 (Cambridge, UK: Cambridge University Press, 2009), 530.

21 **supernatural intelligence:** See Leonard Mlodinow, *The Upright Thinkers: The Human Journey from Living in Trees to Understanding the Cosmos* (New York: Pantheon Books, 2015), 195. Catharine Morris Cox, "The Early Mental Traits of Three Hundred Geniuses," in *Genetic Studies of Genius*, vol. 2, ed. Lewis M. Terman, (Stanford, CA: Stanford University Press, 1926), 399.

21 **"no great quickness":** Charles Darwin, *The Autobiography of Charles Darwin* (London: Collins Clear-Type Press, 1958), 140–41.

22 **data presented itself:** Adam S. Wilkins, "Charles Darwin: Genius or Plodder?" *Genetics* 183 (2009): 773–77.

22 **"The Energies of Men":** William James, "The Energies of Men," *Science* 25 (1907): 321–32.

23 **that our talents vary:** Talents are, of course, plural. For interested readers, see Howard Gardner, *Frames of Mind: The Theory of Multiple Intelligences* (New York: Basic Books, 1983). Also, Ellen Winner, *Gifted Children: Myths and Realities* (New York: Basic Books, 1996). Robert J. Sternberg and James C. Kaufman, "Human Abilities," *Annual Review of Psychology* 49 (1998): 479–502.

23 **twice as likely to single out effort:** Survey of America's Inner Financial Life, *Worth Magazine*, November 1993.

23 **about athletic ability:** "CBS News Poll: Does Practice Make Perfect in Sports?," CBS News website, April 6, 2014, www.cbsnews.com/news/cbs-news-poll-does-practice-make-perfect-in-sports.

23 **endorse "intelligence":** The *60 Minutes/Vanity Fair* Poll, *Vanity Fair*, January 2010.

24 **more likely to succeed:** Chia-Jung Tsay and Mahzarin R. Banaji, "Naturals and Strivers: Preferences and Beliefs About Sources of Achievement," *Journal of Experimental Social Psychology* 47 (2011): 460–65.

24 **naturals were rated higher:** Chia-Jung Tsay, "Privileging Naturals Over Strivers: The Costs of the Naturalness Bias," *Personality and Social Psychology Bulletin* (2015).

24 **favor the natural:** Ibid.

25 **"technical skills can flourish":** "Juilliard Pre-College," The Juilliard School, accessed August 10, 2015, http://www.juilliard.edu/youth-adult-programs/juilliard-pre-college

26 **a self-fulfilling prophecy:** Robert Rosenthal, "Pygmalion Effect," in *The Corsini Encyclopedia of Psychology*, ed. Irving B. Weiner and W. Edward Craighead (Hoboken, NJ: John Wiley & Sons, Inc., 2010), 1398–99.

26 **"I wanted to get better"**: Chia-Jung Tsay, assistant professor at the University College London School of Management, in an interview with the author, April 8, 2015.

26 **"The War for Talent"**: Elizabeth Chambers et al., "The War for Talent," *McKinsey Quarterly* 3 (1998): 44–57.

26 **became a best-selling book**: Ed Michaels, Helen Handfield-Jones, and Beth Axelrod, *The War for Talent* (Boston: Harvard Business School Press, 2001).

26 **"What do we mean by *talent*?"**: Ibid., xii.

27 **"like comparing SAT scores"**: John Huey, "How McKinsey Does It," *Fortune*, November 1993: 56–81.

27 **on being "bright"**: Ibid., 56.

29 *The War on Common Sense*: Duff McDonald, "McKinsey's Dirty War: Bogus 'War for Talent' Was Self-Serving (and Failed)," *New York Observer*, November 5, 2013.

30 **Gladwell has also critiqued**: Malcolm Gladwell, "The Talent Myth," *New Yorker*, July 22, 2002.

30 **largest corporate bankruptcy**: Clinton Free, Norman Macintosh, and Mitchell Stein, "Management Controls: The Organizational Fraud Triangle of Leadership, Culture, and Control in Enron," *Ivey Business Journal*, July 2007, http://iveybusinessjournal.com/publication/management-controls-the-organizational-fraud-triangle-of-leadership-culture-and-control-in-enron/.

30 **firing the bottom 15 percent**: Ibid.

31 **"always a step or two behind"**: Scott Barry Kaufman, director of the Imagination Institute, in an interview with the author, May 3, 2015. Also see www.scottbarrykaufman.com.

32 **"I was so driven"**: Scott Barry Kaufman, "From Evaluation to Inspiration: Scott Barry Kaufman at TEDxManhattanBeach," YouTube video, posted January 6, 2014, https://youtu.be/HQ6fW_GDEpA.

33 **"does achievement trump potential?"**: Ibid.

33 **"I had this grit"**: Kaufman, interview.

33 **deemed insufficiently bright**: I know two other people whose tested aptitude wasn't particularly prognostic of what they would go on to achieve. The first is Darrin McMahon, an eminent historian at Dartmouth College. In Darrin's book, *Divine Fury: A History of Genius* (New York: Basic Books, 2013), he points out that genius incites ambivalence. On one hand, the idea that a few of us stand above the rest by virtue of our God-given gifts holds timeless appeal. On the other hand, we love the idea of equality; we like to think we all have the same chance of succeeding in life. In a recent conversation on this topic, Darrin told me, "What we are seeing play out now is the democratization of genius. Part of us wants to believe that everyone can be a genius." I was never a very good history student, and sometimes I was a very poor one. So I was more than a little surprised that I couldn't put Darrin's book down. It

was beautifully written. The meticulous research and careful argumentation somehow did not get in the way of it telling a story. And then, at the very end, on page 243, I got to the acknowledgments: "I have undoubtedly suffered from many delusions in my life—and undoubtedly suffer from many still. But being a genius is not one of them." Then Darrin says, with humor and affection, that when he was growing up, his parents saw to it that their son "never got too big for his britches." And even more to the point, he recalls being tested as a child for his school's gifted program. There were "shapes and pictures and the like," but the only thing he remembers with certainty is "I didn't pass." Darrin remembers watching his classmates "trundle off each week to special classes for the specially endowed." And then he reflects on whether getting labeled nongifted was, in the end, a blessing or a curse: "At an early age, I was told, with all the objectivity of science, that I was not the recipient of gifts. I might have just thrown in the towel then and there, but I am a stubborn sort, and I spent many years disputing the verdict, working away to prove to myself and to others, dammit, that I had not been slighted at birth." Similarly, Michael Lomax was not easily identifiable as any kind of prodigy. Nevertheless, he has an illustrious résumé: he is president and CEO of the United Negro College Fund, a leadership position he has held for more than a decade. Before that, Michael was president of Dillard University. He has taught English at Emory University, Spelman College, and Morehouse College and was a two-time mayoral candidate for the city of Atlanta. "Honestly, I wasn't considered the smartest kid," Michael told me recently. When he was sixteen, his mother nevertheless wrote to the president of Morehouse College to ask whether her son could be admitted to its prep school. "Of course, there was no prep school at Morehouse!" Michael chuckled. The Morehouse president decided, on the basis of Michael's outstanding grades, to admit him as a freshman to the college. "I got there. I hated it. I wanted to leave. I was number one in my class, but I wanted to transfer. I got it in my head that I would be a better fit at Williams College, so I applied. I had done everything, and they were about to admit me, and then the director of admissions said, 'Oh, by the way, we need an SAT score.'" Because he'd been admitted to Morehouse without a formal application, Michael had never taken the SAT before. "That test was make-or-break for me. I sat down and took it. And I didn't do well. Williams didn't admit me." So Michael stayed at Morehouse and made the best of it, graduating Phi Beta Kappa with a degree in English. Later, he earned his master's degree in English from Columbia University, and his PhD in American and African American literature from Emory University. Now sixty-eight years old, Michael told me, "At my age, I think it's character more than genius. I know all kinds of very talented people who squander their great talents, or who are dissatisfied and unhappy because they think talent is enough. In fact, it ain't even *near* enough. What I tell my kids, what I try to tell my grandchildren, and anybody I get a chance to mentor is this: It's the sweat, it's the hard work, it's the persistence, it's the determination. It is the getting up and dusting yourself off. That's what it's all about." In anticipation of hate mail about this passage on gifted and talented programs, let me say this: I am *wholeheartedly* in favor of giving kids all the intellectual stimulation they can handle. At the same time, I urge opening those programs to all children who might benefit. Thirty years ago, Benjamin Bloom said it best: "We in this country have come to believe that we can tell who's going to be a great musician by giving musical aptitude tests, who's going to be a great mathematician by giving mathematics aptitude tests. Doing that counts some people in and others out far too early. . . . All the children should be given opportunities to explore fields that they might be interested in." Ronald S. Brandt, "On Talent Development: A Conversation with Benjamin Bloom," *Educational Leadership* 43 (1985): 33–35.

CHAPTER 3: EFFORT COUNTS TWICE

36 **"The Mundanity of Excellence":** Daniel F. Chambliss, "The Mundanity of Excellence: An Ethnographic Report on Stratification and Olympic Swimmers," *Sociological Theory* 7 (1989): 70–86.

36 **"dozens of small skills":** Ibid., 81.

36 **"You need to jazz it up":** Ibid., 86.

37 **"we have for athletic success":** Ibid., 78.

37 **"distinguishes the best among our athletes":** Ibid, 78.

37 **"It's easy to do":** Ibid., 79.

37 **"anatomical advantages":** Daniel F. Chambliss, professor of sociology at Hamilton College, in an interview with the author, June 2, 2015.

39 **"how it came to be":** This is an informal translation, Friedrich Nietzsche, *Menschliches, Allzumenschliches: Ein Buch für Freie Geister* (Leipzig: Alfred Kröner Verlag, 1925), 135.

39 **"out of the ground by magic":** Friedrich Nietzsche, *Human, All Too Human: A Book for Free Spirits*, trans. R. J. Hollingdale (Cambridge, UK: Cambridge University Press, 1986), 80.

39 **"grows somewhat cool":** Ibid., 86.

39 **"the cult of the genius":** Ibid.

39 **"active in *one* direction":** Ibid.

40 **"giftedness, inborn talents!":** Ibid.

40 **human flourishing:** Marty Seligman lays out the rationale for Positive Psychology in his presidential address to the American Psychological Association, reprinted in *American Psychologist* 54 (1999): 559–62.

42 **talent is how quickly:** The word *talent* is used differently by different people, but I think the most intuitive definition is the one I've offered here. For evidence that individuals do differ in the rate at which they acquire skills, see Paul B. Baltes and Reinhold Kliegl, "Further Testing of Limits of Cognitive Plasticity: Negative Age Differences in a Mnemonic Skill Are Robust," *Devel-*

opmental Psychology 28 (1992): 121–25. See also Tom Stafford and Michael Dewar, "Tracing the Trajectory of Skill Learning with a Very Large Sample of Online Game Players," *Psychological Science*, 25 (2014), 511–18. Finally, see the work of David Hambrick and colleagues on factors other than practice that likely influence skill acquisition; for example, see Brooke N. Macnamara, David Z. Hambrick, and Frederick L. Oswald, "Deliberate Practice and Performance in Music, Games, Sports, Education, and Professions: A Meta-Analysis," *Psychological Science* 25 (2014): 1608–18. A critique of this meta-analysis by psychologist Anders Ericsson, whose work we explore in depth in chapter 7, is posted on his website: https://psy.fsu.edu/faculty/ericsson /ericsson.hp.html.

43 **"going to be the renaissance people"**: "Oral History Interview with Warren MacKenzie, 2002 October 29," Archives of American Art, Smithsonian Institution, www.aaa.si.edu/collections/interviews/oral-history-interview-warren -mackenzie-12417.

43 **"our true interest lay"**: Ibid.

43 **"40 or 50 pots in a day"**: Warren MacKenzie, potter, in an interview with the author, June 16, 2015.

43 **"continue to engage the senses"**: Warren MacKenzie, Artist's Statement, Schaller Gallery, https://www.schallergallery.com/artists/macwa/pdf/Mac Kenzie-Warren-statement.pdf.

43 **"the most exciting things"**: "Oral History," Archives of American Art.

43 **"in my work today"**: Ibid.

43 **"first 10,000 pots are difficult"**: Alex Lauer, "Living with Pottery: Warren MacKenzie at 90," Walker Art Center blog, February 16, 2014, http://blogs .walkerart.org/visualarts/2014/02/16/living-with-pottery-warren-mackenzie -at-90.

44 **"Garp was a natural storyteller"**: John Irving, *The World According to Garp* (New York: Ballantine, 1978), 127.

44 **"the great storyteller"**: Peter Matthiessen, quoted in "Life & Times: John Iriving," *New York Times*, http://www.nytimes.com/books/97/06/15/lifetimes /irving.html.

44 **Garp "could make things up"**: Irving, *Garp*, 127.

44 **"my lack of talent"**: John Irving, *The Imaginary Girlfriend: A Memoir* (New York: Ballantine, 1996), 10.

44 **SAT verbal score was 475**: Sally Shaywitz, *Overcoming Dyslexia: A New and Complete Science-based Program for Reading Problems at Any Level* (New York: Alfred A. Knopf, 2003), 345–50.

45 **"lazy" and "stupid"**: Ibid., 346.

45 **"frequently misspelled words"**: Irving, *Imaginary Girlfriend*, 9.

45 **"slowly—and with my finger"**: Shaywitz, *Overcoming Dyslexia*, 346.

45 **"you have to overextend yourself"**: Ibid., 347.

45 **"no matter how difficult it is"**: Ibid.

45 **"Rewriting is what I do best":** John Irving, "Author Q&A," Random House Online Catalogue, 2002.

45 **"to have to go slowly":** Shaywitz, *Overcoming Dyslexia*, 347.

46 **"sickening work ethic":** *60 Minutes*, CBS, December 2, 2007, http://www .cbsnews.com/news/will-smith-my-work-ethic-is-sickening. A lyric in one of Will Smith's raps goes: "If you say you're going to run three miles, and you only run two, I don't ever have to worry about losing in nothing to you." See "Will Smith Interview: Will Power," *Reader's Digest*, December 2006.

46 **"or I'm going to die":** Tavis Smiley, PBS, December 12, 2007.

46 **"healthy young men":** Clark W. Heath, *What People Are: A Study of Normal Young Men* (Cambridge, MA: Harvard University Press, 1945), 7.

46 **for only four minutes:** Katharine A. Phillips, George E. Vaillant, and Paula Schnurr, "Some Physiologic Antecedents of Adult Mental Health," *The American Journal of Psychiatry* 144 (1987): 1009–13.

47 **"strength of will":** Heath, *Normal Young Men*, 75.

47 **"becomes too severe":** Ibid., 74.

47 **"with mental health":** Phillips, Vaillant, and Schnurr, "Some Physiologic Antecedents," 1012.

48 **"I'm not all that persistent":** George Vaillant, professor at Harvard Medical School and former director of the Grant Study, in an interview with the author, April 8, 2015.

49 **"never write the play or book":** William Safire, "On Language; The Elision Fields," *New York Times*, August 13, 1989.

49 **"Eighty percent of success in life is showing up":** Ibid.

50 **less than they'd expected:** *Consumer Reports*, "Home Exercise Machines," August 2011.

51 **"beating on your craft":** *Today* show, NBC, June 23, 2008.

CHAPTER 4: HOW GRITTY ARE YOU?

54 **Grit Scale:** The original twelve-item Grit Scale, from which this ten-item version is adapted, was published in Duckworth et al., "Grit." The correlation between these two versions of the scale is $r = .99$. Note also that, as you'll learn in chapter 9, I've revised item 2, adding, "I don't give up easily" to "Setbacks don't discourage me."

56 **how your scores compare:** Data for these norms are from Duckworth et al., "Grit" Study 1. Note that there are numerous limitations of any measure, including self-report questionnaires like the Grit Scale. For an extended discussion, see Angela L. Duckworth and David S. Yeager, "Measurement Matters: Assessing Personal Qualities Other Than Cognitive Ability for Educational Purposes," *Educational Researcher* 44 (2015): 237–51.

58 **"work in East Africa":** Jeffrey Gettleman, East Africa bureau chief for the *New York Times*, in an interview with the author, May 22, 2015.

59 **"it was the easiest to fulfill the requirements"**: Abigail Warren, "Gettleman Shares Anecdotes, Offers Advice," *Cornell Chronicle*, March 2, 2015, http://www.news.cornell.edu/stories/2015/03/gettleman-shares-anecdotes-offers-advice.

59 **"I wanted to make it a part of my life"**: Gettleman, interview.

59 **"who wants to work for a boring newspaper?"**: Max Schindler, "New York Times Reporter Jeffrey Gettleman '94 Chronicles His Time in Africa," *Cornell Daily Sun*, April 6, 2011.

59 **"I was pretty lost academically"**: Gettleman, interview.

61 **"have a life philosophy"**: Pete Carroll, head coach of the Seattle Seahawks, in an interview with the author, June 2, 2015.

61 **they have ever been done before:** For more on Pete's perspective, see Pete Carroll, *Win Forever: Live, Work, and Play Like a Champion* (New York: Penguin, 2010). Some of the quotations in this section, and later in the book, are from interviews with the author between 2014 and 2015. Others are from Pete's book or public talks.

61 **"drive all my actions"**: Carroll, *Win Forever*, 73.

61 **"and filling binders"**: Ibid., 78.

62 **goals in a hierarchy:** Material in this chapter on the hierarchical structure of goals from Angela Duckworth and James J. Gross, "Self-control and Grit: Related but Separable Determinants of Success." *Current Directions in Psychological Science* 23 (2014): 319–25. On goal hierarchies more generally, see Arie W. Kruglanski et al., "A Theory of Goal Systems," in *Advances in Experimental Social Psychology* 34 (2002): 331–78. And, finally, for a review of goal-setting theory, see Edwin A. Locke and Gary P. Latham, "Building a Practically Useful Theory of Goal Setting and Task Motivation: A 35-Year Odyssey," *American Psychologist* 57 (2002): 705–17.

63 **an "ultimate concern"**: Robert A. Emmons, *The Psychology of Ultimate Concerns: Motivation and Spirituality in Personality* (New York: Guildford Press, 1999).

63 **when he retired in 1987:** Ira Berkow, "Sports of the Times; Farewell, Sweet Pitcher," *New York Times*, June 23, 1987.

63 **"day after day, year after year"**: Pat Jordan, "Tom Terrific and His Mystic Talent," *Sports Illustrated*, July 24, 1972, http://www.si.com/vault/1972/07/24/612578/tom-terrific-and-his-mystic-talent.

63 **"then I eat cottage cheese"**: Ibid.

64 **"help me be happy"**: Ibid.

64 **"positive fantasizing"**: Gabriele Oettingen, "Future Thought and Behaviour Change," *European Review of Social Psychology* 23 (2012): 1–63. For a terrific summary, and practical suggestions, on goal setting and planning, see Gabriele Oettingen, *Rethinking Positive Thinking: Inside the New Science of Motivation* (New York: Penguin, 2014).

65 **reportedly gave his personal pilot:** James Clear, "Warren Buffett's 'Two List' Strategy: How to Maximize Your Focus and Master Your Priorities," *Huffington*

Post, originally posted October, 24, 2014, updated December 24, 2014, http://www.huffingtonpost.com/james-clear/warren-buffetts-two-list-strategy-how-to-maximize-your-focus-_b_6041584.html.

69 **a more important end:** For instance, in one study, young adults wrote down their high-level, mid-level, and low-level goals; over the next two weeks, they reported on daily frustrations. People whose goals demonstrated a more organized, hierarchical structure subsequently demonstrated greater resilience in the face of daily frustrations. In particular, when confronted with frustrating experiences, they maintained a sense that they were in control of attaining their goals. In a related study, a more hierarchical goal structure predicted feeling less anger and annoyance in the face of daily frustrations over the next two weeks. See Michael D. Robinson and Sara K. Moeller, "Frustrated, but Not Flustered: The Benefits of Hierarchical Approach Motivation to Weathering Daily Frustrations," *Motivation and Emotion* 38 (2014): 547–59.

70 **"improvise, adapt, overcome":** Michael Martel, *Improvise, Adapt, Overcome: Achieve the Green Beret Way* (Seattle: Amazon Digital Services, Inc., 2012).

71 **"made mine wither":** Robert Mankoff, *How About Never—Is Never Good for You?: My Life in Cartoons* (New York: Henry Holt and Company, 2014), 34.

71 **"I've written this book":** Syd Hoff, *Learning to Cartoon* (New York: Stravon Educational Press, 1966), vii.

71 **"How could anyone do more than twenty-seven cartoons?":** Mankoff, *How About Never*, 38.

72 **"I'm the funniest guy you ever met":** Bob Mankoff, cartoon editor of the *New Yorker*, in an interview with the author, February 10, 2015.

72 **"I'm going to be a cartoonist":** Mankoff, interview.

72 **"wallpaper my bathroom":** Mankoff, *How About Never*, 44.

72 **"you too were one of the best":** Ibid., 46.

72 **"I looked up all the cartoons":** Mankoff, interview.

73 **"I had complete confidence":** Ibid.

74 **"things never work out":** Mankoff, *How About Never*, 114.

74 **301 exceptionally accomplished:** Cox, "Early Mental Traits."

76 **"Cox's First Ten":** Ibid., 181. Presented here in alphabetical order by last name.

78 **"with somewhat less persistence":** Ibid., 187.

CHAPTER 5: GRIT GROWS

79 **worth our attention:** Psychologist Steve Heine has done research showing that if you think something is genetic, then you think it is "natural" and therefore the way things "should be." For example, if you tell obese people that obesity has a genetic basis, they reduce their dieting efforts. See Ilan Dar-Nimrod and Steven J. Heine, "Genetic Essentialism: On the Deceptive Determinism of DNA," *Psychological Bulletin* 137 (2011): 800–18. Perhaps people would not have such a knee-jerk reaction if they understood better that the interplay

between genes and the environment is complex and dynamic. The interested reader might find the work of Elliot Tucker-Drob on this topic especially illuminating; for example, see Daniel A. Briley and Elliot M. Tucker-Drob, "Comparing the Developmental Genetics of Cognition and Personality Over the Life Span," *Journal of Personality* (2015): 1–14.

80 **150 years ago:** Timothy J. Hatton and Bernice E. Bray, "Long Run Trends in the Heights of European Men, 19th–20th Centuries," *Economics and Human Biology* 8 (2010): 405–13.

80 **average is five feet ten inches:** Alison Moody, "Adult Anthropometric Measures, Overweight and Obesity," in *Health Survey for England 2013*, ed. Rachel Craig and Jennifer Mindell (London: Health and Social Care Information Centre, 2014).

80 **gain of more than six inches:** Hatton, "Long Run Trends." Yvonne Schonbeck et al., "The World's Tallest Nation Has Stopped Growing Taller: The Height of Dutch Children from 1955 to 2009," *Pediatric Research* 73 (2013): 371–77.

80 **honesty and generosity:** See Eric Turkheimer, Erik Pettersson, and Erin E. Horn, "A Phenotypic Null Hypothesis for the Genetics of Personality," *Annual Review of Psychology* 65 (2014): 515–40.

80 **Ditto for IQ:** Richard E. Nisbett et al., "Intelligence: New Findings and Theoretical Developments," *American Psychologist* 67 (2012): 130–59.

80 **enjoying the great outdoors:** Niels G. Waller, David T. Lykken, and Auke Tellegen, "Occupational Interests, Leisure Time Interests, and Personality: Three Domains or One? Findings from the Minnesota Twin Registry." In *Assessing Individual Differences in Human Behavior: New Concepts, Methods, and Findings*, ed. David John Lubinski and René V. Dawis (Palo Alto, CA: Davies-Black Publishing, 1995): 233–59.

80 **having a sweet tooth:** Fiona M. Breen, Robert Plomin, and Jane Wardle, "Heritability of Food Preferences in Young Children," *Physiology & Behavior* 88 (2006): 443–47.

80 **end up a chain-smoker:** Gary E. Swan et al., "Smoking and Alcohol Consumption in Adult Male Twins: Genetic Heritability and Shared Environmental Influences," *Journal of Substance Abuse* 2 (1990): 39–50.

80 **getting skin cancer:** Paul Lichtenstein et al. "Environmental and Heritable Factors in the Causation of Cancer—Analyses of Cohorts of Twins from Sweden, Denmark, and Finland," *New England Journal of Medicine* 343 (2000): 78–85.

80 **carry a tune:** Elizabeth Theusch and Jane Gitschier, "Absolute Pitch Twin Study and Segregation Analysis," *Twin Research and Human Genetics* 14 (2011): 173–78.

80 **dunk a basketball:** Lisa M. Guth and Stephen M. Roth, "Genetic Influence and Athletic Performance," *Current Opinion in Pediatrics* 25 (2013): 653–58.

80 **solve a quadratic equation:** Bonamy Oliver et al., "A Twin Study of Teacher-Reported Mathematics Performance and Low Performance in 7-Year-Olds," *Journal of Educational Psychology* 96 (2004): 504–17.

81 **"I could only swim breaststroke":** Chambliss, interview.

81 **"I had horribly bad coaches":** Chambliss, interview. The tremendous importance of teacher quality to trajectories of academic achievement is documented in Eric A. Hanushek, "Valuing Teachers: How Much Is a Good Teacher Worth?" *Education Next* 11 (2011), 40–45.

82 **researchers in London:** Personal communication with Robert Plomin, June 21, 2015. For a review of heritability of personality traits, see Turkheimer, Pettersson, and Horn, "Phenotypic Null Hypothesis." It's worth noting that there are behavioral genetics studies that do not rely on twins, and also that heritability is a topic too complex to fully summarize here. In particular, there are interactions between different genes, between genes and the environment, and epigenetic effects. Relatedly, there is an ongoing debate as to the proportion of environmental influence that can be attributed to parenting. Definitively teasing apart the effects of parenting from genetic heritage is difficult. Chiefly, this is because you can't randomly swap human children to live with different parents. However, you can do exactly that with rat pups and their moms. You can, for example, randomly assign rat pups to grow up with very nurturing mothers or very negligent ones. Neurobiologist Michael Meaney has done exactly that, and he has found that nurturing rats—who lick and groom and nurse their pups more than average—raise pups who are less stressed when dealing with challenging situations. The effects last into adulthood, and in fact, rat pups who are born to low-lick moms but, within twenty-four hours of birth, are switched to be raised by high-lick moms, grow up to be high-lick moms themselves. See Darlene Francis, Josie Diorio, Dong Liu, and Michael J. Meaney, "Nongenomic Transmission Across Generations of Maternal Behavior and Stress Responses in the Rat," *Science* 286 (1999): 1155–58.

82 **traits are polygenic:** Christopher F. Chabris et al., "The Fourth Law of Behavioral Genetics," *Current Directions in Psychological Science* 24 (2015): 304–12.

82 **at least 697 different genes:** Andrew R. Wood et al., "Defining the Role of Common Variation in the Genomic and Biological Architecture of Adult Human Height," *Nature Genetics* 46 (2014): 1173–86.

82 **as many as twenty-five thousand different genes:** "A Brief Guide to Genomics," National Human Genome Research Institute, last modified August 27, 2015, http://www.genome.gov/18016863.

83 **Wechsler Adult Intelligence Scale:** The Wechsler tests are now published by Pearson's Clinical Assessment.

83 **in the last fifty years:** Information on the Flynn effect comes from personal communications with James Flynn from 2006 to 2015. For more information on the Flynn effect, see James R. Flynn, *Are We Getting Smarter?: Ris-*

ing IQ in the Twenty-First Century (Cambridge, UK: Cambridge University Press, 2012).See also Jakob Pietschnig and Martin Voracek, "One Century of Global IQ Gains: A Formal Meta-Analysis of the Flynn Effect (1909–2013)," *Perspectives on Psychological Science* 10 (2015): 282–306. In this analysis of 271 independent samples, totaling almost four million people from thirty-one countries, a few key findings emerged: IQ gains are ubiquitous and positive over the past century; gains have varied in magnitude by domain of intelligence; gains have been less dramatic in recent years; and, finally, candidate causes include, in addition to social multiplier effects, changes in education, nutrition, hygiene, medical care, and test-taking sophistication.

84 **the social multiplier effect:** William T. Dickens and James R. Flynn, "Heritability Estimates Versus Large Environmental Effects: The IQ Paradox Resolved," *Psychological Review* 108 (2001): 346–69.

85 **Grit and age:** These data are originally reported in Duckworth et al., "Grit," 1092.

86 **more conscientious, confident, caring, and calm:** Avshalom Caspi, Brent W. Roberts, and Rebecca L. Shiner, "Personality Development: Stability and Change," *Annual Review of Psychology* 56 (2005): 453–84.

87 **"the maturity principle":** Ibid., 468.

87 **"doesn't come overnight":** Shaywitz, *Overcoming Dyslexia*, 347.

88 **"you're late, you're fired":** Bernie Noe, head of school, Lakeside School, Seattle, in an interview with the author, July 29, 2015.

91 **interest without purpose:** Ken M. Sheldon, "Becoming Oneself: The Central Role of Self-Concordant Goal Selection," *Personality and Social Psychology Review* 18 (2014): 349–65. See psychologist Ken Sheldon's work on enjoyment and importance as the two components of what he calls autonomously motivated goals. Ken points out that all of us have responsibilities we must fulfill out of obligation or necessity. But no matter how much we think we care about externally motivated goals, their accomplishment rarely fulfills us in the way that interesting and purposeful goals do. A lot of the people in Ken's studies are highly educated and very comfortably upper-middle-class yet sorely lacking in autonomously motivated goals. They tell Ken they feel like they're in the passenger seat of their own lives. By following these individuals over time, Ken's learned that they're less likely to accomplish their goals; even when they do achieve them, they derive less satisfaction from having done so. Recently, I collected data from hundreds of adults, ages twenty-five to seventy-five and found that Ken's measure of autonomous motivation correlates positively with grit.

CHAPTER 6: INTEREST

95 **"follow your passion":** Indiana University, "Will Shortz's 2008 Commencement Address," CSPAN, http://www.c-span.org/video/?205168-1/indiana-university-commencement-address.

95 **"to follow my passion"**: Princeton University, "Jeff Bezos' 2010 Baccalaure-ate Remarks," TED, https://www.ted.com/talks/jeff_bezos_gifts_vs_choices.

95 **"won't be able to stick with it"**: Taylor Soper, "Advice from Amazon Founder Jeff Bezos: Be Proud of Your Choices, Not Your Gifts," *GeekWire*, Octo-ber 13, 2013, http://www.geekwire.com/2013/advice-amazon-founder-jeff -bezos-proud-choices-gifts.

96 **asks the same questions:** Hester Lacey, "The Inventory," published weekly in the *Financial Times*.

96 **"I love what I do"**: Hester Lacey, journalist for the *Financial Times,* in an interview with the author, June 2, 2015.

97 **fits their personal interests:** Mark Allen Morris, "A Meta-Analytic Inves-tigation of Vocational Interest-Based Job Fit, and Its Relationship to Job Satisfaction, Performance, and Turnover" (PhD dissertation, University of Houston, 2003).

97 **happier with their lives:** Rong Su, Louis Tay, and Qi Zhang, "Interest Fit and Life Satisfaction: A Cross-Cultural Study in Ten Countries" (manuscript in preparation)."

97 *perform* **better:** Christopher D. Nye, Rong Su, James Rounds, and Fritz Drasgow, "Vocational Interests and Performance: A Quantitative Summary of over 60 Years of Research," *Perspectives on Psychological Science* 7 (2012), 384–403.

98 **very real constraints:** See Cal Newport, *So Good They Can't Ignore You: Why Skills Trump Passion in the Quest for Work You Love* (New York: Hachette Book Group, 2012). Cal points out that getting very good at something and therefore making yourself valuable to others often precedes identifying what you do as your passion.

98 **"strength of [our] interest"**: William James, *Talks to Teachers on Psychology; and to Students on Some of Life's Ideals* (New York: Henry Holt and Company, 1916), 114.

98 **"engaged" at work:** Gallup, *State of the Global Workplace: Employee Engage-ment Insights for Business Leaders Worldwide* (Washington, DC: Gallup, Inc., 2013).

99 **food could be this good:** *Julie & Julia,* dir. Nora Ephron, Columbia Pictures, 2009.

99 **"I was hooked, and for life"**: Marilyn Mellowes, "About Julia Child," PBS, June 15, 2005, http://www.pbs.org/wnet/americanmasters/julia-child-about -julia-child/555.

100 **"I could really fall in love with"**: Rowdy Gaines, Olympic gold medalist swimmer, in an interview with the author, June 15, 2015.

100 **"I'm glad I went this way"**: Marc Vetri, chef, in an interview with the author, February 2, 2015.

101 **writing a cookbook for Americans:** Julia Child with Alex Prud'homme, *My Life in France* (New York: Alfred A. Knopf, 2006).

101 **"zero interest in the stove"**: Ibid., 3.

101 **"to find my true passion"**: Mellowes, "About Julia Child."

101 **"No Career Direction"**: "Fleeting Interest in Everything, No Career Direction," Reddit, accessed June 17, 2015, https://www.reddit.com/r/jobs/comments/1asw10/fleeting_interest_in_everything_no_career.

102 **"They're holding out for perfection"**: Barry Schwartz, Dorwin Cartwright Professor of Social Theory and Social Action at Swarthmore College, in an interview with the author, January 27, 2015.

104 **around middle school:** Douglas K. S. Low, Mijung Yoon, Brent W. Roberts, and James Rounds. "The Stability of Vocational Interests from Early Adolescence to Middle Adulthood: A Quantitative Review of Longitudinal Studies." *Psychological Bulletin* 131 (2005): 713–37.

104 **with the outside world:** Much of the content in this chapter on the development of interests comes from an interview between the author and Ann Renninger, Eugene M. Lang Professor of Educational Studies at Swarthmore College, on July 13, 2015. For an in-depth review, the interested reader is referred to K. Ann Renninger and Suzanne Hidi, *The Power of Interest for Motivation and Engagement* (London: Routledge, 2015).

104 **"to *force* an interest"**: Rob Walker, "25 Entrepreneurs We Love: Jeff Bezos, Amazon.com," *Inc.* magazine, April 2004, 150.

105 **"one piece of information led to another"**: Mike Hopkins, NASA astronaut and colonel in the U.S. Air Force, in an interview with the author, May 12, 2015.

105 **"I started wanting to make that"**: Vetri, interview.

106 **"I'll always need you"**: Marc Vetri, *Il Viaggio Di Vetri: A Culinary Journey* (New York: Ten Speed Press, 2008), ix.

106 **"at the things they love"**: Amy Chua, *Battle Hymn of the Tiger Mother* (New York: Penguin, 2011), 213.

107 **120 people who achieved:** Benjamin Bloom, *Developing Talent in Young People* (New York: Ballantine, 1985).

107 **"the early years"**: Ibid. I would like to point out here that while interest typically precedes the effortful practice we will discuss in the next chapter, it's also been shown that investing effort into an endeavor can reciprocally increase passion. See Michael M. Gielnik et al., "'I Put in Effort, Therefore I Am Passionate': Investigating the Path from Effort to Passion in Entrepreneurship," *Academy of Management Journal* 58 (2015): 1012–31.

107 **Encouragement during the early years:** For related work, see Stacey R. Finkelstein and Ayelet Fishbach, "Tell Me What I Did Wrong: Experts Seek and Respond to Negative Feedback," *Journal of Consumer Research* 39 (2012): 22–38.

107 **"perhaps the major quality"**: Bloom, *Developing Talent*, 514.

107 **erode intrinsic motivation:** Robert Vallerand, Nathalie Houlfort, and Jacques Forest, "Passion for Work: Determinants and Outcomes," in *The Oxford*

Handbook of Work Engagement, Motivation, and Self-Determination Theory, ed. Marylène Gagné (Oxford, UK: Oxford University Press, 2014), 85–105.

108 **injured physically and to burn out:** Jean Côté, Professor of Psychology at Queen's University, in an interview with the author, July 24, 2015. See also, Jean Côté, Karl Erickson, and Bruce Abernethy, "Play and Practice During Childhood," in *Conditions of Children's Talent Development in Sport*, ed. Jean Côté and Ronnie Lidor (Morgantown, WV: Fitness Information Technology, 2013), 9–20. Côté, Baker, and Abernethy, "Practice and Play in the Development of Sport Exercise," in *Handbook of Sport Psychology*, ed. Gershon Tenenbaum and Robert C. Eklund (Hoboken, NJ: John Wiley & Sons, 2007), 184–202.

108 **different motivational needs:** Robert J. Vallerand, *The Psychology of Passion: A Dualistic Model* (Oxford, UK: Oxford University Press, 2015). Vallerand has found that passion leads to deliberate practice, and that autonomy support from teachers and parents leads to passion.

108 **"I just wanted to make my own":** Will Shortz, crossword puzzle editor for the *New York Times*, in an interview with the author, February 28, 2015.

109 **"my first crossword":** Elisabeth Andrews, "20 Questions for Will Shortz," *Bloom Magazine*, December 2007/January 2008, 58.

109 **"I sold my first puzzle":** Shortz, interview.

110 **"what I was supposed to do":** Jackie Bezos, in an interview with the author, August 6, 2015. Jackie also told me that Jeff's early love of space has never waned. His high school valedictory speech was about colonizing space. Decades later, he created Blue Origin to establish a permanent presence in space: www.blueorigin.com.

112 **"because they're so diverse":** Shortz, interview.

112 **"call them short-termers":** Jane Golden, founder and executive director of the Mural Arts Program, in an interview with the author, June 5, 2015.

114 **"it's a basic drive":** Paul Silvia, associate professor of psychology at the University of North Carolina at Greensboro, in an interview with the author, July 22, 2015.

114 **enduring interests:** Paul J. Silvia, "Interest—the Curious Emotion," *Current Directions in Psychological Science* 17 (2008): 57–60.

114 **"how eager to learn":** See www.templeton.org.

114 **"they're not sure what it's all about":** Silvia, interview.

115 **"How to Solve the New York Times Crossword Puzzle":** Will Shortz, "How to Solve the *New York Times* Crossword Puzzle," *New York Times Magazine*, April 8, 2001.

116 **"with a slightly new turn":** James, *Talks to Teachers*, 108.

CHAPTER 7: PRACTICE

117 **grittier kids at the National Spelling Bee:** Duckworth et al., "Grit."

118 **"be better than the last":** Lacey, interview.

118 **world expert on world experts:** Anders Ericsson and Robert Pool, *Peak: Secrets from the New Science of Expertise* (New York: Houghton Mifflin Harcourt, 2016). See also, K. Anders Ericsson, "The Influence of Experience and Deliberate Practice on the Development of Superior Expert Performance," in *The Cambridge Handbook of Expertise and Expert Performance*, ed. K. Anders Ericsson et al. (Cambridge, UK: Cambridge University Press, 2006). K. Anders Ericsson, Ralf Th. Krampe, and Clemens Tesch-Römer, "The Role of Deliberate Practice in the Acquisition of Expert Performance," *Psychological Review* 100 (1993): 363–406.

119 **their rate of improvement slows:** See K. Anders Ericsson and Paul Ward, "Capturing the Naturally Occurring Superior Performance of Experts in the Laboratory," *Current Directions in Psychological Science* 16 (2007): 346–50. See also Allen Newell and Paul S. Rosenbloom, "Mechanisms of Skill Acquisition and the Law of Practice," in *Cognitive Skills and Their Acquisition*, ed. John R. Anderson (Hillsdale, NJ: Lawrence Erlbaum Associates, 1981), 1–56. Grit paragons tell me, in so many words, that if you had a magnifying glass, you'd see that learning curves are not smooth at all. Instead, there are "mini" plateaus—getting stuck on a problem for hours, days, weeks or even longer, and then suddenly a breakthrough. Ninety-six-year-old MacArthur Fellow and poet Irving Feldman put it to me this way: "Learning isn't an evenly rising slope, but a series of leaps from plateau to plateau."

119 **ten thousand hours of practice:** Ericsson et al., "The Role of Deliberate Practice."

119 **"make a mature dancer":** Martha Graham, "I Am a Dancer," on Edward R. Murrow's *This I Believe*, CBS, circa 1953. Republished on NPR, "An Athlete of God," January 4, 2006, http://www.npr.org/templates/story/story.php?storyId=5065006.

119 **"seasoned press dispatcher":** Bryan Lowe William and Noble Harter, "Studies on the Telegraphic Language: The Acquisition of a Hierarchy of Habits," *Psychological Review* 6 (1899): 358. Also relevant is John R. Hayes, "Cognitive Processes in Creativity," in *Handbook of Creativity*, ed. John A. Glover, Royce R. Ronning, and Cecil R. Reynolds (New York: Springer, 1989), 135–45.

120 **is just a rough average:** See K. Anders Ericsson, "The Danger of Delegating Education to Journalists: Why the APS Observer Needs Peer Review When Summarizing New Scientific Developments" (unpublished manuscript, 2012), https://psy.fsu.edu/faculty/ericsson/ericsson.hp.html.

120 **"*not* doing deliberate practice":** K. Anders Ericsson, professor of psychology at Florida State University, in conversation with the author, December 2005.

121 **intentionally seek out challenges:** Ericsson et al., "The Role of Deliberate Practice."

121 **"I'd try to hold 1:14":** Gaines, interview.

121 **"that needs problem solving":** Roberto Díaz, president and CEO of the Curtis Institute of Music, in an interview with the author, October 7, 2015.

122 **"every single piece of my game":** An additional 15 percent of his time, he says, is for playing pick-up, either one-on-one or three-on-three, so that the microrefinements he has worked on can be integrated into team play. And, finally, the last 15 percent is for organized games. "Kevin Durant," *The Film Room Project*.

122 **"there we were, stuck":** Ulrik Juul Christensen, executive chairman of Area9 and senior fellow at McGraw-Hill Education, in an interview with the author, July 15, 2015.

123 **first studied in chess players:** Herbert A. Simon and William G. Chase, "Skill in Chess: Experiments with Chess-Playing Tasks and Computer Simulation of Skilled Performance Throw Light on Some Human Perceptual and Memory Processes," *American Scientist* 61 (1973): 394–403. See also: Ericsson et al., "The Role of Deliberate Practice."

123 **"and corrected them":** *The Autobiography of Benjamin Franklin: With an Introduction and Notes* (New York: MacMillan Company, 1921), 14.

124 **"no gains without pains":** Benjamin Franklin, "The Way to Wealth," in *Memoirs of Benjamin Franklin* (New York: Harper & Brothers, 1839), 7.

124 **"a small number of practices":** Peter F. Drucker, *The Effective Executive: The Definitive Guide to Getting the Right Things Done* (New York: HarperCollins, 2006), ix.

124 **"for years on end":** Atul Gawande, "The Learning Curve: Like Everyone Else, Surgeons Need Practice. That's Where You Come In," *New Yorker*, January 28, 2002.

124 **"that's what magic is to me":** David Blaine, "How I Held My Breath for 17 Minutes," TED video, filmed October 2009, http://www.ted.com/talks/david _blaine_how_i_held_my_breath_for_17_min. See also Roy F. Baumeister and John Tierney, *Willpower: Rediscovering the Greatest Human Strenth* (New York: Penguin, 2011).

125 **pored through published books:** Barrie Trinkle, Carolyn Andrews, and Paige Kimble, *How to Spell Like a Champ: Roots, Lists, Rules, Games, Tricks, and Bee-Winning Tips from the Pros* (New York: Workman Publishing Company, 2006)

125 **"studying as hard as I can":** James Maguire, *American Bee: The National Spelling Bee and the Culture of Word Nerds* (Emmaus, PA: Rodale, 2006), 360.

126 *deliberate* **practice predicted:** Angela Duckworth et al., "Deliberate Practice Spells Success: Why Grittier Competitors Triumph at the National Spelling Bee," *Social Psychological and Personality Science* 2 (2011): 174–81. Getting quizzed also predicted doing well in competition, but when comparing kids who got quizzed the same amount of time to each other, I found that those who did more deliberate practice did better. In contrast, when compar-

ing kids who did the same amount of deliberate practice to each other, I found that more quizzing produced no advantage.

126 **benefits to being quizzed:** Henry L. Roediger and Jeffrey D. Karpicke, "The Power of Testing Memory: Basic Research and Implications for Educational Practice," *Perspectives on Psychological Science* 1 (2006): 181–210.

127 **ten hours per week:** Duckworth et al., "Spells Success," 177.

127 **come to a different conclusion:** On the effortfulness of learning, see also Elizabeth L. Bjork and Robert Bjork, "Making Things Hard on Yourself, but in a Good Way: Creating Desirable Difficulties to Enhance Learning," in *Psychology and the Real World: Essays Illustrating Fundamental Contributions to Society,* ed. Morton A. Gernsbacher et al. (New York: Worth Publishers, 2011), 56–64. See also Sidney K. D'Mello and Arthur C. Graesser, "Confusion" in *International Handbook of Emotions in Education,* ed. Reinhard Pekrun and Lisa Linnenbrink-Garcia (New York: Routledge, 2014), 289–310.

127 **experienced as supremely effortful:** Ericsson et al., "The Role of Deliberate Practice."

127 **"daily small deaths":** Graham, "I Am a Dancer."

128 **"you're concentrating and you're exhausted":** Judd Apatow, interviewed by Charlie Rose, *Charlie Rose,* July 31, 2009, republished in Apatow, *Sick in the Head: Conversations About Life and Comedy* (New York: Random House, 2015), 26.

128 **to keep doing it:** K. Anders Ericsson, "How Experts Attain and Maintain Superior Performance: Implications for the Enhancement of Skilled Performance in Older Individuals," *Journal of Aging and Physical Activity* 8 (2000): 366–72.

128 **"a feeling of spontaneity":** Karen Stansberry Beard, "Theoretically Speaking: An Interview with Mihaly Csikszentmihalyi on Flow Theory Development and Its Usefulness in Addressing Contemporary Challenges in Education," *Educational Psychology Review* 27 (2015): 358. Csikszentmihalyi has emphasized that what matters to the quality of our momentary experience is the *subjective* level of challenge and the *subjective* level of skill.

129 **"just flows out by itself":** Mihaly Csikszentmihalyi, "Play and Intrinsic Rewards," *Journal of Humanistic Psychology* 15 (1975): 50.

129 **"automatically without thinking":** Mihaly Csikszentmihalyi, "Flow: The Joy of Reading," in *Applications of Flow in Human Development: The Collected Works of Mihaly Csikszentmihalyi* (Dordrecht, Netherlands: Springer, 2014), 233.

129 **"incompatible with deliberate practice":** K. Anders Ericsson and Paul Ward, "Capturing the Naturally Occurring Superior Performance of Experts in the Laboratory," *Current Directions in Psychological Science* 16 (2007): 349.

129 **"by no means self-evident":** Csikszentmihalyi, *Applications of Flow,* xx.

129 **"but its fruits are sweet":** Ibid.

129 **"achieve what you desire":** Ibid.

130 **"passion and world-class performance"**: Mihaly Csikszentmihalyi and K. Anders Ericsson, "Passion and World-Class Performance" (presentation, University of Pennsylvania, Philadelphia, PA, August 2006).

131 **flow and grit:** In this study, flow was measured using a previously validated six-item questionnaire whose possible scores ranged from a minimum of 1 and a maximum of 5. Example item: "Whether at work or play, I am usually 'in a zone' and not conscious of myself." See Katherine R. Von Culin, Eli Tsukayama, and Angela L. Duckworth, "Unpacking Grit: Motivational Correlates of Perseverance and Passion for Long-term Goals," *Journal of Positive Psychology* 9 (2014): 1–7.

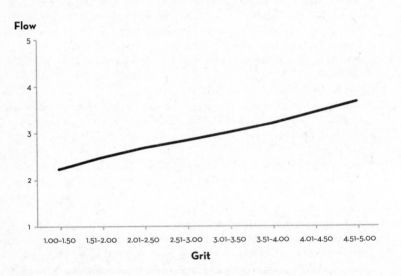

132 **"I swam around the world"**: Gaines, interview.

133 **"It's about hard work"**: Mads Rasmussen, Danish rower and Olympic gold medalist, in an interview with the author, June 28, 2015.

133 **"testament to the work"**: Rod Gilmour, "Ledecky Betters Own 1500m Freestyle World Record," Reuters, August 3, 2015, http://in.reuters.com /article/2015/08/03/swimming-world-1500m-idINKCN0Q813Y20150803.

133 **"shows off in the meet"**: Ashley Branca, "Katie Ledecky: 'I've Just Always Felt Comfortable in the Water from Day One,'" *Guardian*, March 10, 2015.

136 **said they enjoyed it more:** Duckworth et al., "Spells Success."

136 **"she has that attitude"**: Bruce Gemmell, USA National Team swimming coach, in an interview with the author, August 24, 2015.

137 **"and getting it done"**: Kerry Close, 2006 Scripps National Spelling Bee champion, in an interview with the author, August 10, 2015.

137 **basic requirements of deliberate practice:** K. Anders Ericsson, "The Influence of Experience and Deliberate Practice on the Development of Superior Expert Performance," in *Cambridge Handbook of Expertise and Expert Performance* ed. K. Anders Ericsson et al. (Cambridge, UK: Cambridge University Press), 685–706. For a fascinating study of the importance of practicing "strategically," see Robert Duke, Amy Simmons, and Carla Davis Cash, "It's Not How Much; It's How: Characteristics of Practice Behavior and Retention of Performance Skills," *Journal of Research in Music Education* 56 (2009): 310 21.

138 **it's not hours of brute-force:** Rasmussen, interview.

138 **until he was twenty-two:** Noa Kageyama, performance psychologist at The Julliard School, in an interview with the author, September 21, 2015.

138 **challenging, effortful practice:** Lauren Eskreis-Winkler et al., "Using Wise Interventions to Motivate Deliberate Practice," *Journal of Personality and Social Psychology* (in press).

139 **You just do:** Judith A. Ouellette and Wendy Wood, "Habit and Intention in Everyday Life: The Multiple Processes by Which Past Behavior Predicts Future Behavior," *Psychological Bulletin* 124 (1998): 54–74. See also, Charles Duhigg, *The Power of Habit: Why We Do What We Do in Life and Business* (New York: Random House, 2012).

140 **rose at dawn:** Mason Currey, *Daily Rituals: How Artists Work* (New York: Alfred A. Knopf, 2013), 217–18.

140 **a "tiny mean" hotel room:** Ibid., 122.

140 **"beginning of every bit of work":** William James, "The Laws of Habits," *The Popular Science Monthly* 30 (1887): 447.

140 **"with your nose":** Robert Compton, "Joyce Carol Oates Keeps Punching," *Dallas Morning News*, November 17, 1987.

141 **"feel great while you're doing it":** Terry Laughlin, head coach and chief executive optimist (not kidding, that's his real title) of Total Immersion Swimming, in an interview with the author, July 24, 2015.

141 **toddlers don't mind at all:** Elena Bodrova and Deborah Leong, creators of the Tools of the Mind curriculum for early childhood education, in an interview with the author, July 15, 2015. See also Adele Diamond and Kathleen Lee, "Interventions Shown to Aid Executive Function Development in Children 4 to 12 Years Old," *Science* 333 (2011): 959–64. Clancy Blair and C. Cybele Raver, "Closing the Achievement Gap Through Modification of Neurocognitive and Neuroendocrine Function," *PLoS ONE* 9 (2014): 1–13.

141 **"give their best effort":** Gemmell, interview.

CHAPTER 8: PURPOSE

143 **"have a lemonade stand":** Alex's Lemonade Stand, http://www.alexslemon ade.org.

144 **this three-phase progression:** Bloom, *Developing Talent*.

NOTES

144 **"the larger purpose and meaning":** Bloom, *Developing Talent*, 527.

145 **"new perspective on life":** Golden, interview.

145 **Election Day never comes:** Melissa Dribben, "Gracing the City Jane Golden Has Made Mural Arts the Nation's Top Public Arts Program," *Philadelphia Inquirer*, July 27, 2008, http://articles.philly.com/2008-07-27/news/25245217_1_jane-seymour-golden-globes-philadelphia-s-mural-arts-program.

145 **"so I find ways to get energized":** Ibid.

145 **"it's a moral imperative":** Golden, interview.

146 **"beautiful bottle of wine":** Antonio Galloni, wine critic and founder of *Vinous*, in an interview with the author, July 24, 2015

146 **"a million lightbulbs":** "Liv-Ex Interview with Antonio Galloni, Part One," *Liv-Ex Blog*, December 13, 2013, www.blog.liv-ex.com/2013/12/liv-ex-interview-with-antonio-galloni-part-one.html.

146 **"sense of purpose":** Galloni, interview.

146 **purpose, pleasure, and age:** These data are originally reported in Von Culin, Tsukayama, and Duckworth, "Unpacking Grit."

146 **well-being of others:** Different scholars use the word *purpose* in slightly different ways. Often it is emphasized that a goal, to be purposeful, has to be meaningful to the self and, at the same time, beneficial to others. Here I emphasize the beyond-the-self aspect of purpose because we already covered the more self-oriented motivation of interest in the last chapter.

146 **the eudaimonic life:** Aristotle, *The Nicomachean Ethics*, trans. David Ross (Oxford, UK: Oxford University Press, 2009), 5.

146 **"pleasure principle":** Sigmund Freud, "Formulations Regarding the Two Principles in Mental Functioning," in *The Standard Edition of the Complete Psychological Works of Sigmund Freud*, vol. 12, trans. James Strachey and Anna Freud (London: Hogarth Press, 1958), 218–26.

147 **evolved to seek meaning:** See John T. Cacioppo and William Patrick, *Loneliness: Human Nature and the Need for Social Connection* (New York: W.W. Norton & Company, 2008). See also Roy F. Baumeister and Mark R. Leary, "The Need to Belong: Desire for Interpersonal Attachments as a Fundamental Human Motivation," *Psychological Bulletin* 117 (1995): 497–529. Finally, see Edward L. Deci with Richard Flaste, *Why We Do What We Do: Understanding Self-Motivation* (New York: Penguin, 1995). Note that recent primate studies show that longevity and reproductive success depend on the ability to form strong, enduring social bonds with others. The desire to connect is as basic a human—even mammalian—need as the need for pleasure. See Robert M. Seyfarth and Dorothy L. Cheney, "The Evolutionary Origins of Friendship," *Annual Review of Psychology* 63 (2012): 153–77.

147 **than we care about pleasure:** Richard M. Ryan and Edward L. Deci, "On Happiness and Human Potential: A Review of Research on Hedonic and Eudaimonic Well-Being," *Annual Review of Psychology* 52 (2001): 141–66.

149 **which of the three bricklayers:** Amy Wrzesniewski, Clark McCauley, Paul Rozin, and Barry Schwartz, "Jobs, Careers, and Callings: People's Relations to Their Work," *Journal of Research in Personality* 31 (1997): 25.

150 **their occupations a calling:** We collected this data in 2015.

150 **than those with a job:** Wrzesniewski et al., "Jobs, Careers, and Callings," 25.

150 **survey of 982 zookeepers:** J. Stuart Bunderson and Jeffery A. Thompson, "The Call of the Wild: Zookeepers, Callings, and the Double-Edged Sword of Deeply Meaningful Work," *Administrative Science Quarterly* 54 (2009): 32–57.

150 **"Monday through Friday sort of dying":** Studs Terkel, *Working: People Talk About What They Do All Day and How They Feel About What They Do* (New York: Pantheon Books, 1974), xi. Note that the names of the workers in Terkel's book were pseudonyms.

151 **"I don't think I have a calling":** Ibid., 521–24.

151 **"find a savor in their daily job":** Ibid., xi.

151 **"It's meaningful to society":** Ibid., 103–6.

152 **when she studied secretaries:** Wrzesniewski et al., "Jobs, Careers, and Callings."

153 **"waiting to be discovered":** Amy Wrzesniewski, professor of organizational behavior at Yale School of Management, in an interview with the author, January 27, 2015.

153 **all the way to Chicago:** Metropolitan Transit Authority, "Facts and Figures," accessed March 10, 2015, http://web.mta.info/nyct/facts/ffsubway.htm.

154 **"and I got hired":** Joe Leader, senior vice president at New York City Transit, in an interview with the author, February 26, 2015.

155 **"experience I've ever had":** Michael Baime, clinical associate professor of medicine at the University of Pennsylvania and director of the Penn Program for Mindfulness, in an interview with the author, January 21, 2015.

158 **having fun at the same time:** The next year, we doubled in size and, to better support our students, developed an after-school enrichment program. The following year, the program won the Better Government Award for the state of Massachusetts. Around the same time, professors at the Harvard Kennedy School of Government wrote up the story of Summerbridge Cambridge as a case study in social entrepreneurship.

158 **hundreds of students every year:** For more information on Breakthrough Greater Boston, see www.breakthroughgreaterboston.org.

159 **"you can have both":** Adam Grant, Class of 1965 Wharton Professor of Management, in an interview with the author, July 15, 2015.

160 **prosocial interests in mind do better:** Adam Grant, *Give and Take: Why Helping Others Drives Our Success* (New York: Penguin, 2014).

160 **interest in the work itself:** Adam Grant, "Does Intrinsic Motivation Fuel the Prosocial Fire? Motivational Synergy in Predicting Persistence, Performance, and Productivity," *Journal of Applied Psychology* 93 (2008): 48–58.

160 **raised more money:** Ibid.

160 **about a hundred adolescents:** David S. Yeager and Matthew J. Bundick, "The Role of Purposeful Work Goals in Promoting Meaning in Life and in Schoolwork During Adolescence," *Journal of Adolescent Research* 24 (2009): 423–52. Relatedly, it's been shown that affirming values can boost perfor- ·mance for other reasons, particularly by maintaining a sense of personal ade- quacy. Geoffrey L. Cohen and David K. Sherman, "The Psychology of Change: Self-Affirmation and Social Psychological Intervention," *Annual Review of Psy- chology* 65 (2014): 333–71.

161 **"didn't give in to obstacles":** Aurora and Franco Fonte, wife and husband founders and directors of Assetlink, in an interview with the author, March 13, 2015.

162 **"something you're interested in":** Bill Damon, professor of psychology at Stanford Graduate School of Education, in an interview with the author, July 20, 2015.

163 **personal loss or adversity:** For example, detectives who have themselves been the victim of a crime are grittier and, in turn, more engaged in their work. See Lauren Eskreis-Winkler, Elizabeth P. Shulman, and Angela L. Duckworth, "Survivor Mission: Do Those Who Survive Have a Drive to Thrive at Work?" *Journal of Positive Psychology* 9 (2014): 209–18.

163 **"became family to her":** Kat Cole, president of Cinnabon, in an interview with the author, February 1, 2015.

164 **exceeded one billion dollars:** Charlotte Alter, "How to Run a Billion Dollar Brand Before You're 35," *Time*, December 2, 2014.

165 **"My passion is to help people":** Jo Barsh, in an interview with the author, July 31, 2015.

165 **"like they are that person":** Kat Cole, "See What's Possible, and Help Oth- ers Do the Same," from Kat Cole's blog, *The Difference*, August 7, 2013, http:// www.katcole.net/2013/08/see-whats-possible-and-help-others-do.html.

166 **"be a better place?":** David S. Yeager et al., "Boring but Important: A Self- Transcendent Purpose for Learning Fosters Academic Self-Regulation," *Atti- tudes and Social Cognition* 107 (2014): 559–80.

166 **calls this idea *job crafting*:** Amy Wrzesniewski and Jane E. Dutton, "Craft- ing a Job: Revisioning Employees as Active Crafters of Their Work," *Academy of Management Review* 26 (2001): 179–201. See also www.jobcrafting.org and Grant, *Give and Take*, 262–63. This section also reflects personal correspon- dence between the author and Amy Wrzesniewski, professor of organizational behavior at Yale School of Management, October 20, 2015.

166 **"be a better person":** Interested readers can find a more complete list of questions that Bill Damon uses in his book, *The Path to Purpose: How Young People Find Their Calling in Life* (New York: Free Press, 2008), 183–86.

CHAPTER 9: HOPE

169 **getting up again:** For a more expansive discussion of how hope can be conceptualized, see Kevin L. Rand, Allison D. Martin, and Amanda M. Shea, "Hope, but Not Optimism, Predicts Academic Performance of Law Students Beyond Previous Academic Achievement," *Journal of Research in Personality* 45 (2011): 683–86. Also see Shane J. Lopez, *Making Hope Happen: Create the Future You Want for Yourself and Others* (New York: Atria Books, 2013).

169 *major* **in—neurobiology:** At Harvard until 2006, you actually declared your "concentration" (which is Harvard's terminology for "major"), in the spring of your freshman year and at the same time mapped out every class you intended to take. My official concentration was the neurobiology track within biology, since neurobiology as a separate concentration was not created until years later.

172 **the punishments to stop:** Steven F. Maier and Martin E. Seligman, "Learned Helplessness: Theory and Evidence," *Journal of Experimental Psychology* 105 (1976): 3–46. The seminal studies on learned helplessness actually had a triadic design, meaning that there was a third condition: dogs who received no shock at all. In general, these dogs behaved similarly to those who were subjected to stress *with* control. Some of the material in this chapter is from an interview between Seligman and the author, July 20, 2015. See also Martin E. P. Seligman, *Learned Optimism: How to Change Your Mind and Your Life* (New York: Pocket Books, 1990).

173 **practical antidotes for depression:** For more information on Aaron Beck, see www.beckinstitute.org.

174 **distinguish optimists from pessimists:** Christopher Peterson et al., "The Attributional Style Questionnaire," *Cognitive Therapy and Research* 6 (1982): 287–300. See also Lyn Y. Abramson, Gerald I. Metalsky, and Lauren B. Alloy, "Hopelessness Depression: A Theory-Based Subtype of Depression," *Psychological Review* 96 (1989): 358–72.

174 **suffer from depression and anxiety:** Peter Schulman, Camilo Castellon, and Martin E. P. Seligman, "Assessing Explanatory Style: The Content Analysis of Verbatim Explanations and the Attributional Style Questionnaire," *Behavioural Research and Therapy* 27 (1989): 505–9.

174 **drop out of school:** Leslie P. Kamen and Martin E. P. Seligman, "Explanatory Style Predicts College Grade Point Average" (unpublished manuscript, 1985). Christopher Peterson and Lisa C. Barrett, "Explanatory Style and Academic Performance Among University Freshman," *Journal of Personality and Social Psychology* 53 (1987): 603–7.

174 **stay healthier:** Toshihiko Maruto, Robert C. Colligan, Michael Malinchoc, and Kenneth P. Offord, "Optimists vs. Pessimists: Survival Rate Among Medical Patients Over a 30-Year Period," *Mayo Clinic Proceedings* 75 (2000): 140–43. Christopher Peterson, Martin E. P. Seligman, "Pessimistic Explanatory

Style Is a Risk Factor for Physical Illness: A Thirty-Five-Year Longitudinal Study," *Journal of Personality and Social Psychology* 55 (1988): 23–27.

174 **satisfied with their marriages:** Karen J. Horneffer and Frank D. Fincham, "Construct of Attributional Style in Depression and Marital Distress," *Journal of Family Psychology* 9 (1995): 186–95. See also, Horneffer and Fincham, "Attributional Models of Depression and Distress," *Personality and Social Psychology Bulletin* 22 (1996): 678–89.

174 **sell about 25 percent more insurance:** On optimism and sales, see Martin E. P. Seligman and Peter Schulman, "Explanatory Style as a Predictor of Productivity and Quitting Among Life Insurance Sales Agents," *Journal of Personality and Social Psychology* 50 (1986): 832–38. Shulman, "Explanatory Style." See also Peter Schulman, "Applying Learned Optimism to Increase Sales Productivity," *Journal of Personal Selling & Sales Management* 19 (1999): 31–37.

175 **swim in his or her best event:** Martin E. P. Seligman, "Explanatory Style as a Mechanism of Disappointing Athletic Performance," *Psychological Science* 1 (1990): 143–46.

175 **"I will just carry on":** Lacey, interview.

175 **could be the target of therapy:** Aaron T. Beck, A. John Rush, Brian F. Shaw, and Gary Emery, *Cognitive Therapy of Depression* (New York: Guilford Press, 1979). Also note that, in the same era, Albert Ellis developed a similar approach. So Beck and Ellis are jointly recognized as pioneers in what is now commonly referred to as cognitive behavioral therapy.

176 **longer-lasting in its effects:** Robert J. DeRubeis et al., "Cognitive Therapy vs Medications in the Treatment of Moderate to Severe Depression," *Archives of General Psychiatry* 62 (2005): 409–16. Steven D. Hollon et al., "Prevention of Relapse Following Cognitive Therapy vs Medications in Moderate to Severe Depression," *Archives of General Psychiatry* 62 (2005): 417–22. Some patients struggle with the aspect of CBT that involves trying to talk themselves out of their negative self-talk. These patients say things like: "In my head, I know it's not fair to call myself a loser. I'm labeling myself, I'm engaging in all-or-nothing thinking. But in my heart, part of me still feels like a loser—like I'll never be good enough." A new form of CBT, acceptance and commitment therapy (ACT), addresses these concerns. In ACT, the goal is simply to notice any negative self-talk and accept that it exists, while not letting it control your actions.

176 **"Relentless pursuit":** Information on Teach For America's mission and history can be found at www.teachforamerica.org.

177 **optimistic teachers were grittier:** Claire Robertson-Kraft and Angela L. Duckworth, "True Grit: Perseverance and Passion for Long-term Goals Predicts Effectiveness and Retention Among Novice Teachers," *Teachers College Record (1970)* 116 (2014): 1–24.

178 **one of Carol's first studies:** Carol S. Dweck, "The Role of Expectations and Attributions in the Alleviation of Learned Helplessness," *Journal of Personality and Social Psychology* 31 (1975): 674–85.

179 **assess a person's theory of intelligence:** This measure was developed by Carol Dweck, Sheri Levy, Valanne MacGyvers, C.Y. Chiu, and Ying-yi Hong. For interested readers, I highly recommend Carol Dweck, *Mindset: The New Psychology of Success* (New York: Ballantine Books, 2008).

181 **positive social relationships:** See Carol S. Dweck, "Mindsets and Human Nature: Promoting Change in the Middle East, the Schoolyard, the Racial Divide, and Willpower," *American Psychologist* (2012): 614–22.

181 **persist through college:** Brian Galla et al., "Intellective, Motivational, and Self-Regulatory Determinants of High School Grades, SAT Scores, and College Persistence" (manuscript under review, 2015).

181 **KIPP Schools:** For more information on KIPP, see www.kipp.org.

182 **Promotes Growth Mindset and Grit:** This thesaurus was originally developed by psychologist David Yeager, whom I thank for this age-general revision. On generic statements, see Daeun Park et al., "How Do Generic Statements Impact Performance? Evidence for Entity Beliefs," *Developmental Science* (in press, 2015). And finally, on the importance of a "genuine" growth mindset, see Carol S. Dweck, "Carol Dweck Revisits the 'Growth Mindset'" *Education Week*, September 22, 2015.

183 **"never failed to imitate them":** James Baldwin, *Nobody Knows My Name* (New York: Vintage Books, 1993), 61–62.

183 **inadvertently inculcated a fixed mindset:** Daeun Park et al., "Young Children's Motivational Frameworks and Math Achievement: Relation to Teacher-Reported Instructional Practices, but Not Teacher Theory of Intelligence," *Journal of Educational Psychology* (in press, 2015).

183 **parents react to mistakes:** Kyla Haimovitz and Carol S. Dweck, "What Predicts Children's Fixed and Growth Mindsets? Not Their Parent's Views of Intelligence But Their Parents' Views of Failure" (manuscript under review, 2015).

183 **apply in a corporate setting:** Harvard Business Review Staff, "How Companies Can Profit from a 'Growth Mindset'" *Harvard Business Review*, November 2014.

185 **"tracked senior leaders":** Bill McNabb, CEO of Vanguard, in an interview with the author, August 20, 2015.

187 **"makes me stronger":** Friedrich Nietzsche, *The Anti-Christ, Ecce Homo, Twilight of the Idols: and Other Writings*, ed. Aaron Ridley, trans. Judith Norman (Cambridge, UK: Cambridge University Press, 2005), 157.

187 **croon the same words:** Kanye West, "Stronger," *Graduation*, 2007. Kelly Clarkson sings a popularized version of the phrase, "What doesn't kill you makes you stronger," in "Stronger (What Doesn't Kill You)," *Stronger*, 2011.

187 **more confident:** In fact, the idea that suffering can make us more capable is timeless. Every major religious tradition includes a parable where suffering is necessary for enlightenment. The Latin root of the word *passion* is *pati*, which means "to suffer." *OED* Online, Oxford University Press, September 2015.

187 **"tenacity in pursuit":** For more information on Outward Bound, see www
.outwardbound.org.

187 **benefits tend to increase:** John A. Hattie, Herbert W. Marsh, James T.
Neill, and Garry E. Richards, "Adventure Education and Outward Bound:
Out-of-Class Experiences That Make a Lasting Difference," *Review of Educa-tional Psychology* 67 (1997): 43–87.

187 **were much more vulnerable:** Maier and Seligman, "Learned Helplessness."

187 **Steve Maier and his students:** Kenneth H. Kubala et al., "Short- and Long-
Term Consequences of Stressor Controllability in Adolescent Rats," *Behav-ioural Brain Research* 234 (2012): 278–84.

189 **"respond to stress":** Steven F. Maier, professor of psychology and director of
the Center for Neuroscience at the University of Colorado at Boulder, in an
interview with the author, April 2, 2015.

190 **Milton Hershey School:** Not coincidentally, Milton Hershey himself exemplified grit, having started several unsuccessful companies before developing,
through trial and error, a formula for milk chocolate that would soon make
his company the largest confectionary in the world. He and his wife could
not have children and therefore created the Hershey School, which owns a
controlling interest in Hershey stock. For more information on the Milton
Hershey School and its founder, visit www.mhskids.org.

191 **always learning and growing:** If you want to hear Kayvon's music, visit
www.kayvonmusic.com.

192 **increased their IQ scores:** Sue Ramsden et al., "Verbal and Non-Verbal
Intelligence Changes in the Teenage Brain," *Nature* 479 (2011): 113–16.

193 **ability to grow myelin:** Carol S. Dweck, "The Secret to Raising Smart
Kids," *Scientific American* 23 (2015). Lisa S. Blackwell, Kali H. Trzesniewski,
and Carol S. Dweck, "Implicit Theories of Intelligence Predict Achievement
Across an Adolescent Transition: A Longitudinal Study and in Intervention,"
Child Development 78 (2007): 246–63. Joshua Aronson, Carrie B. Fried and
Catherine Good, "Reducing the Effects of Stereotype Threat on African
American College Students by Shaping Theories of Intelligence," *Journal of
Experimental Psychology* 38 (2002): 113–25. David Paunesku et al., "Mind-
Set Interventions Are a Scalable Treatment for Academic Underachieve-
ment," *Psychological Science* (2015): 1–10. Allyson P. Mackey, Kirstie J.
Whitaker, and Silvia A. Bunge, "Experience-Dependent Plasticity in White
Matter Microstructure: Reasoning Training Alters Structural Connectiv-
ity," *Frontiers in Neuroanatomy* 6 (2012): 1–9. Robert J. Zatorre, R. Douglas
Fields, and Heidi Johansen-Berg, "Plasticity in Gray and White: Neuroimag-
ing Changes in Brain Structure During Learning," *Nature Neuroscience* 15
(2012): 528–36.

193 **"resilience training":** The Penn Resilience Program was developed by Jane
Gillham, Karen Reivich, and Lisa Jaycox. This school-based program teaches

cognitive-behavioral and social-emotional skills to students using role plays, games, and interactive activities. See J. E. Gillham, K. J. Reivich, L.H. Jaycox, and M. E. P. Seligman, "Preventing Depressive Symptoms in Schoolchildren: Two Year Follow-up," *Psychological Science* 6 (1995): 343–51. Martin E. P. Seligman, Peter Schulman, Robert J. DeRubeis, and Steven D. Hollon, "The Prevention of Depression and Anxiety," *Prevention and Treatment* 2 (1999). Note that a more recent meta-analytic review confirmed benefits of the program over twelve months post-intervention in comparison to no treatment, but not active treatment, control conditions: Steven M. Brunwasser, Jane E. Gillham, and Eric S. Kim, "A Meta-Analytic Review of the Penn Resiliency Program's Effect on Depressive Symptoms," *Journal of Consulting and Clinical Psychology* 77 (2009): 1042–54.

193 **cognitive behavioral therapy:** For more information on cognitive therapy, see www.beckinstitute.org.

194 **"I get back on my feet":** Rhonda Hughes, Helen Herrmann Professor of Mathematics Emeritus at Bryn Mawr College and cofounder of the EDGE Program, in conversation with the author, May 25, 2013.

194 **"Don't give up!":** Sylvia Bozeman, professor emeritus of mathematics at Spelman College, in correspondence with the author, October 14, 2015. Sylvia has made similar remarks in Edna Francisco, "Changing the Culture of Math," *Science*, September 16, 2005. I should also note that sometimes there's nobody available to tell you to keep going. Psychologist Kristin Neff suggests thinking about what you would say to a friend who was struggling with a similar situation, and then to practice saying similar compassionate, understanding things to yourself.

CHAPTER 10: PARENTING FOR GRIT

200 **"can quite overwhelm him":** John B. Watson, *Psychological Care of Infant and Child* (London: Unwin Brothers, 1928), 14.

200 **"give them a pat on the head":** Ibid., 73.

202 **"my parents were my foundation":** Don Amore, "Redemption for a Pure Passer," *Hartford Courant*, January 29, 1995.

202 **"I'd like to come home":** *Grit: The True Story of Steve Young*, directed by Kevin Doman (Cedar Fort, KSL Television, and HomeSports, 2014), DVD.

202 **"You're not coming back here":** Ibid.

203 **"I threw over 10,000 spirals":** Steve Young with Jeff Benedict, "Ten Thousand Spirals," chapter in forthcoming book, 2015, http://www.jeffbenedict.com/index.php/blog/389-ten-thousand-spirals.

203 **"I couldn't get a hit":** Doman, *Grit: The True Story*.

203 **"you cannot quit":** Christopher W. Hunt, "Forever Young, Part II: Resolve in the Face of Failure," *Greenwich Time*, February 2, 2013.

203 **"and I'd be hitting them":** Doman, *Grit: The True Story*.

203 **"Endure to the end, Steve":** The Pro Football Hall of Fame, "Steve Young's Enshrinement Speech Transcript," August 7, 2005.

204 **"The name really fits him":** Doman, *Grit: The True Story.*

204 **ten thousand sit-ups in a row:** Kevin Doman, "Grit: The True Story of Steve Young," *Deseret News*, April 4, 2014.

204 **"Our Steve is a great kid!":** Sherry and Grit Young, parents of Steve Young, in an interview with the author, August 23, 2015.

206 **"Everything is contextual":** Steve Young, former quarterback of the San Francisco 49ers, in an interview with the author, August 18, 2015.

207 **funniest comics in Britain:** *Observer*, "The A-Z of Laughter (Part Two)," *Guardian*, December 7, 2003.

208 **"came from my family":** Francesca Martinez, comedian, in an interview with the author, August 4, 2015.

208 **"then you can reassess":** Francesca Martinez, *What the **** Is Normal?!* (London: Virgin Books, 2014), 185.

208 **"leave formal education":** Martinez, interview. In her book, Francesca gives a similar account.

209 **"the throwing of objects":** Martinez, *What the **** Is Normal?!*, 48.

211 **"authoritative parenting":** Wendy S. Grolnick and Richard M. Ryan, "Parent Styles Associated with Children's Self-Regulation and Competence in School," *Journal of Educational Psychology* 81 (1989): 143–54. Earl S. Schaefer, "A Configurational Analysis of Children's Reports of Parent Behavior," *Journal of Consulting Psychology* 29 (1965): 552–57. Diana Baumrind, "Authoritative Parenting Revisited: History and Current Status," in *Authoritative Parenting: Synthesizing Nurturance and Discipline for Optimal Child Development*, ed. Robert E. Larzelere, Amanda Sheffield Morris, and Amanda W. Harrist (Washington, D.C.: American Psychological Association, 2013), 11–34.

212 **a moratorium on further research:** Laurence Steinberg, "Presidential Address: We Know Some Things: Parent-Adolescent Relationships in Retrospect and Prospect," *Journal of Research on Adolescence* 11 (2001): 1–19.

213 **warm, respectful, and demanding parents:** Laurence Steinberg, Nina S. Mounts, Susie D. Lamborn, and Sanford M. Dornbusch, "Authoritative Parenting and Adolescent Adjustment Across Varied Ecological Niches," *Journal of Research on Adolescence* 1 (1991): 19–36.

213 **across a decade or more:** Koen Luyckx et al., "Parenting and Trajectories of Children's Maladaptive Behaviors: A 12-year Prospective Community Study," *Journal of Clinical Child & Adolescent Psychology* 40 (2011): 468–78.

213 **messages their children receive:** Earl S. Schaefer, "Children's Reports of Parental Behavior: An Inventory," *Child Development* 36 (1965): 413–24. Nancy Darling and Laurence Steinberg, "Parenting Style as Context: An Integrative Model," *Psychological Bulletin* 113 (1993): 487–96.

213 **parenting assessment:** Adapted with permission from Nancy Darling and Teru Toyokawa, "Construction and Validation of the Parenting Style Inventory II (PSI-II)," (unpublished manuscript, 1997).

215 **as virtual "carbon copies":** Albert Bandura, Dorothea Ross, and Sheila Ross, "Imitation of Film-Mediated Aggressive Models," *Journal of Abnormal and Social Psychology* 66 (1963): 3–11.

216 **"work toward distant goals":** Bloom, *Developing Talent*, 510.

216 **"parents' own interests":** Ronald S. Brandt, "On Talent Development: A Conversation with Benjamin Bloom," *Educational Leadership* 43 (1985): 34.

217 **the next generation:** Center for Promise, *Don't Quit on Me: What Young People Who Left School Say About the Power of Relationships* (Washington, D.C.: America's Promise Alliance, 2015), www.gradnation.org/report/dont -quit-me.

217 **"fifty-something, grizzled rocker":** Tobi Lütke, "The Apprentice Programmer," Tobi Lütke's blog, March 3, 2013, http://tobi.lutke.com/blogs/news /11280301-the-apprentice-programmer.

218 **emerging research on teaching:** Kathryn R. Wentzel, "Are Effective Teachers Like Good Parents? Teaching Styles and Student Adjustment in Early Adolescence," *Child Development* 73 (2002): 287–301. Douglas A. Bernstein, "Parenting and Teaching: What's the Connection in Our Classrooms?" *Psychology Teacher Network*, September 2013, http://www.apa.org/ed/precollege /ptn/2013/09/parenting-teaching.aspx.

218 **1,892 different classrooms:** Ronald F. Ferguson and Charlotte Danielson, "How Framework for Teaching and Tripod 7Cs Evidence Distinguish Key Components of Effective Teaching," in *Designing Teacher Evaluation Systems: New Guidance from the Measures of Effective Teaching Project*, ed. Thomas J. Kane, Kerri A. Kerr, and Robert C. Pianta (San Francisco: Jossey-Bass, 2014), 98–133.

218 **David Yeager and Geoff Cohen:** David Scott Yeager et al., "Breaking the Cycle of Mistrust: Wise Interventions to Provide Critical Feedback Across the Racial Divide," *Journal of Experimental Psychology* 143 (2013): 804–24. For the research on highly effective tutors that originally inspired this intervention, see Mark R. Lepper and Maria Woolverton, "The Wisdom of Practice: Lessons Learned from the Study of Highly Effective Tutors," in *Improving Academic Achievement: Impact of Psychological Factors on Education*, ed. Joshua Aronson (New York: Academic Press, 2002), 135–58.

218 **"have very high expectations":** Yeager et al., "Breaking the Cycle"

220 **Cody Coleman:** Cody Coleman, PhD candidate in computer science at Stanford University, in conversation with the author, May 24, 2013.

221 **Chantel Smith:** Chantel Smith, mathematics teacher at Winslow Township High School, in conversation with the author, March 15, 2015.

222 **"Stay positive":** Cody Coleman, interview by Stephanie Renée, 900AM-WURD, October 31, 2014.

CHAPTER 11: THE PLAYING FIELDS OF GRIT

225 *both* **challenged and having fun:** Reed W. Larson and Douglas Kleiber, "Daily Experience of Adolescents," in *Handbook of Clinical Research and Practice with Adolescents*, ed. Patrick H. Tolan and Bertram J. Cohler (Oxford, UK: John Wiley & Sons, 1993), 125–45. Reed W. Larson, "Positive Development in a Disorderly World," *Journal of Research on Adolescence* 21 (2011): 317–34. Data are originally from Reed W. Larson, Giovanni Moneta, Maryse H. Richards, and Suzanne Wilson, "Continuity, Stability, and Change in Daily Emotional Experience Across Adolescence," *Child Development* 73 (2002): 1151–65.

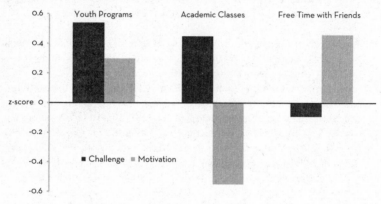

Adapted with permission from Young et al. poster

See also David J. Shernoff, Mihaly Csikszentmihalyi, Barbara Schneider, and Elisa Steele Shernoff, "Student Engagement in High School Classrooms from the Perspective of Flow Theory," *School Psychology Quarterly* 18 (2003): 158–76. David J. Shernoff and Deborah Lowe Vandell, "Engagement in After-School Program Activities: Quality of Experience from the Perspective of Participants," *Journal of Youth and Adolescence* 36 (2007): 891–903. Kiyoshi Asakawa and Mihaly Csikszentmihalyi, "The Quality of Experience of Asian American Adolescents in Academic Activities: An Exploration of Educational Achievement," *Journal of Research on Adolescence* 8 (1998): 241–62.

225 **involved in extracurriculars:** Reed W. Larson, "Toward a Psychology of Positive Youth Development," *American Psychologist* 55 (2000): 170–83. See also Robert D. Putnam, *Our Kids: The American Dream in Crisis* (New York: Simon & Schuster, 2015), 174–82.

225 **predicts better outcomes:** For example, see Jennifer Fredricks and Jacquelynne S. Eccles, "Extracurricular Participation Associated with Benefi-

cial Outcomes? Concurrent and Longitudinal Relations," *Developmental Psychology* 42 (2006): 698–713.

225 **playing video games:** Bureau of Labor Statistics, "American Time Use Survey," Average Hours Spent Per Day in Leisure and Sports Activities, by Youngest and Oldest Populations Graph, 2013, http://www.bls.gov/TUS/CHARTS /LEISURE.HTM. See also Vanessa R. Wight, Joseph Price, Suzanne M. Bianchi, and Bijou R. Hunt, "The Time Use of Teenagers," *Social Science Research* 38 (2009): 792–809.

226 **success in adulthood:** Margo Gardner, Jodie Roth, and Jeanne Brooks-Gunn, "Adolescents' Participation in Organized Activities and Developmental Success 2 and 8 Years After High School: Do Sponsorship, Duration, and Intensity Matter?" *Developmental Psychology* 44 (2008): 814–30.

226 **Willingham was the director:** Warren H. Willingham, *Success in College: The Role of Personal Qualities and Academic Ability* (New York: College Entrance Examination Board, 1985). Around the time Warren Willingham was conducting this study, his teenage son Dan went off to college to study psychology. Dan is now a professor of psychology at the University of Virginia and, in the spirit of his father's legacy, dedicated to helping kids benefit from advances in cognitive psychology. My favorite of his books is *Why Don't Students Like School?* (San Francisco: Jossey-Bass, 2009).

227 **beyond standardized tests:** The predictive validity of standardized achievement tests for academic and professional outcomes is well-documented. See the work of psychologists Paul Sackett and Nathan Kuncel in particular. My claim here is not that achievement tests are invalid, per se, but rather that they are an incomplete and imperfect metric for what students know and can do. See Angela L. Duckworth, Patrick D. Quinn, and Eli Tsukayama, "What *No Child Left Behind* Leaves Behind: The Roles of IQ and Self-Control in Predicting Standardized Achievement Test Scores and Report Card Grades," *Journal of Educational Psychology* 104 (2012): 439–51. See also James J. Heckman, John Eric Humphries, and Tim Kautz, ed., *The Myth of Achievement Tests: The GED and the Role of Character in American Life* (Chicago: University of Chicago Press, 2014).

228 **"purposeful, continuous commitment":** Willingham, *Success in College*, 213.

228 **"winning an important meet":** Michael Wines, "Extracurricular Work Spurs Success in College," *Los Angeles Times*, October 17, 1985.

230 **"productive follow-through":** Willingham, *Success in College*, 193. For a review of the advantages and disadvantages of various approaches to measuring qualities like grit, see Duckworth and Yeager, "Measurement Matters."

230 **at very different rates:** Brian M. Galla et al., "Cognitive and Noncognitive Determinants of High School Grades, SAT Scores, and College Persistence," *Journal of Educational Psychology* (under review, 2015).

231 **the Grit Grid:** Alyssa J. Matteucci et al., "Quantifying Grit from Extracurricular Activities: A Biodata Measure of Passion and Perseverance for Long-Term Goals" (manuscript in preparation, 2015).

232 **extracurriculars of novice teachers:** Robertson-Kraft and Duckworth, "True Grit"

233 *corresponsive principle*: Brent W. Roberts and Avshalom Caspi, "The Cumulative Continuity Model of Personality Development: Striking a Balance Between Continuity and Change in Personality Traits Across the Life Course," in *Understanding Human Development: Dialogues with Lifespan Psychology*, ed. Ursula M. Staudinger and Ulman Lindenberger (Norwell, MA: Kluwer Academic Publishers, 2003), 183–214.

233 **"set like plaster":** William James claimed in 1890 that by age thirty, personality is "set like plaster." Quoted in Brent W. Roberts and Wendy F. DelVecchio, "The Rank-Order Consistency of Personality Traits from Childhood to Old Age: A Quantitative Review of Longitudinal Studies," *Psychological Bulletin* 126 (2000): 6.

233 **change after childhood:** Ibid. Avshalom Caspi, Brent W. Roberts, and Rebecca L. Shiner, "Personality Development: Stability and Change," *Annual Review of Psychology* 56 (2005): 453–84. Brent W. Roberts, Kate E. Walton, and Wolfgang Viechtbauer, "Patterns of Mean-Level Change in Personality Traits Across the Life Course: A Meta-Analysis of Longitudinal Studies," *Psychological Bulletin* 132 (2006): 1–25.

234 **tendency toward sociability:** Brent W. Roberts, Avshalom Caspi, and Terrie E. Moffitt, "Work Experiences and Personality Development in Young Adulthood," *Journal of Personality and Social Psychology* 84 (2003): 582–93.

235 **"It's never far from reach":** William R. Fitzsimmons, dean of admissions and financial aid at Harvard College, in an interview with the author, February 17, 2015.

235 **"plain old hard work":** William R. Fitzsimmons, "Guidance Office: Answers from Harvard's Dean, Part 3," *New York Times*, September 14, 2009, http://thechoice.blogs.nytimes.com/tag/harvarddean.

235 **"all that grit":** Fitzsimmons, interview.

237 **dropping precipitously:** Kaisa Snellman, Jennifer M. Silva, Carl B. Frederick, and Robert D. Putnam, "The Engagement Gap: Social Mobility and Extracurricular Participation Among American Youth," *The Annals of the American Academy of Political and Social Science* 657 (2015): 194–207.

238 **Harlem Children's Zone:** For more information on Geoffrey Canada and the Harlem Children's Zone, visit www.hcz.org.

238 **"a decent childhood":** Geoffrey Canada, founder and president of the Harlem Children's Zone, in conversation with the author, May 14, 2012.

238 **"I actually like kids":** Geoffrey Canada, "Our Failing Schools. Enough Is Enough!" TED Talks Education video, filmed May 2013, https://www.ted.com/talks/geoffrey_canada_our_failing_schools_enough_is_enough?language=en.

238 **Bob Eisenberger:** For a summary of his research, see Robert Eisenberger, "Learned Industriousness," *Psychological Review* 99 (1992): 248–67 and Eisenberger's book *Blue Monday: The Loss of the Work Ethic in America* (New York: Paragon House, 1989).

240 **playing fields for grit:** Even for those of us who are beyond our high school and college years, there are many activities we can sign up for that offer challenge and support. For example, I've learned a lot about grit from Joe De Sena, founder of the Spartan Race. Here's a story from our interview: "We live in Vermont. It gets very icy. My son is on the ski team. One day, he comes in an hour before lunch. He tells me he came in early because he was cold." It turns out that the rest of the team was still out practicing. "Okay," Joe said to his son, "I understand you're cold. But you're on the team, and the team is skiing, so now you're on my team, and my team doesn't take the chairlift." Father and son then proceed outside and hike up the mountain on foot, the son upset and complaining the whole way. And then they skied down. Lesson over. "Sounds like torture," I said, half-joking. "The point was not to torture him," Joe replied. "The point was to show him it could be a lot worse. We never had that issue again because now he had a frame of reference that said, 'Okay, this is uncomfortable, but it could be a lot worse.'" Then Joe paused. "You know, I've quit a race before. I learned there's a lot worse than dealing with the pain in front of me. That's a lesson you need help learning. You're not born knowing that."

CHAPTER 12: A CULTURE OF GRIT

243 **"really have *grit*":** Pete Carroll, interviewed by Eric Wayne Davis, *NFL AM*, posted by the Seattle Seahawks, "Pete Carroll: 'We're Looking for Grit,'" February 3, 2014, http://www.seahawks.com/video/2014/02/03/pete-carroll-were-looking-grit.

244 **"be great competitors":** Pete Carroll, head coach of the Seattle Seahawks, in a phone call with the author, May 13, 2013.

246 **"join a great team":** Chambliss, interview.

247 **thinking a different way:** Lee Ross and Richard E. Nisbett, *The Person and the Situation: Perspectives of Social Psychology* (London: McGraw-Hill, 1991). This book sums up all this research beautifully.

248 **James March:** James G. March, "How Decisions Happen in Organizations," *Human-Computer Interaction* 6 (1991): 95–117.

248 **"I am a West Pointer":** Tom Deierlein, cofounder and CEO of ThunderCat Technology, in an email with the author, October 29, 2011.

249 **"they got used to it":** Deierlein, in an email to the author, September 17, 2015.

251 **"*the Finnish spirit*":** *Time*, "Northern Theatre: Sisu," January 8, 1940.

251 **"he can stand worse":** Hudson Strode, "Sisu: A Word That Explains Finland," *New York Times*, January 14, 1940.

251 **asked a thousand Finns:** Emilia Lahti, "Above and Beyond Perseverance: An Exploration of Sisu" (Masters Capstone, University of Pennsylvania, 2013).

252 **"I wear this jersey":** Betty Liu, *Work Smarts: What CEOs Say You Need to Know to Get Ahead* (Hoboken, NJ: John Wiley & Sons, 2014), 7.

252 **"No one here is insignificant":** Thomas II, Amazon review of "Last Man Standing: The Ascent of Jamie Dimon and JP Morgan Chase," October 8, 2009, http://www.amazon.com/Last-Man-Standing-Ascent-JPMorgan/dp/B003 STCKN0.

253 **"grytte":** Ben Smith, "Master Howard Dean," *Observer*, December 8, 2003, http://observer.com/2003/12/master-howard-dean.

253 **senior year at Browning:** Duff McDonald, *Last Man Standing: The Ascent of Jamie Dimon* (New York: Simon and Schuster, 2009), 5.

253 **"I call it fortitude":** Jamie Dimon, chairman, president, and CEO of JPMorgan Chase, in conversation with the author, April 14, 2015.

253 **"the ultimate thing":** Dimon, interview.

254 **"how they treat people":** Nick Summers and Max Abelson, "Why JPMorgan's Jamie Dimon is Wall Street's Indispensable Man," *Bloomberg Businessweek*, May 16, 2013.

254 **"let my kids work for them?":** Dimon, interview.

254 **"actually in the arena":** Theodore Roosevelt, "The Man in the Arena. Citizenship in a Republic," address delivered at the Sorbonne, Paris, 1910.

254 **"not reasons to quit":** JPMorgan Chase & Co., *How We Do Business*, 2014, http://www.jpmorganchase.com/corporate/About-JPMC/document/20140 711_Website_PDF_FINAL.pdf.

255 **"that as a compliment":** Tim Crothers, *The Man Watching: Anson Dorrance and the University of North Carolina Women's Soccer Dynasty* (New York: Thomas Dunne, 2006), 37.

255 **"final measure of greatness":** Ibid., 106.

255 **"It's our culture":** Anson Dorrance, head coach of the University of North Carolina's women's soccer team, in an interview with the author, August 21, 2015.

255 **the Beep Test:** Luc A. Léger, D. Mercier, C. Gadoury, and J. Lambert, "The Multistage 20 Metre Shuttle Run Test for Aerobic Fitness," *Journal of Sports Sciences* 6 (1988): 93–101.

256 **"this is a test of your mentality":** Dorrance, in an interview with the author, September 30, 2015.

256 **"language is everything":** Dimon, interview.

258 **"making you happy":** George Bernard Shaw, *Man and Superman: A Comedy and a Philosophy* (New York: Penguin, 1903), 32. The original passage reads: "This is the true joy in life, the being used for a purpose recognized by yourself as a mighty one . . . the being a force of Nature instead of a feverish selfish little clod of ailments and grievances complaining that the world will not devote itself to making you happy."

258 **the Bugle Notes:** West-Point.org, "Bugle Notes," accessed February 10, 2015, http://www.west-point.org/academy/malo-wa/inspirations/buglenotes .html.

258 **"than to make an army":** Major General John M. Schofield, former superintendent of the United States Military Academy, address to cadets, August 11, 1879.

259 **"the yelling and screaming":** Lieutenant General Robert L. Caslen, superintendent of the United States Military Academy, in an interview with the author, September 4, 2015.

259 **less than 2 percent:** Data provided by the United States Military Academy.

262 **"allows you to get there":** Carroll, *Win Forever*, 183.

262 **"they can demonstrate passion":** "Pete Carroll Returns to USC, Full Interview, 2014," YouTube video, 1:57:42, posted March 20, 2014, https://youtube /jSizvISegnE.

263 **"they're helping me to get better":** Earl Thomas, "Take Nothing for Granted," Earl Thomas's blog, January 25, 2014, http://www.earlthomas.com /2014/01/25/take-nothing-granted.

264 **"the worst call in NFL history":** Don Banks, "The Worst Play Call in NFL History Will Continue to Haunt Seahawks in 2015," *Sports Illustrated*, July 21, 2015.

264 **"failure is never fatal":** "The Wizard's Wisdom: 'Woodenism,'" ESPN, June 5, 2010.

268 **"And use it. *Use it!*":** Greg Bishop, "Pete Carroll, NFL's Eternal Optimist, Is Ready to Turn Heartbreak into Triumph," *Sports Illustrated*, August 3, 2015, http://www.si.com/nfl/2015/07/28/pete-carroll-seattle-seahawks-2015-season -super-bowl-xlix.

CHAPTER 13: CONCLUSION

270 **hand in hand with well-being:** Victoria Young, Yuchen Lin, and Angela L. Duckworth, "Associations Between Grit and Subjective Well-Being in a Large Sample of US Adults," poster presented at the 16th Annual Convention of the Society for Personality and Social Psychology, Long Beach, CA, February 2015.

272 **between the extremes:** Aristotle, *Nicomachean Ethics*. Adam M. Grant and Barry Schwartz, "Too Much of a Good Thing: The Challenge and Opportunity of the Inverted U," *Perspectives in Psychological Science* 6 (2011): 61–76.

273 **wanted to be grittier:** This data was collected in 2015 and is not yet published.

273 **honesty trumps all:** Geoffrey P. Goodwin, Jared Piazza, and Paul Rozin, "Moral Character Predominates in Person Perception and Evaluation," *Journal of Personality and Social Psychology* 106 (2014): 148–68.

273 **character is plural:** I wish I could take credit for the expression, "character is plural." I cannot. Many others have made the same observation, including Christopher Peterson and Martin Seligman in *Character Strengths and Virtues* (New York: Oxford University Press, 2004), 10.

273 **dimensions of character:** Daeun Park et al., "A Tripartite Taxonomy of Character: Evidence for Interpersonal, Intrapersonal, and Intellectual Competencies in Youth," (manuscript under review, 2015). Note that these same three virtue clusters correspond, roughly, to the Big Five personality dimensions of conscientiousness, agreeableness, and openness to experience.

274 **tend to be self-controlled:** I see self-control as related but distinct from grit. You can be self-controlled about a goal that is not your top-level, ultimate concern. And self-control isn't directly related to overcoming setbacks and failures. However, both grit and self-control are about achieving valued goals. See Angela L. Duckworth and James J. Gross, "Self-Control and Grit: Related but Separable Determinants of Success," *Current Directions in Psychological Science* 23 (2014): 319–25. I personally believe that self-control is an extraordinarily important virtue, and to learn more about strategies that facilitate it and their benefits, see Walter Mischel, *The Marshmallow Test: Mastering Self-Control* (New York: Little, Brown, 2014), and Roy F. Baumeister and John Tierney, *Willpower: Rediscovering the Greatest Human Strength* (New York: Penguin, 2011).

274 **"resume virtues"; "eulogy virtues":** David Brooks, *The Road to Character* (New York: Random House, 2015), xi.

274 **world of ideas:** I haven't touched upon creativity in this book. In many endeavors, creativity is absolutely essential, and I direct the interested reader to Scott Barry Kaufman and Carolyn Gregoire, *Wired to Create: Unraveling the Mysteries of the Creative Mind* (New York: Perigee Books, 2015).

274 **predict different outcomes:** Park et al., "Tripartite Taxonomy."

276 **"nothing was coming out":** "Advice on Writing from the *Atlantic*'s Ta-Nehisi Coates," Atlantic video, September 27, 2013, http://www.theatlantic.com /video/archive/2013/09/advice-on-writing-from-i-the-atlantic-i-s-ta-nehisi -coates/280025.

276 **"writing is failure":** "Journalist Ta-Nehisi Coates, 2015 MacArthur Fellow," MacArthur Foundation video, posted September 28, 2015, https://www.mac found.org/fellows/931.

AFTERWORD: SEVEN QUESTIONS I GET ASKED ABOUT GRIT

281 **young adults who kept daily diaries:** Alexander E. Wong and Robin R. Vallacher, "Reciprocal feedback between self-concept and goal pursuit in daily life," *Journal of Personality* (in press).

281 **doctors and nurses report alarming levels of burnout:** Matthew D. McHugh, Ann Kutney-Lee, Jeannie P. Cimiotti, Douglas M. Sloane, and Linda H. Aiken,

"Nurses' Widespread Job Dissatisfaction, Burnout, and Frustration with Health Benefits Signal Problems for Patient Care," *Health Affairs* 30 (2011): 202–10.

283 **it's well-documented that poverty:** see Gary W. Evans, Edith Chen, and Greg E. Miller, "How Poverty Gets Under the Skin: A Life Course Perspective," in *Oxford Handbook of Poverty and Child Development*, ed. Valerie Maholmes and Rosalind Berkowitz King (New York: Oxford University Press, 2012): 13–36; Jeanne Brooks-Gunn and Greg J. Duncan, "The Effects of Poverty on Children," *Future of Children* 7 (1997): 55–71; The effects of chronic stress on development are pernicious—and the effects of a stable, supportive family entirely positive. For a sociological critique of using grit to blame victims, see Anindya Kundu, "Roses in concrete: A perspective on how agency and grit can foster the success of all students, especially those most disadvantaged," *Journal of School & Society* 3 (2016): 18–31.

283 **tested the idea that "talent needs trauma" to bloom:** Dave Collins, Áine MacNamara, and Neil McCarthy, "Super Champions, Champions, and Almosts: Important Differences and Commonalities on the Rocky Road," *Frontiers in Psychology* 6 (2016): 1.

283 **"no evidence was found for the necessity of major trauma":** Ibid.

284 **"They were supportive":** Ibid, 7.

284 **"Once there [on my own at university]":** Ibid, 8.

284 **"Sometimes, we aren't willing":** Anson Dorrance, *Training Soccer Champions* (U.S.A: Echo Point Books & Media, 1996): 21.

286 **Glick noticed that high school and college dropouts:** Karl E. Bauman, "The Relationship Between Age at First Marriage, School Dropout, and Marital Instability: An Analysis of the Glick Effect," *Journal of Marriage and Family* 29 (1967): 672–80.

286 **men and women who score higher on conscientiousness also have marriages that last longer:** Brent W. Roberts, Nathan R. Kuncel, Rebecca Shiner, Avshalom Caspi, and Lewis R. Goldberg, "The Power of Personality: The Comparative Validity of Personality Traits, Socioeconomic Status, and Cognitive Ability for Predicting Important Life Outcomes," *Perspectives on Psychological Science* 2 (2007): 313–45.

286 **and the longevity of romantic relationships:** Lauren Eskreis-Winkler, Elizabeth P. Shulman, Scott A. Beal, and Angela L. Duckworth, "The Grit Effect: Predicting Retention in the Military, the Workplace, School and Marriage," *Frontiers in Psychology,* 5 (2014): 1–12.

286 **less-gritty men are more likely to be divorced or separated:** Lauren Eskreis-Winkler, Elizabeth P. Shulman, Scott A. Beal, and Angela L. Duckworth, "The Grit Effect: Predicting Retention in the Military, the Workplace, School and Marriage," *Frontiers in Psychology* 5 (2014): 1–12.

287 **"*soul mate* isn't a preexisting condition":** Pamela Druckerman, "What You Learn in Your 40s," *New York Times*, Feb. 28, 2014, https://www.nytimes.com/2014/03/01/opinion/sunday/what-you-learn-in-your-40s.html.

287 **immediate gratification:** Adam Alter, *Irresistible: The Rise of Addictive Technology and the Business of Keeping Us Hooked* (New York: Penguin Press, 2017).

288 **voluntarily administered electric shocks to themselves:** Matthew Hutson, "People Prefer Electric Shocks to Being Alone with Their Thoughts," *Atlantic*, July 3, 2014. Also see Timothy D. Wilson et al., "Just think: The challenges of the disengaged mind," *Science* 345 (2014): 75–77.

289 **both professional and Olympic athletes don't specialize early:** Suzie Riewald and Chris Snyder, "The Path to Excellence: A View on the Athletic Development of U.S. Olympians Who Competed From 2000–2012," *Initial Report: Results of the Talent Identification and Development Questionnaire to U.S. Olympians* (2014).

289 **they spend much of their youth sampling:** John P. DiFiori et al., "Debunking Early Single Sport Specialisation and Reshaping the Youth Sport Experience: An NBA Perspective," *British Journal of Sports Medicine* 51 (2017): 142–43.

290 **"the most meticulous cook who ever lived":** Amanda Hesser, "A Baking Bible, Installment No. 2," *New York Times*, December 16, 1998, http://www.nytimes.com/1998/12/16/dining/by-the-book-a-baking-bible-installment-no-2.html.

291 **grit isn't as important as self-control:** Angela L. Duckworth and James J. Gross, "Self-Control and Grit: Related but Separable Determinants of Success," *Current Directions in Psychological Science* 23 (2014): 319–25.

291 **whether the endeavor in question is physical, mental, entrepreneurial, civic, or artistic:** Also see Kennon M. Sheldon et al., "Personality, Effective Goal-Striving, and Enhanced Well-Being," *Personality and Social Psychology Bulletin* 41 (2015): 575–85.

INDEX

INDEX

ABOUT THE AUTHOR

Angela Duckworth is a professor of psychology at the University of Pennsylvania and a 2013 MacArthur Fellow. She studies grit and other attributes that predict success in life. A former middle and high school math teacher, Angela founded the Character Lab, a nonprofit whose mission is to advance the science and practice of character development in children.